BLACK AND WHITE IN SCHOOL

Praeger Studies in Ethnographic Perspectives on American Education

General editor: **Ray C. Rist**

BLACK AND WHITE IN SCHOOL

Trust, Tension, or Tolerance?

Janet Ward Schofield

PRAEGER

PRAEGER SPECIAL STUDIES • PRAEGER SCIENTIFIC

Library of Congress Cataloging in Publication Data

Schofield, Janet Ward.
  Black and white in school.

  (Praeger studies in ethnographic perspectives on
American education)
  Bibliography: p.
  Includes index.
  1. School integration—United States—Case studies.
2. Interpersonal relations—Case studies. 3. Social
interaction—United States—Case studies. I. Title.
II. Series.
LC214.S36 1982   370.19'342   82-9117
ISBN 0-03-056977-X   AACR2

Published in 1982 by Praeger Publishers
CBS Educational and Professional Publishing
a Division of CBS Inc.

© 1982, by Praeger Publishers

23456789 052 987654321

Printed in the United States of America

*For Alanya and all children of her generation in the
hope that the world which they inherit will be
a better place our having lived*

SERIES FOREWORD

Our understanding of American education is undergoing profound and swift change. Instrumental in this process is the turning away from a nearly exclusive reliance on quantitative research methods as the only acceptable means by which to analyze and interpret the realities of education. In fact, one of the basic themes of this shift now under way is that there are multiple ways of "knowing" and no one method can answer all our questions or offer all the necessary perspectives.

As those interested in education begin to explore alternative frameworks and approaches, one that is gaining increased attention and utilization is ethnographic research. This intensive, in-depth investigation by means of direct naturalistic observation has a long and honored tradition within the social sciences, especially sociology and anthropology. Only in the past decade, however, has this method gained new adherents who are applying it to the study of education. The impact has been immediate. The call for ethnographic case studies now comes from the academic community, from practitioners, and from policy makers. All are interested in the explication of the day-to-day realities of education, the micro-level issues that influence the lives of teachers, administrators, and students, and in the understanding of the school as a social system.

This present book is one in a series, *Ethnographic Perspectives on American Education*. The series is aimed at bringing together an exemplary set of recent studies employing ethnographic methods. What makes this collection of singular importance is that it will constitute perhaps the first "critical mass" of such studies of American education. Further, the focus of the various volumes will span the formal organizational structure of the educational experience — from the early grades through higher education. The topics to be covered will be among the most pressing now confronting our educational system, such as school desegregation, bilingual education, social class stratification, the future of rural education, and the preparation of teachers.

This series comes at a most opportune time. As the popularity of ethnographic research continues to increase, it is important for those concerned with education to have ready access to an outstanding collection of books employing this methodology, both to become more familiar with the approach and to study the insights it can provide. These studies seek not only to chronicle current conditions, but to articulate explanations of why the situations are as they are. Each moves beyond the descriptive to the analytic. Their contributions reconfirm the absolute necessity of our continuing to observe American education as it is and where it occurs.

I am especially pleased to include *Black and White in School: Trust, Tension, or Tolerance* as the seventh book in this series. Written by Dr. Janet Schofield, this book is a vitally important contribution to our understanding of school desegregation. Focusing on Wexler School, a newly opened middle school that sought to exemplify what a "model" desegregated school might accomplish, Schofield analyzes for us the inner workings of the school to chart the dynamics and processes of interracial interaction. *Black and White in School* comes after a number of years of careful and painstaking field work at Wexler. The depth of understanding and insight exhibited here should stand as a model to others who would wish to read or conduct an exemplary qualitative study of American education.

The study constantly demonstrates the linkages of events in individual classrooms to the policies of the school board and the politics of the city. Indeed, the very process by which this $12 million school came into being in a city hard-pressed financially to sustain its educational system is provocative. Throughout the study are insights on the role of race and social class in the politics of an American city and how these forces are constantly shaping the views and responses of the public sector. Equipping a new middle school with an olympic-sized swimming pool and a complete television production studio had to do less with the relation of these resources to pedagogy than to the substantive and symbolic politics of race relations. It is a singular contribution of Schofield to tie together disparate bits of information in analyzing how this school came to be and what political and pedagogical agendas it was supposed to address.

Yet another important contribution here comes through Dr. Schofield and her associates' long-term, intimate work with students in the sixth, seventh, and eighth grades. The literature on youth in these middle school years is sparse. Here we are presented with sensitive and detailed descriptions of their behaviors, aspirations, confusions, and anxieties. Youth in these years develop social behaviors, values, and attitudes toward sexuality, race relations, and authority. They test out interactions that will carry them into peer groups and relations with those of the other sex. That so little has been written to describe the young in this stage of their development is curious, given the policy trend in the United States toward more middle schools. Such schools are advocated as institutions uniquely able to respond to the maturational and social-emotional needs of early adolescent youth, yet these needs are little known. Thus the importance of this book.

What Schofield tells us here of the attempt at Wexler to achieve viable school desegregation is sobering. It was an effort made with the best of intentions and supported by superior facilities, staff morale, and community backing. Why the school was soon diverted from its original objective raises important questions with respect to the trade-offs between racial integration and separatism, between social class politics and racial politics, and between implementation versus improvisation in creating educational change. The answers to these questions provide important insights as to why school desegregation is faring as it is. The message in this book is loud and clear: No school is a political island immune to the constant political waves that erode and reshape its contours. In the instance of Wexler, politics conceived the school, brought it into being, and determined its future.

On a personal note, I am gratified to see the publication of this book. The study was initially begun in 1975 with support from the National Institute of Education. I headed the division within the NIE that awarded the grant to Dr. Schofield. Culminating here in the manner it has, I consider it one of my important successes at the NIE. I commend this book to the reader with a final observation: There is every indication this study will become a landmark effort in our understanding of school desegregation.

Ray C. Rist
Washington, D.C.

ACKNOWLEDGMENTS

The placement of these acknowledgments near the beginning of this book is most appropriate since it symbolizes the important role that others have played in making the book possible. Chief among these individuals is H. Andrew Sagar, who, over the course of several years while a graduate student in social psychology at the University of Pittsburgh, was of invaluable help in virtually every stage of the research from conducting observations and interviews to performing statistical analyses and synthesizing and interpreting the data. Also essential to many phases of this research over more than two years was Elaine McGivern, then a graduate student in sociology, whose hard work, interpersonal skills, and research acumen made a major contribution to this project. The participation of a number of other graduate students, including Donna Durant, Barbara Hall, Chuck Hopkins, Sandra Leath, and David Schaeffer, also enriched the study in a variety of ways.

An intensive research project such as the one reported here generates a vast amount of data to be typed, indexed, and analyzed. The mammoth job of transcribing literally thousands of pages of dictated notes and taped interviews fell primarily on the capable shoulders of Peter Rubinsky and Karen Ginley. I am sincerely grateful to both of them for the dedication, patience, intelligence, and good humor with which they approached this Herculean task. Others who made a major contribution to this work in its later stages were Nancy Zak, Debbie Connell, and Darlene Luppino-Grant all of whom approached this work with superb skills, initiative, and a sense of professionalism for which I am most grateful.

A number of undergraduates at the University of Pittsburgh also contributed to this project by capably assisting in analysis of the interview data. They are Bob Bittel, Paul Carosi, Monica Kreuger, Bill Seidel, Karen Snider, and Kim Strayer. Other graduate and undergraduate students, including Yvette Cook, Sue Gorna, Laurie Ney, Jim Rodgers, Nancy Short, and Leslie Steele, assisted in the research in various ways too numerous to mention. Special thanks go to Debbie Guydish for applying her administrative and accounting skills so effectively and thus relieving me of many time-consuming tasks.

The research reported here was funded by the Desegregation Studies Unit at the National Institute of Education, and I would like to express my appreciation to Ray Rist and Ron Henderson, who served as head of that unit at different stages of the project, for their encouragement and support, financial and otherwise. Thanks also go to a number of my colleagues and students at the Learning Research and Development Center and in the Psychology Department at the University of Pittsburgh for their valuable comments on draft chapters of this manuscript and to Sarah Ward for her editorial assistance.

The research on which the book is based would not have been possible without the very generous cooperation of those at Wexler Middle School as well as of the administrative staff at the Waterford Board of Education. I thank Wexler's students and staff for their time, their willingness to share their thoughts and observations, and for the courage they showed in allowing us to observe them day in and day out in the best and worst of conditions. Only concern about maintaining the confidentiality of data keeps me from singling out by name for particular thanks those administrators, teachers, and students who made a special contribution to this research by serving on interview panels or participating in the observational phases of the study.

A project that spans six or seven years, as has the research for and the writing of this book, and that makes intense demands on one's time, emotions, and intellect cannot help but profoundly affect one's development as an individual. The people I have met, the experiences I had as an observer at Wexler, the things I read, and the reflection involved in the preparation of this volume have greatly enriched my life. Thus I would like to thank my parents, who, by providing a warm and supportive home environment that valued intellectual endeavors, and financial support throughout my undergraduate and graduate years, set the stage for my undertaking such a project. So fundamental that it hardly needs mention but much too important to omit is my gratitude to my husband, Douglas, for his confidence in my abilities, his encouragement of my work, and his willingness to make those adjustments and compromises inevitable in a two-career family. All of these things helped make possible the undertaking and completion of this work, which I hope the reader will find both enlightening and provocative.

Small portions of the text have appeared previously in the three books listed below. This material is reprinted by permission of the publishers concerned.

Janet W. Schofield, "Cooperation as social exchange: Resource gaps and reciprocity in academic work." In Shlomo Sharan et al. (eds.) *Cooperation in Education*. Provo, Utah: Brigham Young University Press, 1980, parts of pp. 162, 167-77.

——— . "Complementary and conflicting identities: Images and interaction in an interracial school." In Steven Asher and John Gottman (eds.) *The Development of Children's Friendships*. New York: Cambridge University Press, 1981, parts of pp. 62-66, 68-71, 73-80.

Janet W. Schofield and H. Andrew Sagar, "The social context of learning in an integrated school." In Ray C. Rist (ed.) *Desegregated Schools: Appraisals of an American Experiment*. New York: Academic Press, 1979, parts of pp. 159, 161-68, 172, 175-76, 181-86, 188-90, 192, 195, 197.

CONTENTS

LIST OF TABLES

1

WEXLER MIDDLE SCHOOL:
PROMISE AND PROBLEMS

Wexler Middle School opened amid great fanfare and high hopes.*
The new school was touted as a model of both high-quality education and thoroughgoing integration. Indeed, the major local newspaper rhapsodized:

> If anything, Wexler may be too good. . . . That is, it could skim off
> the cream and make more difficult later plans to establish [middle]
> schools. . . . But the administration is putting its best foot forward
> and worrying later about future successes.

*Pseudonyms are used throughout this book in place of actual proper
names in order to provide confidentiality. For the same reason, occasional
changes have been made in the names of specific programs or positions within
the school when it was possible to do this without creating confusion about
their nature. Finally, in a very few instances, such as the quotations from newspaper articles, complete source information has not been provided because it
could compromise the other efforts made to insure confidentiality.

The research on which this book is based was funded by the National
Institute of Education (NIE) under contract no. 400-76-0011. Some of the other
expenses related to the preparation of the book were funded by grant number
MH31602-01 from the National Institute of Mental Health (NIMH) and by the
Learning Research and Development Center of the University of Pittsburgh,
which is supported in part by funds from NIE. However, all opinions expressed
herein are solely those of the author, and no endorsement of the ideas by NIE or
NIMH is implied or intended.

Less than four years after this propitious start, another major paper characterized Wexler, which was by then heavily black, as "a racial timebomb ticking toward disaster."

As indicated in the foreword, this book focuses on the relations that developed between black and white students at Wexler and analyzes the social processes that accounted for the development, maintenance, and change of these relations during the school's first three years. It also examines the evolution of Wexler as an institution, since the extraordinary changes in the school and its public image were important in setting the context in which relations between students evolved as well as being instructive in and of themselves. This chapter provides an introduction to Wexler and an assessment of the extent to which it held promise of meeting its goals of providing an environment conducive to interracial harmony and academic excellence. It also briefly introduces the reader to the data-gathering and analysis strategies that were used in the study on which this book is based.

WEXLER'S COMMUNITY AND EDUCATIONAL CONTEXT

Wexler Middle School is located in a large, industrial, northeastern city that will be called Waterford. The city contains a rich variety of ethnic groups including substantial numbers of Irish and Italians as well as sizable communities of Poles, Slovaks, and other eastern European groups. Roughly one-quarter of the city's population is black. About 10 percent is Jewish. Residential patterns in Waterford are strongly influenced by both ethnicity and race. Many neighborhoods have been associated with specific ethnic groups for well over a century. However, rather abrupt population shifts after World War II left some previously integrated neighborhoods both heavily segregated and economically depressed. A large proportion of Waterford's blacks live in such neighborhoods. There are also sizable numbers of middle- and working-class blacks. Some race-related civil disorders, which resulted in considerable property loss in spite of the efforts of the National Guard, occurred in the 1960s. However, they were not severe compared to those in cities like Los Angeles or Washington, D.C. Waterford's schools have experienced relatively few serious, overtly race-related conflicts, but violence did erupt in the late 1960s, especially in one very visible high school.

A brief discussion of the recent history of the Waterford school system will help to point out the events that eventually led to the decision to open Wexler as a racially balanced school. There is no question that the de facto segregation in Waterford's schools increased in the years after the historic 1954 *Brown* vs. *Board of Education* decision, which led to such heated controversies over desegregation elsewhere. However, it was not until the latter half of the 1960s that desegregation of the city's schools became a real focus of public attention. At that time, black parents and community groups began to protest overcrowded conditions in some of the predominantly black schools. Partially in response to this pressure, the Board of Education issued a report that admitted that in the past decade the number of schools with a black enrollment exceeding 80 percent had more than doubled, while the proportion of black students in the system had increased only moderately. The report also indicated that there were large differences between the achievement levels of students from predominantly white and predominantly black schools. These findings suggested that the Board's earlier efforts to improve education in the heavily black schools through the use of compensatory education programs had been far from completely effective.

The Board's report took a strong, almost emotional, position in favor of integration. The letter to the public accompanying it stated, "We will disturb those, both Negro and White, who think that the social revolution of 1965 will pass over soon. . . ." The report itself asserted, "We have stated without qualification that we believe in integrated schools," and referred to the Board's "feverish efforts to bring about improved integration." However, the report also foreshadowed the very slow progress that actually followed in the next decade. For example, after making strong positive statements about integration, the letter to the public accompanying the report went on to state, "We believe that a lifetime of work remains to be done," giving little encouragement to those who expected prompt, far-reaching action. Furthermore, the report included no new plans to bring about integration and committed the Board to avoiding "forced, unnatural, or irrational" ways of achieving desegregation.

The Board did take a number of actions in the 1960s consistent with the basic commitment to desegregation made in the report. For example, it adopted an open enrollment plan that let students voluntarily transfer to another school if that school was not operating at full capacity and if the transfer improved the racial balance there. It also redrew some attendance boundaries and chose the locations for some new schools with an eye toward achieving racially mixed student bodies. Other steps taken included hiring increased numbers of black staff and adopting some biracial and multiethnic textbooks. Although such actions were welcomed by many proponents of desegregation, they did little to actually desegregate the school system.

Toward the end of the 1960s, the state in which Waterford is located made its first formal demands that the district desegregate. In the decade following, the school system continued its gradualist approach, building a few racially mixed schools and hiring more black teachers and administrators. However, it consistently failed to come up with the overall plan that the state required. Time and time again, state deadlines passed without the Board having put forward an acceptable plan. For example, in the early 1970s the Board appointed a citizen's committee to work out a proposal. However, it then refused to accept this group's plan, which required busing fewer than 20 percent of the system's students to achieve racial balance, and missed yet another state deadline.

Under increasing pressure in the early 1970s because of a judicial order to comply with the state's request for a plan, the Board finally accepted a proposal that called for voluntary transfers to desegregate the system's middle schools over a period of several years. The state, however, rejected this plan, saying it was inadequate. Not surprisingly, the Board subsequently failed to implement it. However, it did continue its piecemeal efforts to keep segregation from increasing and, in fact, the percentage of black students in essentially all-black schools decreased modestly in the 1970s from roughly 55 percent at the beginning of the decade to about 45 percent in 1974.

In the decade before the opening of Wexler in 1975, the Board repeatedly made public pronouncements reaffirming its commitment to desegregating the schools. On the other hand, it also consistently refused to consider seriously any plan that required busing a substantial number of students solely for the purpose of desegregation. Such busing, especially if it were not limited to students who volunteered to transfer, was considered as "forced" and "unnatural" and hence not consistent with the Board's policy. Given residential patterns in Waterford, it was virtually impossible to achieve any thoroughgoing desegregation of the schools without such busing. So the Board was still thinking in terms of piecemeal efforts rather than an overall desegregation plan when it made decisions about Wexler.

The Board's public commitment to desegregation and the increasingly strong state pressures on the system in the 1970s made it virtually inevitable that a new school of any size would have to be racially mixed. The emphasis on middle schools as a vehicle for desegregation that characterized much of the Board's thinking in the early 1970s made this doubly true in Wexler's case. The Board's commitment to avoiding "forced" desegregation led it to adopt an open enrollment policy for Wexler. Specifically, it decided that the student body would consist of those students from twenty-four elementary schools in one section of the city who wished to enroll. Students from the city's numerous private schools were also eligible and several dozen did indeed enroll. Students were to be admitted on a first-come, first-served basis within predetermined quotas set to achieve racial and sexual balance.

The Board held public meetings to obtain reaction to the proposed open enrollment plan for Wexler. It hoped to obtain a student body approximately 58 percent white and 42 percent black, which would mirror the black/white ratio in the entire school system. As indicated by articles in Waterford's major newspapers, response to the plan was more positive than that shown to any previous desegregation effort. Yet black and white community groups both advocated changing the quotas to increase the percentage of students from their own group attending the school. There was special concern in the black community over the fate of those children who would be prevented from attending the school by the racial quotas. Black parents had long been waiting for a new middle school, since some of the schools serving their children were old and comparatively run down. Now a new and attractive middle school was being built, but the majority of the places were reserved for whites. Many blacks nonetheless supported the open enrollment plan since their children did not attend the schools whose students would be assigned to Wexler under the alternate assigned enrollment plan. Finally, after considerable debate and discussion, the Board adopted an open enrollment plan, sticking with the initially proposed racial quotas.

Once the quota issue was settled, applications were accepted from students wishing to attend Wexler. Blacks applied at a much more rapid rate than whites. Over three-fourths of the applications received during the first three days were from blacks. On the first day, 433 blacks and 74 whites applied; on the second, 226 blacks and 43 whites; and on the third day, approximately 100 from each group. The black community's enthusiasm for the school was vividly demonstrated by the fact that by noon of the first day on which applications were accepted, the slots for eighth grade black girls were entirely filled.

Less than a year after Wexler first opened, the Waterford Board of Education made a decision that had far-reaching consequences for the school. The open enrollment policy was replaced by a plan in which children graduating from eleven elementary schools were required to attend Wexler. Other children were permitted to enroll only under a few special circumstances, such as having a sibling who had entered the school under the earlier open enrollment plan. The reasons for this change and its impact on the school are discussed in Chapter 7. However, it must at least be noted here that this policy change had two important effects. First, the number of children in Wexler's sixth grade increased from approximately 450 to just over 600. Second, the new sixth grade was over two-thirds black rather than half black.

WEXLER'S PHYSICAL PLANT, ORGANIZATIONAL STRUCTURE, AND ACADEMIC PROGRAM

When Wexler first opened its doors, in the fall of 1975, the student body was almost exactly 50 percent white and 50 percent black. The deviation from the Board's goal of 58 percent white reflected the fact that many whites were dubious about enrolling their children in a racially mixed school. Few people were surprised by the large number of applications from black students. Historically, a high proportion of the black population has favored desegregation, although many of Waterford's black citizens were not enthusiastic about busing. Also, and perhaps more importantly, some of the black schools available as alternatives to Wexler were widely perceived as relatively poorly staffed and equipped. Although Wexler did not attract as many whites as it had hoped to, it came relatively close to meeting its goal.

The question arises as to how Wexler was able to attract the white students that it did. Certainly the fact that Waterford's predominantly white school board had been unable to come up with a desegregation plan in spite of state pressures for one suggests that there was relatively little popular support in the white community for desegregated schooling. Interviews suggested that two major factors motivated white students to attend Wexler: (1) its outstanding physical facilities and equipment, which made possible an unusually broad array of nonacademic activities, and (2) its strong academic program. These factors also played an important role in black students' decisions. In fact, when asked why they had come to Wexler, over half of all the students interviewed mentioned physical aspects of the school, like the carpeting and the swimming pool, or special programs made possible by the physical facilities.

Wexler cost over twelve million dollars to build, and its high cost was clearly reflected in its fine physical facilities. For example, its swimming pool and tennis courts were comparable to or better than those at most high schools in the city, let alone the middle schools. Also illustrative of the school's unusual facilities and programs was a $200,000 media center — three rooms, including a production studio and a control room, in which students used regular TV cameras, lights, and sound equipment to produce programs for transmission throughout the school on a closed circuit system. These facilities, according to one of Waterford's major newspapers, "would be the envy of some commercial TV studios." Exceptionally well-equipped rooms for teaching fine arts and for introducing students to the skills needed in various vocational and technical fields made possible well-publicized and attractive courses that supplemented Wexler's highly touted academic program.

In addition to being lavish, the physical plant was well suited to the administrative structure of the school. Administratively, Wexler was divided by grade level into three "schools within a school."* Each grade, called a house, was headed by a vice-principal who had considerable autonomy, and was separated physically from the others. By way of illustration, although the seventh and eighth grade houses shared a floor in the building, they were separated by a large library. Within each house, faculty and students were divided into teams. The faculty teams consisted of five teachers each of whom was responsible for one subject area: English, social studies, math,

---

*Wexler is described in this chapter as it was during its first year. Numerous changes in organizational structure and in the use of physical space occurred during the study. The most significant of these are discussed in Chapter 7.

reading, or science. Students on each team, divided into five classes of approximately twenty-five each, rotated through the classrooms of their five academic teachers. They generally stayed with other students from their team, but not necessarily with students in their particular class, for nonacademic courses such as gym, art, or home economics. Within the houses, the classrooms of each team were grouped together. Many of the classrooms were separated by partitions, which could be removed when teachers desired to work with the team as a group rather than with individual classes.

Two basic strategies were adopted to make Wexler an institution that could attract students by providing, in one administrator's words, "a better education than [is available] anywhere else in Waterford." First, a number of rather innovative teaching techniques were adopted. For example, as mentioned above, academic teachers were organized into multidisciplinary teams, with each team jointly having responsibility for a specific group of students. Teachers' schedules were organized so that teams regularly had the opportunity to meet during the school day. Although these planning periods were often used as opportunities for casual gossip or for activities like correcting tests, they also encouraged curricular coordination and facilitated consultation among teachers about the needs of particular children.

Wexler's principal strongly encouraged individualized instruction aimed at providing every child with work at the most appropriate level of difficulty. He and others also highlighted the existence of "open space" at Wexler. Neither of these two innovations was utilized as thoroughly as one might have expected, given the fanfare concerning them. Yet both had some impact on students' experiences. For example, in March of the school's first year, one team of teachers took out the partitions between some of their rooms and set up a plan whereby students could work at their own pace on a variety of activities in locations called learning stations spread around the large open area. Other teachers set up work contracts that allowed children to progress through a specified amount of material by themselves as long as they completed their work by an agreed-upon time.

To many people, an even more attractive part of the academic program was the existence of special accelerated programs. Wexler was the home for one part of the city of a prestigious accelerated academic program for eighth graders with measured IQs exceeding

130. When arguing in favor of locating this program at Wexler, the superintendent of schools pointed out specifically that this would help the school to attract students. There was also a less extensive enriched academic program for academically talented sixth and seventh graders. As indicated earlier, many students, especially white students, reported that these programs had strongly influenced them or their parents to choose Wexler.

WEXLER AS A SETTING FOR THE DEVELOPMENT OF INTERGROUP RELATIONS

Wexler was designed not only to provide an outstanding academic program but also to serve as a model of integrated schooling. Somewhat cynical observers in Waterford believed that an exemplary Wexler was the Board's way of attempting to show that it really was doing its best in spite of its continuing failure to develop an acceptable plan for the desegregation of the entire system. Other more trusting individuals argued that it was not a sop to those forces pushing for desegregation, but an exemplar, which, if successful, could pave the way for greater public acceptance of the idea of desegregated schools. The crucial fact for this discussion though is that the Board, whatever the motivations of its members, did make unusually strong efforts to provide an environment that would make Wexler a model of interracial harmony.

Contact Theory: A Perspective on Improving Intergroup Relations

In order to lay the groundwork for describing Wexler in a way that illuminates its potential for improving intergroup relations, I will briefly discuss some aspects of current thinking on the factors that are important to achieving this goal. As is frequently the case, there is no one completely accepted theory to which virtually all scholars subscribe. Thus one could approach the task of describing Wexler from a variety of perspectives. I believe that a particularly fruitful approach is based on the work of Gordon Allport and of later theorists and researchers who have been influenced by his ideas. As will become apparent in the following discussion, even within this one tradition there is some disagreement about the precise nature of the conditions that will lead to improved intergroup relations. Since most of these disputes cannot be completely resolved with the research evidence now available and the differences between points of view are generally not fundamental, I will not try to build a case for some of these theoretical positions rather than for others. Rather, I will briefly present these various views to sensitize the reader to the complexity of the issues involved. Although the research on which this book is based was not specifically designed to provide a clear test of the theoretical differences outlined below, later chapters have distinct implications for at least some of these disputes.

Social scientists have been aware since Allport's (1954) classic book, *The Nature of Prejudice*, that contact between two previously isolated and hostile groups per se may do little or nothing to improve relations between them. Indeed, such contact may exacerbate pre-existing tensions and prejudice. Allport and others like Pettigrew (1969), Amir (1969, 1976), and Cook (1969, 1978) have argued that the specific nature of the contact situation is crucial in determining what the effects of contact will be on intergroup relations. Pettigrew, building on Allport's work, calls the mere mixing of students *desegregation* and distinguishes it from *integration*, mixing under the circumstances that Allport argued are conducive to positive outcomes. These conditions, briefly stated, are equal status for both groups within the contact situation, a cooperative rather than competitive atmosphere, and the support of the relevant authorities for positive intergroup relations. Allport's work has influenced thinking about intergroup relations for over a quarter of a century, and it remains a basic orienting perspective used by many scholars today.

Although Allport (1954) argues that equal status is crucial to the development of positive intergroup relations, he does not discuss at length precisely what he means by the term *equal status*. Close reading of his work suggests that he appears to be referring primarily to equality of status in basic formal roles. Quite a number of researchers have considered the equal status criterion met when members of both groups have access to the same very fundamental roles, such as student or teacher, in the same institution. Pettigrew (1969, 1975) expands this rather minimal definition, arguing that true equal status is not obtained unless both groups have access not only to the most basic formal roles but to a plethora of other formal and informal ones. He stresses the importance of equal status and power *within* the contact situation and argues that this can be achieved by careful planning even when there is a marked difference in the socioeconomic background of black and white students.

Other researchers, however, take a somewhat different view. St. John (1975) and Armor (1972) emphasize the ways in which unequal external status tends to undercut the attainment of equal status within the contact situation. For example, St. John writes (1975, p. 98):

> Black and white children may be unequally prepared to be successful students or may be accorded unequal status in the peer group because of differential family background.

According to this view, inequalities due to differential socioeconomic status or academic performance are likely to create serious problems in desegregated schools by undermining even the most determined efforts to provide the broadly construed sort of equal status within the school that Pettigrew sees as important.

Cohen (1975) takes an even more pessimistic position. She argues that even if blacks and whites are accorded equal formal status *and* have similar background characteristics, race itself operates as what she terms a diffuse status characteristic to create the expectation that whites are more competent. She argues that unless these expectations are changed in both black and white students, undesirable unequal status behavior patterns will emerge, with whites tending to dominate interracial interaction. Cohen's view of equal status is notably different from Pettigrew's on two important dimensions. First, she focuses more heavily upon actual interaction patterns. (Indeed, one could argue that the type of equal status behavior Cohen discusses could reasonably be conceptualized as an *outcome* of carefully planned interracial contact as well as a possible mediating variable leading to other outcomes, such as a reduction in stereotyping.) Second, whereas Pettigrew emphasizes that the equal status can prevail within a contact situation in spite of major differences in family background between black and white students, Cohen argues that being black or white in and of itself creates expectations that lead to unequal participation and influence and hence, in her terms, to unequal status.

The purpose of the foregoing discussion was to outline three somewhat different conceptions as to what it means to say that a school provides its students with equal status, for, although some theorists have argued that it may not be an absolutely indispensable prerequisite to improved intergroup relations, there is considerable evidence that equal status, as variously defined by different researchers, is helpful in achieving that goal (Amir 1969, 1976; Cook 1978; Riordan 1978). As will become apparent later in this chapter, Wexler tried in a variety of ways to provide blacks and whites with the sort of equal status within the contact situation that Pettigrew discusses. But it could do little about either their rather unequal social, economic, and academic status or the expectations about each other that they brought to school with them.

Allport (1954) also stresses the importance of cooperation between individuals of different backgrounds in improving intergroup relations, contending that cooperative striving for shared goals will be effective in improving intergroup relations to the extent that it results in the perception of "common interests and common humanity" (p. 267). Furthermore, he argues that competition is likely to mobilize and intensify already existing prejudices.

There has been a great deal of research suggesting that cooperation can and often does have quite positive effects on interpersonal and intergroup relations, as Worchel (1979, p. 264) points out.

> Research has demonstrated that cooperation results in increased communication, greater trust and attraction, greater satisfaction with group production [and] greater feelings of similarity between group members. . . .

Similarly, there is good reason to believe that competition reinforces tensions and produces dislike and other negative reactions to one's competitors (Cook 1980; Dion 1979; Johnson and Johnson 1974; Sherif et al. 1961). Indeed, theoretical elaboration on both the nature of cooperation and competition and on how and why they influence intergroup relations is relatively developed compared to the more rudimentary distinctions made concerning equal status, although many important issues remain to be resolved. Readers interested in detailed discussions of these topics are referred to other sources (Aronson, Bridgeman, and Geffner 1978; Cook 1978; Deutsch 1949; Dion 1979; Johnson and Johnson 1974; Levine 1981; Miller and Hamblin 1963; Sharan 1980; Slavin 1980; Worchel 1979). The goal of this brief discussion is not to summarize the voluminous research done on the effect of cooperation and competition on intergroup relations, but to lay the groundwork for describing the ways in which Wexler's programs and policies were likely to influence relations between blacks and whites. Thus, only a few of the more relevant distinctions will be introduced here.

First, cooperation and competition can occur between either individuals or groups. Generally, in school settings, the former is more common than the latter. Thus one might expect cooperation and competition to have their major impact on interpersonal rather than intergroup relations. Yet in many settings, including schools, the racial or gender group membership of individuals is likely to be very salient to those with whom they are interacting. Thus, to the extent that changes in reactions to individuals influence reactions to the groups to which those individuals belong, one might expect some change in intergroup relations to occur. Even if little or no such generalization occurs, one would expect cooperation to improve relations between individual members of different racial groups, a not unimportant outcome.

When discussing cooperation, competition, and intergroup contact in schools, theorists have often remarked upon the importance of classroom reward structures. Slavin (1980, p. 634) writes:

> The *reward structure* of a classroom refers to the rules under which students are rewarded. . . . If one student's receipt of rewards diminishes the probability that another will also be rewarded, the students are operating under a *competitive reward structure*. . . . If the probability of one student's receiving a reward is unrelated to the probability that any other student receives a reward, the students are in an *independent reward structure*, as in individualized instruction. . . . Finally if an increase in the performance level of any student increases the probability that another will receive rewards, the students are in a *cooperative reward structure*.

There is good evidence that classroom practices that emphasize cooperative reward structures are conducive to improved relations between students from different backgrounds who cooperate in order to jointly obtain desired rewards (Johnson and Johnson 1974; Sharan 1980; Slavin 1980). This conclusion is consistent with Sherif and his colleagues' conclusion that cooperation in obtaining shared, highly valued goals *that could not be obtained without cooperation* can mitigate hostility brought about by intergroup competition, whereas other types of cooperation may not have this effect (Sherif et al. 1961).

Taking a somewhat different view, Amir (1976) has argued that cooperation by individuals from different groups in pursuit of their own individual goals may have a positive impact on peer relations, even though a cooperative reward structure does not exist. Thus, for example, students who are graded individually but who cooperate by sharing information or other resources would be expected to come to like each other more than previously, just as would students who work together on a project for which they jointly receive a grade. Amir's position is not inconsistent with Allport's, for although the latter emphasizes the positive effects of cooperating in situations, such as athletic teams or military units, where the group strives as a unit to achieve a shared goal, he also mentions the importance of common participation, which allows people to come to know each other as individuals.

There is considerable evidence consistent with Amir's contention that task interdependence improves relations between students of different backgrounds even when the reward structure is not cooperative (Aronson et al. 1978). However, it must be noted that much of the evidence relevant to the impact of cooperation induced either by task interdependence or by a cooperative reward structure comes from research in which great care has been taken to insure that individual or group differences in academic achievement have a minimal impact on each person's ability to contribute to the task at hand or to group success. Cooperative situations in which there is task or reward interdependence might be expected to have a less positive impact on peer relations if the members of one racial or ethnic group are consistently perceived as impeding attainment of desired rewards because of inappropriate behavior, poor skills, or lack of effort. Indeed, there is some experimental evidence suggesting that in cooperative situations, liking and respect for other group members is related to their competence (Blanchard and Cook 1976).

As with the various views of equal status, the different views on the precise type of cooperation necessary to improve intergroup relations are generally complementary rather than competitive. That is, virtually all theorists would agree that situations that embody equal status or cooperation in their strongest forms (Cohen's conception of equal status and Sherif's conception of cooperation) are likely to have a positive impact on intergroup relations. Further, there is wide agreement that competition is very likely to have a negative impact on intergroup and interpersonal relations. The disagreement is over whether the other, weaker types of cooperation or equal status contact are also quite certain to have a positive impact. Although I would not argue that all forms of equal status, cooperation, and competition will necessarily have predictable effects on intergroup relations, the evidence for the impact of even their weaker forms is strong enough to warrant examining the extent to which they were present at Wexler.

Compared to the amount of discussion and research relating to the effects of equal status, cooperation, and competition on relations between members of different racial and ethnic groups, there has been relatively little theoretical or empirical work explicitly investigating the final criterion that Allport (1954) specifies, the support of authorities for positive intergroup relations. Perhaps one reason for this is the complexity of clarifying precisely which authorities are relevant to a particular situation, of specifying the numerous ways in which their support could be made manifest, and of delineating how such support will lead to improved intergroup relations.

Existing research relevant to the impact of authorities' attitudes and behavior on intergroup relations between children in desegregated schools focuses primarily on the role of three types of authorities — principals, teachers, and parents. Very briefly summarized, it suggests that the attitudes and behaviors of individuals occupying all three of these roles can have a substantial impact on relations between black and white students (Schofield 1980). The importance of the principal is emphasized by Noblit (1979) and St. John (1975, p. 98). According to the latter:

> Administrative sanction is probably the most important precondition of prejudice-reducing contact in schools. If [the school's] central office staff is determined that integration shall be complete, the status of all school children made equal, and racial competition avoided, the other necessary ingredients of healthy biracial schools probably will follow.

Other research highlights the impact of teachers and parents on intergroup relations in desegregated schools. For example, Gerard, Jackson, and Conolley (1975) found a relation between teachers' prejudice and white children's acceptance of minority group children as friends. This relation may well be due to teachers' classroom practices. Indeed, the same study found that teachers who were quite prejudiced were less likely than others to assign children to work in small groups, a practice conducive to cooperation. Allport (1954, p. 279) contends that "conformity with the home atmosphere is undoubtedly the most important single source of prejudice. . . ." Thus one would expect parental attitudes to have a significant impact on children's responses to out-group members. Quite a number of studies show just such a linkage. For example, Patchen's (1982) research suggests that parents' racial attitudes are an important determinant of several aspects of intergroup relations. Specifically, it found that the racial attitudes of both black and white parents were related to their children's racial attitudes as well as to their propensity to have friends of the other race and to be involved in unfriendly interracial contacts.

In summary, although there has been relatively little attention paid to fleshing out systematically Allport's rather unelaborated argument about the role of the authorities in promoting positive intergroup relations, there is enough empirical evidence supporting the general argument to suggest that it is worthwhile to examine the extent to which Wexler met this as well as the other criteria that he specified as important intergroup relations. The next three sections of this chapter will do just that.

Equal Status at Wexler

Wexler's commitment to promoting the most basic sort of equal formal status for blacks and whites is well illustrated in its staffing patterns. The high-level administrative positions were evenly divided between the two groups. The school's principal, Mr. Reuben, who was white, had previously been the well-regarded principal of a black school after teaching in a variety of predominantly black schools. The eighth grade vice-principal, Mr. Callahan, was also white, whereas the vice-principals of the sixth and seventh grades, Ms. Kent and Mr. Cooper, were black. Each house had two counselors, one white and one black. The school's commitment to *maintaining* this sort of staffing pattern is clear in the following excerpt from field notes on a meeting with Vice-principal Cooper during Wexler's second year.

The vice-principal said, "You know, when they laid out this school, they were really careful about the staffing. You had to get it divided white/black, male/female, and that sort of thing. . . . Both of the counselors that worked with me last year were really good, and both of them are interested in coming back; but I can't hire them because the person we have now is a white female, so I have to get a black male."

Wexler's faculty was approximately 25 percent black. The principal tried to get more black teachers for the school so that the black/white ratio of the faculty would be closer to that of the student body. However, the Board of Education was unwilling to allow this since the proportion of black faculty in the entire school system was markedly below 25 percent, and they did not want to rob other schools of too many of their black teachers.

Although the school went a long way toward providing the most basic sort of equal status to blacks and whites, it must be noted that there were many ways, some obvious and others less so, in which even the weakest definition of equal status was not completely satisfied. For example, the four top administrative positions were divided between blacks and whites, but white males held the two most prestigious positions — principal, and vice-principal for the eighth grade, which had both the oldest students and the elite academic honors program. Similarly, the black faculty were not evenly distributed throughout the different types of teaching positions. For example, about 15 percent of the sixth grade academic faculty were black compared to about 30 percent of the faculty for certain non-academic subjects. The school also had a number of teachers' aides, virtually all of whom were black. The aides were clearly subordinate to the teachers, but they did notably increase the number of blacks involved in the instructional process since much of their time was spent tutoring students on an individual or small-group basis in the regular classrooms. Relatively few of the academic teachers who were appointed by the principal as team leaders were black. When one black team leader was appointed, some white teachers were heard to grumble about preferential treatment for black staff in spite of the fact that the new team leader had a widespread reputation for high competence.

Wexler tried in a variety of ways to go well beyond providing the minimal sort of equal status that stems from making roles such as student, teacher, and administrator available to both blacks and whites. Many of its features were conducive to promoting the broader, more inclusive sort of equal status discussed by Pettigrew (1969, 1975). For example, school desegregation typically involves sending black children to previously all-white schools. This immediately puts black children at a disadvantage because they are outsiders in the community surrounding the school and newcomers in an already established social system. Wexler differed from this situation in two important ways. First, it was not located on traditionally white or black territory. The school sits on a large tract of land bounded by a factory, a government building, a park, and small stores that are on the periphery of one of the most desegregated shopping areas in the city. Beyond these immediate racially rather neutral boundaries, a white residential area fans out in one direction and a black area in another. In fact, one of the reasons the Board of Education purchased this particular tract of land was its easy access from both black and white communities.

In addition to being located on land that was not clearly white or black territory, the school was interracial from the day it opened. Hence children of one group were not confronted with having to make a place for themselves in an already functioning social system dominated by the other group and permeated with its attitudes and values. This is a very important factor in making possible equal status relations of the type that Pettigrew and Cohen discuss. For example, in some previously all-white schools, black students have had to resort to litigation to end the use of traditional but racially insulting school songs or cheers (Bell 1975). The process through which the Wexler mascot was adopted illustrates the equal footing of black and white students in the creation of symbols to represent their school. First, all students were informed by the principal that the school mascot would be chosen. All interested children were asked to submit a drawing and a name. A biracial committee of administrators chose three finalists from all submissions, and every student could vote for his or her favorite.

The nearly equal representation of blacks and whites in Wexler's student body was clearly conducive to the development of equal status relations between black and white students, for if either group forms too large a majority it becomes much easier for that group to gain a monopoly on desirable positions. Of course, the mere fact that a student body is about half black does not guarantee that formal and informal status will be equally distributed. For example, in many desegregated schools, students are sorted into specific classes on the basis of standardized test scores and grades, with black students frequently being disproportionately represented in the less advanced classes. A school that is 50 percent black but has most of its black students in the slow classes can hardly be said to provide both groups of students with equal status.

At Wexler, the formal organization of students into teams and classroom groups generally avoided making such distinctions between groups of students. For example, in the sixth grade, students were assigned to teams essentially randomly with respect to their achievement test scores. Then, within each team, students were initially grouped into classes in a way that guaranteed moderate heterogeneity, that is, students with the lowest scores were grouped with students with average scores to form a class. Students with the next lowest scores were grouped with others who were slightly above average, and so on. Hence, the range of scores within each class was restricted somewhat, but there were no obvious "slow" or "fast" classes.

In March of Wexler's first year, one team of sixth grade teachers decided to regroup their classes in order to reduce the range of abilities within each classroom. They felt that the adoption of a plan that grouped students on the basis of similarity in academic achievement would make it easier to teach effectively. However, the vice-principal for the sixth grade, Ms. Kent, refused to let them go ahead primarily because their plan would have tended to resegregate students within the team. A similar reorganization plan on the part of another sixth grade team was also dropped about this time because of the vice-principal's opposition. This plan would have resulted in two "slow" classes, one "fast," and two "intermediate" ones. The "slow" classes would have been almost 90 percent black and the "fast" class about 80 percent white.

Wexler generally did not use a tracking system to divide students into academically homogeneous classes, but there were some exceptions to this rule. Such groups tended to be either predominately white or black. For example, over 75 percent of the students in the prestigious accelerated academic program in the eighth grade were white. This was so in spite of the fact that somewhat lower cut-off points on standardized tests were used for black students than for white.* The enriched academic program in the sixth and seventh

---

*I have no official verification of this statement from school authorities. However, teachers and other school staff in a good position to know about the selection procedure maintain that this is the case.

grades also had a disproportionate number of whites. However, the imbalance was not as obvious as in the eighth grade since children were in these classes for the equivalent of just one day a week. In sharp contrast to the various accelerated classes, classes for the educable mentally retarded were typically over 70 percent black.

Although Wexler was different from many desegregated schools in providing an environment that encouraged relatively equal formal status for blacks and whites, it was quite similar to many others in that its white students were, on the average, of markedly higher socioeconomic status than its black students. Because individual school records with information pertaining to socioeconomic status were not available for inspection, it is difficult to be precise about the extent of this difference. However, a number of rather crude measures of this disparity will be mentioned to give the reader some idea of the difference between the two populations. These comparisons are based on a randomly selected group of 350 sixth graders. Similar information gathered on other groups of Wexler students suggests that the differences outlined below are quite typical of those found between the school's black and white students more generally. The black and white students, on the average, came from communities with very different characteristics. Census block statistics show that the average level of education was noticeably higher in the white children's communities than in those of the black children. Specifically the former were characterized by an average level of education of about 13.3 years compared to 11.3 in the latter. This difference is quite significant since it means, of course, that in the black children's communities the average level of education was less than graduation from high school, whereas in the white children's neighborhoods the average adult had had a significant amount of post-high school education. Income differentials between the areas were even more striking, with the average income in the white areas being almost 150 percent of that in the black areas. Enrollment figures in the school lunch program suggested that these overall community differences were reflected in the financial position of the children's families themselves. Over 60 percent of the black children qualified for the school's free or reduced-price lunch program compared to roughly 25 percent of the whites. Indeed, it is not inaccurate to say that many of the white children at Wexler were the sons and daughters of Waterford's professional and intellectual elite. Affluent, generally liberal, and often Jewish, many of these children's parents were doctors, lawyers, and professors. Although there were certainly black children at the school from similarly well-educated and financially secure families, the proportion was small. A much greater proportion came from poor or working-class families.

In view of the rather marked differences in average socioeconomic status between whites and blacks at Wexler, it should not be surprising that whites, on the average, tended to outperform their black classmates academically. During the school's first year, nearly 40 percent of the sixth graders were classified as gifted on the basis of standardized tests. The school's principal reported that "virtually all" of these students were white. Whites as a group consistently scored roughly one standard deviation above the black students on a variety of standardized tests of intellectual ability and achievement.

Since both academic performance and socioeconomic background were quite highly correlated with race at Wexler, as is the case in many U.S. schools, it was difficult to judge the extent to which race per se functioned as Cohen has demonstrated it can to affect power and influence patterns. However, it was clear that whether because of race, class, academic performance, or some combination of these three factors, whites were in a rather advantaged position in Wexler's classrooms.

In summary, Wexler's staffing policy, location, newness, and its racially balanced student body were all conducive to providing relatively equal status for blacks and whites within the school. However, there were rather striking differences in the background characteristics and average level of academic performance of the black and white students, which meant that they clearly did not bring equal status characteristics with them to Wexler. The impact of this fact on peer relations is explored at some length in Chapter 3.

Cooperation and Competition at Wexler

To examine cooperation and competition at Wexler, it is crucial to distinguish between the academic and the nonacademic spheres. In the academic sphere, the school's philosophy emphasized individualized instruction, which neither encourages competition nor requires cooperation among students. The principal stated his goals clearly in an interview during the first year.

We want a more open approach, an individual approach. . . . Someday the teams will have all the walls open, learning centers throughout their areas. The teacher [will be] a resource person, a guide — not standing up and lecturing. The idea is to get kids motivated to move at their own pace. . . . This is what I want to see happen. An open education program — open, humanistic, and individualized.

As is clear from the principal's almost visionary statement, individualized instruction was far from an accomplished fact at Wexler. Rather it was a goal that the principal valued highly and kept in mind in selecting and training the staff. A certain amount of individualization of instruction did occur. More frequent, though, were traditional teaching methods that were quite conducive to encouraging competition between students. For example, teachers often posed questions to the entire class and then selected one student to answer. Frequently, in this type of situation, the children vied to be called upon.

The teacher says, "If you have 400 and 90 and 7½, how much would that be total?" He calls on Dan (black), whose hand is not raised. Dan doesn't know the answer. Three children, all white, are waving their hands in the air. Mr. Little persists with Dan and writes the three figures on the board. By this time there are six white and two black children waving their hands in the air. You can hear little moans of excitement and pleas like, "Call on me." Finally, Dan gets the answer. This class is roughly two-thirds black.

Another practice conducive to promoting competition was the posting of honor rolls and the public reading of grades. Although the principal discouraged the use of honor rolls in Wexler's first years because of his concern over potentially invidious comparisons between students, many teachers felt such public acknowledgment of achievement was an important motivational tool. So, for example, one black teacher made a poster upon which he wrote the names of students who did especially well on tests. The poster was headed "Super Mathematicians" in large block letters and was placed prominently in the front of his room. Other teachers, who did not believe in fostering competition, nonetheless, at least occasionally, behaved in ways that seemed bound to promote it.

Interviewer: How important is competition as a motivation for students? When do you like to use it and when wouldn't you?
Ms. Winters (white): Sometimes it gets obnoxious. Some of the better

students use it as a social popularity kind of thing. . . . So, I don't like to play up the competition. I feel that in too many cases it is more detrimental than it is beneficial. The students that are able seem to have natural competition . . . or they have gotten it from . . . their parents or one of the schools they were in. They just seem to have a drive to compete. But it works against the . . . slower students. . . .

Interviewer: Would you say competition is the same for blacks and whites or do you see more comparing in one group or the other?

Ms. Winters: No, it is the same. . . . The happiest day is when I publicly read the list of grades. They just love it. They want to know what everybody did. . . . Like if I'm grading a test . . . I read off the grades. . . . They don't want to do something unless there's going to be a grade.

Interviewer: Is that the same for poor students as well as the good ones?

Ms. Winters: Yes. . . . They are very conscious of success.

Interviewer: Well now, the kids who got a "D" or an "E" on today's test. . . .

Ms. Winters: I wouldn't read that out. . . . I don't read out D's or E's. . . . I read out a list of grades and say, "People whose names I didn't call out know what they got." That way they aren't identified.

A few teachers specifically set out to find ways of promoting cooperation between children. Some of these teachers tried to create opportunities for cooperation between blacks and whites. For example, Mr. Little assigned his students to racially and sexually mixed groups of six, each of which shared a small table. Oftentimes he actively encouraged cooperation in pursuit of individual academic goals. In addition, he sometimes fostered cooperation toward a shared goal by devices as simple as dismissing children at each table as a group when all of them were ready to go.

Mr. Little says, "Well, it's almost time to go. Which table is ready?" Students from all tables look up at him and about half . . . are frantically waving their hands in the air. Mr. Little says, "OK, it's table A first today. You look cleaned up."

In summary, Wexler's staff used a wide variety of teaching techniques, which varied greatly in the extent to which they fostered cooperation between black and white students. Nonetheless, it seems fair to say that with the emphasis on individualized instruction and the conscious attempt to downplay competition on the part of at least some teachers, Wexler provided an environment that was less likely to foster competition than many schools. As will become apparent in Chapter 3, in which the impact of various teaching techniques on intergroup relations is discussed in more detail, academic competition was still quite noticeable in most classrooms.

The school did a great deal to foster cooperation between children outside their academic classes. Some of the activities planned for Wexler's students required cooperation like that discussed by Sherif — joint activity to achieve otherwise unobtainable but highly valued goals. For example, a large number of students were involved in fund raising activities to purchase equipment for extracurricular activities. Children in the band, for instance, sold candles to buy uniforms. Also, approximately 75 percent of the black and white students in two homerooms observed in this study participated actively in a candy sale by selling anywhere from 1 to 19 boxes of candy in order to raise money for supplies for a broad range of club activities. The fact that the school was new greatly increased the number of opportunities for students to be cooperatively involved in working for such shared goals.

Wexler built time into its school day for in-school clubs and special nonacademic activities designed to help students get acquainted with each other. Several times a week, students went to these "club" periods to participate in activities ranging from blue jeans decorating to poetry reading. Some of these groups were segregated, or nearly so, reflecting both prior friendship patterns and culturally influenced differences in the interests of black and white students. However, since some of the expenses for these activities, as well as the extracurricular program, were paid for by a local foundation interested in promoting positive race relations, strong efforts were made to insure that most of the groups were racially mixed.

Although students worked on individual projects in some of these clubs, most clubs had at least some activities in which cooperation was necessary. In some cases, a minimal amount of cooperation, such as that required for taking turns in using a shared resource to work on individual projects, was all that was required. However, many activities fostered much more intensive cooperation to achieve shared goals. A notable example was the preparation and presentation of a Broadway musical. Small groups of students took responsibility for making costumes, arranging props, planning the lighting, learning the music, and so on. Their combined efforts resulted in several well-received public performances that could never have occurred without the work of a great many individuals.

In summary, then, Wexler's in-school clubs and its after-school program provided unusually good opportunities for black and white children to be involved in various types of cooperative activities. All students participated in the in-school clubs, and enrollment in the after-school program was high, with over 40 percent of all students typically participating. Wexler's academic program downplayed competition more than is typical in many schools, yet with few exceptions could hardly be said to emphasize cooperation to an unusual degree.

Support of Authorities for Positive Intergroup Relations at Wexler

There were four categories of individuals of obvious importance as authorities whose attitudes and behavior were likely to have an impact on peer relations at Wexler: (a) Waterford School Board members and other visible community leaders whose words appeared on TV and in newspapers, (b) school-level administrators such as the principal and vice-principals, (c) teachers, and (d) the parents of students attending the school. The research allowed assessment of the stance of some of these types of individuals more precisely than that of others. All, however, seemed to show at least some support for positive intergroup relations at Wexler.

School Board members made numerous highly publicized pronouncements about Wexler's excellence as an academic institution and as a milieu that would promote interracial harmony. This emphasis on the part of school authorities and visible community members was captured vividly at the ceremony held to dedicate the school shortly after it opened. The proceedings were opened by a rabbi who expressed in his invocation the hope that the school would foster social justice and equality between blacks and whites. After brief remarks by the principal, a flag, donated to the school by a local American Legion post, was accepted for the school by a white girl, a black boy and an oriental boy. Some musical selections by a racially mixed chorus followed. The second song was introduced by a black girl who said, "This song was sung by teenagers in California in 1955 . . . by teenagers of all races and origins, so it is especially appropriate to our new school. The words of the song are, 'Let there be peace on earth and let it begin with me.' " Other excerpts from the notes taken at the ceremony show how the theme of positive intergroup relations was emphasized again and again.

> The widowed husband of Mrs. Wexler [a white woman known for her dedication to civil rights activities, after whom the school was named] continued: "I can picture my wife looking down from on high and casting a blessing on what we are doing today. Her whole life was dedicated to people of all races and creeds. . . . This school is a living memorial to what she stood for — equality of the races, equality of education, and equality of hope and understanding." Next the Superintendent of Schools listed "The Ten Golden Rules" he wanted Wexler's faculty and staff to remember. . . . Rule number eight was, "Planned intergroup activities are essential."

Perhaps the clearest example at the dedication ceremony of the joint efforts on the part of black and white authorities to make the school a success came in the speech of Reverend Howell, a widely respected black who was president of the School Board.

> Reverend Howell then went on to say that he had been on the naming committee for the school. When he was thinking about names, he asked his wife for suggestions. His wife, he related jocularly, said, "Be sure it's a woman! How about Harriet Wexler or Susan Truman?" After reflecting on the matter, he submitted Mrs. Wexler's name. He said, "I was very glad when I heard they decided to call it the Harriet Wexler School. I felt that I had a part. I worked with her for years."

Then, reflecting the twin themes of academic excellence and intergroup acceptance, Reverend Howell continued:

> This building is just wonderful, but it is only concrete and brick. What makes it important is what we do here. You, the students, must learn and the teachers must teach. The second thing that is important about this school is that you have to learn to live with diversity. America is not a melting pot, it never has been, and it shouldn't be. We want teachers and students to appreciate this diversity.

Students appeared to understand that school system authorities were supportive of positive intergroup relations. For example, when asked why the Board of Education arranged a three-day camp experience for prospective Wexler students in the summer before school opened, three-fourths of the students interviewed stated spontaneously that they believed the Board wanted them to make new friends. However, more salient for students' everyday lives were individuals like their principal and their teachers. The principal, Mr. Reuben, made clear time and again his commitment to fostering positive intergroup relations. For example, in the very first faculty meeting held after the school opened, he emphasized this point.

> Mr. Reuben started the meeting by reading from a book about the middle school concept and then reading excerpts from a handbook on affective education (AE) classes. He said the purpose of the AE's is to help children get to know each other, making quite a point of his belief that this sort of goal is perhaps even more important than learning "complicated algebra equations." He said . . . that learning to get along with different groups of people . . . might well never be picked up if it isn't learned by Wexler's students now. . . . He charged the teachers with the responsibility for planning activities which would let the black and white students come to know each other.

Mr. Reuben not only exhorted the teachers to help promote positive relations between black and white children but also conveyed the importance of this goal to students by his actions. In an interview at the end of the third month of school, the usually mild-mannered principal said:

> I have only seen one racial fight. . . . Two kids were fighting out in the hall during lunchtime and the white kid ended up calling the black kid a nigger several times at the top of his lungs. He and I were the only two whites in the hall with about fifty black kids. . . . I got pretty violent with the kid. . . . I grabbed him by the throat. I had to do something very strong. I brought him in the office and talked to him. He was pretty ashamed about calling the kid a name. . . . He knew he was wrong for bringing names in.

The teachers at Wexler were virtually unanimous in believing that racially motivated negative behavior should not be tolerated. They did vary markedly, however, in the extent to which they were actively committed to fostering positive intergroup relations. As will be discussed in more detail in the next chapter, the majority felt that their major and perhaps only responsibility was teaching academic material as efficiently and effectively as possible and that any special emphasis on positive relations between blacks and whites was either unnecessary or unwise. This attitude was typified by a statement made by Mr. Dunne, a white mathematics teacher, in an interview about his teaching goals and philosophy.

> Being a teacher, I guess academics is more important [than personal or social development] . . . . I think we were told once that we shouldn't be concerned that much in sixth grade with the academics of the children who aren't too socialized yet, you know. . . . It was presented to us that socialization, them getting along with each other, black, white or from other areas, is the important skill development right now and the academic is secondary. . . . I think teachers say, "Yea, yea, right, sure," and then they go and teach, try to teach.

Some teachers, both black and white, took a view more consistent with Mr. Reuben's stance. However, quite a number of these teachers felt uncertain as to how to achieve their nonacademic goals in the classroom.

> Ms. Winters (white), referring to teaching black and white children to get along with each other, remarked, "Some of the socialization processes are really needed. . . . A lot of times I'm at a loss as to how to get across."

Parents are also authorities whose attitudes toward intergroup relations are likely to be important. The extent to which the parents of Wexler's students valued interracial schooling as opposed to tolerating it varied widely. For example, on a local television special about Wexler aired in November of the school's first year, just one of the five parents speaking, a black woman, specifically gave the fact that the school was interracial as a major reason for enrolling her child there. The other parents, both black and white, stressed the academic programs. One of the white parents said that she had been "locked into" sending her child to Wexler because she wanted her daughter, who had been admitted to the accelerated program in the eighth grade, to participate in it. Rather ironically, as illustrated by the following excerpt from an interview with a sixth grader, quite a number of sixth and seventh graders appeared to have enrolled in this "model" integrated school so that they could gain access to the highly regarded and predominantly white accelerated classes when they were eighth graders.

Interviewer: Was there anything in particular that appealed to you about Wexler?

Bill (white): Well, my mother wanted me to [come] because there's an accelerated program here [in the eighth grade].

In summary, although parental attitudes toward Wexler were not systematically studied, the evidence we did gather suggests that whereas some parents, both black and white, were very supportive of interracial schooling because of the social experiences it would provide for their children, the interracial student body was not a major attraction for all or perhaps even most parents. The fact remains, though, that all of these parents were sufficiently positive toward interracial schooling to send their children to Wexler in spite of the fact that essentially segregated public schools were readily available to most of them.

METHODOLOGY

Before moving on to trace the development of peer relations at Wexler, it seems appropriate to introduce the reader to the data-gathering and analysis procedures employed. The study began a few months before the school opened with observation of some of the summer preservice training sessions held for its teachers, and continued intensively for almost three years until the students who entered Wexler as sixth graders the year it opened graduated and headed off to high school. Whole books have been written on the complex methodological issues encountered in observational research of the sort described here. Similarly, there are many papers on specific aspects of such research, ranging from ethical issues, such as informed consent in field research (Thorne 1980; Wax 1980), to conceptual and methodological issues relating to reliability and validity (Cole, Hood, and McDermott 1978; LeCompte and Goetz 1982; Tikunoff and Ward 1978). Because of space limitations, it is impossible to discuss here all of these issues and the decisions made about how to deal with them, although brief mention will be made of some to illustrate the ways in which such problems were handled. A considerable amount of guidance is available to a researcher facing these issues. Books that had an important impact on the design and conduct of this research include Bogdan and Taylor (1975), Glaser and Strauss (1967), Lofland (1971), and Schatzman and Strauss (1973).

Observation

The primary data-gathering strategy was *intensive* and *extensive* observation in Wexler's classrooms, hallways, playgrounds, and cafeteria. Decisions about what to observe were made with three general goals in mind: (1) getting a broad picture of the experiences that students and staff had in the school; (2) exploring the extent to which Wexler attempted to meet Allport's criteria for true integration and the problems it encountered in this endeavor; and (3) mapping the developing patterns of association and friendship between black and white students and pinpointing factors that influenced those patterns.

Our observations were planned to yield a fairly comprehensive picture of what the Wexler experience was like. However, because goals two and three were so vitally important, we did not adopt strategies like time sampling to obtain observations on events in strict proportion to their frequency of occurrence or their duration. Rather, Glaser and Strauss's (1967) strategy of theoretical sampling was adopted. Hence events that appeared likely to clarify our developing understanding of social processes and relationships in the school were actively sought out and greatly "oversampled."

Information on pertinent aspects of the classes routinely observed is presented in Table 1. As can be seen, the study focused the majority of its attention on the experiences of Wexler's first sixth grade class as it progressed through the school. A secondary focus was Wexler's second group of sixth graders, especially during their first year in the school. The change in enrollment policy mentioned earlier meant that this second group of students did not volunteer to attend the school. Rather, they were assigned to it because they had attended one of about a dozen elementary schools.

During the course of the study, we routinely observed a wide variety of academic classes including social studies, math, English, and science. In addition, we observed very diverse nonacademic settings including classes such as gym, health, home economics, and art. Also routinely observed were in-school club activities and affective education periods. (Called AEs, these classes were designed to help students get to know each other, to orient them to the school, and so on.) Finally, other classes not listed on the table were observed from time to time to increase the researchers' familiarity with the broad range of experiences the students had at Wexler.

TABLE 1
Routinely Observed Classes

Year of study	Grade	Teacher's name	Teacher's race	Typical number of observation periods a week
1st	6	Mr. Hughes	Black	1½
		Ms. Monroe	Black	2½[a]
		Mr. Little	White	3[a]
		Ms. Winters	White	1
2nd	6	Mr. Hughes	Black	1
		Mr. Little	White	1/2
		Ms. Winters	White	1/2
	7	Ms. Graham	Black (VOC)[b]	1/2[c]
		Ms. Hopkins	Black	2
		Ms. Partridge	Black	2
		Ms. Campbell	White (VOC)[b]	1/2
		Mr. Cousins	White	1 1/2
		Mr. Jamison	White	1
		Mr. Mueller	White (VOC)[b]	1
3rd	8	Ms. Carone	Black (regular)	2/3
			(accelerated)	2/3
		Mr. Socker	White (regular)	2/3
			(accelerated)	2/3
		Mr. Vladimir	White (VOC)	1

Note: The ten academic teachers in whose classes we observed were distributed quite equally across math, language arts, science, and social studies.

[a]Two different types of classes, academic classes and affective education periods, were observed. This accounts for the relatively large number of observations per week in this classroom.

[b]VOC is the term used to refer to occupational, vocational, and technical classes such as shop and home economics. Also included in this category for purposes of the table are gym and health classes.

[c]Ms. Graham and Ms. Campbell were often jointly responsible for a relatively large group of students.

Source: Compiled by author.

Several factors were weighed in deciding which particular classes to observe. First, it seemed important to observe systematically a reasonably large number of groups of students so that our conclusions would not rest on events occurring in a small number of possibly atypical groups. Yet we also wanted to observe few enough classes to be able to get to know individual children's behavior patterns quite well. Second, it seemed desirable to observe at least some groups of students with more than one teacher. Third, we wanted to observe in the classrooms of a relatively large number of teachers, both white and black, and to observe in a variety of academic and nonacademic classes. Fourth, in studying the seventh grade, we decided to observe those classes containing many of the children who had been observed the prior year as sixth graders to increase our ability to assess changes in attitudes and behavior over time. This was made possible by the school's policy of keeping the composition of a particular team of students relatively stable as the students moved from sixth to seventh grade. Finally, practical considerations like the efficient use of observers' time and teachers' willingness to participate in the study also had some influence on scheduling decisions. As Table 1 shows, during the course of the study, routine observations were conducted in the classrooms of six black and eight white teachers. A total of more than twenty different groups of children were systematically observed in the study's three years, although some children and groups of children were in more than one of these groups.

Observation of teachers meeting with each other and with administrators was also carried out intensively. For example, during the first year of study, an observer regularly attended the weekly planning meeting of one sixth grade team as well as the sixth grade house meetings and the all-school faculty meetings. Seventh and eighth grade house meetings were also observed on a less regular basis, as were a great many special events ranging from teachers' workshops to parents' nights.

With occasional exceptions, observers took extensive notes as they sat in a classroom or meeting. Shortly after each observation session, these notes were dictated and transcribed. One clear problem with the use of such notes as a data base is that an observer cannot hope to record literally everything that happens. Hence a major source of potential bias is the possibility of selective recording of certain types of events. Although this problem is impossible to surmount completely in qualitative observation, there are some steps that can be taken to minimize its negative effect. For example, we found it useful to have two researchers observe a particular setting both simultaneously and separately. Thorough discussion of differences between the two observers' notes helped to point out individual biases or preconceptions. Another technique that seemed useful in reducing the effect of such biases was to seek out data that undercut the developing assessment of a situation.

Unwarranted inferences made by the observer can also be a potentially serious source of bias. To deal with this problem, care was taken to make the field notes as factual and as concretely descriptive as possible. For example, instead of or in addition to saying that a child is angry, one can record the behavioral manifestations of anger such as a loud voice and a frown. Transcribed field notes were continuously monitored to keep observers aware of the importance of such procedures.

A third source of potential problems in research like that described here is that the people who are being observed will act differently because of the observer's presence. To minimize the probability of an observer's presence causing important changes in the very social processes that that researcher is attempting to record and analyze, we gave careful attention to developing a role in the school's social system that caused as little interference as possible. We presented ourselves to students as individuals from a university who were interested in what happens in school and how children like school. We took great pains not to be seen by the students as authority figures because it was felt this would inhibit their openness and spontaneity. Hence we made it a rule never to interfere with or comment on a student's behavior unless we felt that clear physical danger for a child was imminent. Our success in cultivating a relatively unobtrusive role is attested to in the following excerpt from the field notes:

> Today as I entered the sixth grade house as classes were changing, I saw Richard and another black male whom I don't know tussling. After glancing at me, Richard's companion drew away from him and leaned over as if to pick up his books on the floor. Richard said, "Aw, come on, she just writes. She never does anything." He then gave his companion a light shove and they were at it again.

Similarly, considerable effort was expended in building rapport with the teachers and gaining their trust so that they would speak and act freely in our presence. Several factors appeared crucial to achieving this goal, including noninterference in events in the classroom, a nonjudgmental and sympathetic attitude, careful guarding of confidentiality, and reciprocity. Again, the success we had in building and maintaining a role that gave us access to crucial information is best attested to by the type of information teachers made available to us. For example, one teacher told us that she had purposely miscounted votes in a closely contested student election so that a "responsible child" (a white boy) was declared the winner rather than an "unstable child" (a black girl). The teacher said that she was uncertain about the appropriateness of this action and therefore did not plan to tell even other teachers about it. Another time, an observer attended a meeting at which teachers planned how to handle a difficult situation with a parent. Together the teachers arranged a story that varied widely from what they had just told the observer had actually happened. The story, concocted in hushed whispers after one teacher had checked to make certain no one was in the hallways, presented the teachers in a more favorable light than did the actual events as related to the observer and revealed in the teachers' discussion.

In spite of our efforts to influence the behavior of Wexler's students and staff as little as possible, there were times, especially in the first months of the research, when it was obvious that the presence of a researcher influenced or disrupted the normal flow of events. Careful note was taken of such situations for three reasons. First, it was often possible to find ways to disrupt normal behavior patterns less markedly. Second, study of such situations suggested topics about which individuals or groups at Wexler were especially sensitive and thus raised interesting research issues. Finally, noting that specific behaviors appeared to occur because of an observers' presence lessened the likelihood that such behaviors would be confused later in the data analysis phase of the research with behaviors that appeared to be quite uninfluenced by the presence of a researcher.

The research team conducting the observations and the other data-gathering activities varied somewhat from year to year. Two social psychologists, the author and Andrew Sagar, a white graduate student, were active observers during the entire study. Strong efforts were made to insure that the research team in any given year included both black and white graduate students and that at least some of the team members were from fields such as sociology or education. Since blacks did not constitute a full 50 percent of the research team, the time of the black team members was disproportionately devoted to the interviews, most especially to the student interviews, since it seemed reasonable to expect that the data obtained in face-to-face interviews, often on explicitly race-related issues, would be more influenced by the researcher's race than would that obtained through observation in desegregated classrooms.

Interviews

Observers, no matter how omnipresent or insightful, are at a great disadvantage if they do not test their emerging ideas through direct inquiry with those whom they are observing. Because interviews can be so useful in providing the participants' perspectives on events, both formal and informal interviews were used extensively. For instance, the five teachers on each of the two teams being observed in Wexler's first year were each formally interviewed individually. Similarly, in the second year, interviews were conducted with eight seventh grade teachers and eight sixth grade teachers. The depth and breadth of these interviews are suggested by the fact that the average single-spaced typed transcript of these interviews is over twenty pages long. Other school personnel, such as the principal, the sixth and seventh grade vice-principals, the social worker in charge of all club and after-school activities, and non-academic teachers, were interviewed formally at least once each year. These interviews were structured to insure that specific topics were covered. However, the questions were generally open-ended in format to maximize each respondent's freedom to discuss the question precisely as he or she saw it.

Two panels of students were also interviewed intensively. The first panel of 20 students was chosen from those who entered Wexler's sixth grade when the school first opened. These students were interviewed at the beginning and end of their first year and at the end of their second and third years. The second panel, of 24 students, was chosen from the children who entered Wexler as sixth graders under the new enrollment policy in the school's second year. These students were interviewed in the fall and the spring of sixth grade and in the spring of seventh grade. Both groups of children were randomly selected from the students in whose classes we observed, using a sampling system designed to obtain equal representation of blacks and whites as well as boys and girls. All children were interviewed by a person of their own race. All formal interviews were tape recorded and then transcribed.

Other Data-Gathering Methods

The detailed observation of social processes and repeated interviews with students and staff were supplemented by a wide variety of other data-gathering techniques designed to yield information on the broader context in which intergroup relations developed. To illustrate, copies of the school's daily bulletin as well as of the letters Wexler sent home to parents were carefully collected. Also, officially sanctioned wall decorations like posters and mottoes, as well as unofficial ones like bathroom graffiti, were systematically noted.

DATA ANALYSIS

Space does not allow full discussion of the many varied techniques employed in collecting and analyzing the data on which this book is based. However, three general principles that guided the research must be mentioned. First, both data-gathering and analysis were as rigorous and systematic as possible. For example, sampling techniques were employed where appropriate; trained coders who were unaware of the race and sex of particular respondents coded the open-ended interviews using reliable systems developed for this research; field notes were carefully indexed so that all notes relevant to a given topic could be examined.

Second, we took very seriously the importance of triangulating the data (Webb et al. 1966). That is, great care was taken to gather many different types of information bearing on the same issue, to minimize the potential problems with each data source, and to be sensitive in analyzing and interpreting the data to biases that could not be completely eliminated. To illustrate this point, some of the types of data underlying the point made in Chapter 4 that blacks were seen by both black and white children as tougher and as more likely to break rules than whites will be briefly mentioned. First, there were the data mentioned in that chapter drawn from systematic coding of the responses of 80 randomly selected black and white sixth grade boys to questions about what differences, if any, they saw between black and white children. Several other pieces of evidence came from interviews with the over 40 sixth and seventh graders who were part of the two panels of students interviewed in the study's second year. Open-ended responses to questions like "What kinds of kids are most likely to fight?" were coded and analyzed. Appropriate statistical analyses were also performed on relevant quantitative data obtained directly from students in these interviews, such as students' estimates of the number of black and white children suspended each year from school.

Since suspensions are a reflection of the school's disciplinary procedures as well as students' behaviors, these interviews also explored whether students felt the disproportionate suspension of black students, of which they were well aware, stemmed from black students' behavioral tendencies or from unfair school practices. Actual suspension rates, teachers' perceptions of these rates, and teachers' thoughts about why rates were higher for blacks than whites were also investigated. Finally, the field notes were systematically examined for (1) incidents of serious rule-breaking and rough physical play and (2) discussion of such topics by children, including threats made by students either to peers or to teachers.

The third general principle that we took very seriously was that data analysis should be an on-going and iterative process. As the field notes and other data accumulated, they were indexed, read, and reread. Informal working memos were written, and data relevant to ideas emerging from the early stages of analysis were actively sought in planned and systematic ways. A good illustration of this process comes from the search for data relevant to the "taboo" theme, which will be discussed in the next chapter. This theme emerged as I worked to organize the data from the project's first year although I had certainly not anticipated the emergence of a norm virtually prohibiting reference to race in the school. As the potential importance of this norm in influencing the development of relations between students became more and more apparent, we set about gathering further data on the topic. Both quantitative and qualitative questions on this theme were added to the formal student interviews. Similarly, teachers' opinions on the use of racial references were further probed in formal interviews as well as in everyday conversations. Finally, the first rather informal analysis of when and where the taboo appeared to be broken was expanded and systematized as we searched the complete set of field observations for every relevant instance.

A NOTE ON READING THIS BOOK

The data analysis described above was basically a search for patterns and for connections between them. The rest of this book explores these patterns and their linkages. Since race and gender were so salient to Wexler's students and influenced both behavioral styles and modes of interaction, many of the patterns discussed in succeeding chapters contrast white and black students or boys and girls. Although race- and gender-linked patterns clearly emerged, it is important to recognize that each child had a unique set of experiences at Wexler and brought a unique personality to that set of experiences. Thus, although there is strong evidence to support the patterns outlined, it must be emphasized that each student undoubtedly reacted and behaved in an individual manner and that the general statements made do not, of course, apply with equal force to every member of a particular group. The same caveat applies to statements made about adults connected with Wexler such as teachers and parents. I have attempted throughout the book to keep the reader aware of this diversity by mentioning exceptions to patterns and discussing the varied responses of students to particular situations.

2

THE TEACHERS' IDEOLOGY

The primary focus of this book is the development of social relations among Wexler's students. Yet in order to understand these relations it is necessary to be aware of the context in which they evolved. Chapter 1 provided one type of context by briefly describing the history of desegregation efforts in Waterford as well as by discussing the extent to which Wexler provided a milieu that, according to social psychological theory, might be expected to be conducive to positive intergroup relations. This chapter further sets the context for the coming exploration of interaction patterns between black and white students by discussing in some detail a set of beliefs, value positions, and assumptions widely shared by Wexler's teachers that I shall characterize as the teachers' ideology. Not all of the teachers, of course, subscribed to all parts of the ideology described here. Furthermore, since the major concerns of this book are the attitudes and behaviors of students, I have not attempted to characterize comprehensively all of the beliefs, values, and assumptions shared by the teachers. Rather, I have concentrated on four aspects of the teachers' ideology that appeared to be especially important in shaping the evolution of peer relations through their impact on the teachers' everyday words and behavior.

THE ACADEMICS FIRST, LAST, AND ONLY ORIENTATION

Wexler was presented to the public as a model of both academic excellence and carefully planned integration. Since the faculty were carefully selected on the basis of judgments about their ability to work effectively in a desegregated setting as well as their teaching skills, most of them were basically in favor of desegregated schooling. The vast majority of the teachers took their responsibilities in the academic sphere very seriously.* In contrast, a much smaller proportion felt they had any major role to play in shaping positive relations between blacks and whites beyond keeping their classrooms reasonably orderly, as they would strive to do in any school. It is hardly surprising that Wexler's teachers felt their first responsibility was to teach academic material. That is, after all, an understanding of their role that is reflected in its very name. Indeed, teachers who do not take their academic responsibilities seriously would not be suitable staff for any school, let alone one that purports to be a model of academic excellence. However, important consequences for the evolution of intergroup relations resulted from the fact that many of the teachers focused virtually exclusively on academic achievement and tended to see maximizing achievement as potentially in conflict with or, at the very least, as unrelated to the school's second goal of fostering positive relations between black and white students. Before analyzing these consequences I will discuss more thoroughly the teachers' attitudes toward achievement and the origins of these attitudes.

Although Wexler's principal often stressed the importance of the social outcomes of schooling, a large majority of its faculty, as indicated above, clearly saw teaching academic or other task-related skills as their overriding, indeed even their only, mission. Mr. Dunne, quoted in Chapter 1, exemplifies this point of view, as does the following excerpt from an interview with a sixth grade reading teacher.

---

*A distinction was made at Wexler between teachers of traditional academic subjects like English, math, and science and those in other fields such as health, shop, and music. The orientation described in this section was present in both types of teachers with regard to the subject matter that they taught. Thus, the term *academic* is used broadly here to apply to the material covered in Wexler's classes regardless of its specific nature. I have adopted this practice to avoid cumbersome repetition of phrases like "academics and other course-related skills." The only caveat that needs to be kept in mind is that the external pressure reinforcing this orientation from sources such as students and parents appeared to be somewhat stronger in the basic academic courses than in the others.

Ms. Sharp (white): I really feel that the school is an academic setting. Quite frankly I think that's what its primary function is. I think it is good for the children to interact socially . . . but I'm coming from an academic point of view. My emphasis is on academics. I believe a school should have an academic orientation.

Some teachers like Mr. Dunne and Ms. Sharp gave top priority to academics and paid little attention to the impact of their decisions on relations between black and white children because they believed that total concentration on the traditional curriculum is the only appropriate behavior for a teacher. Others emphasized academics primarily because they saw success in this area as vitally important in and of itself, but secondarily because they believed success or failure in this realm has an important impact on children's personal and social development. Ms. Shore, another white teacher, articulated this view.

Quite frankly, on our team the kids who are the poorest readers and the poorest academic students are the same children that are always being suspended. . . . I am not saying that they are mentally retarded, but their achievement level is very low. And if they are constantly frustrated in class day in and day out, and many times they are, they take all their problems out on other kids around them. You see it in the halls where these kids are hitting on other kids or trying to boost them out of their lunch tickets just to show how tough they are . . . to achieve some status . . . or prestige.

Ms. Shore and others emphasized the importance of academic failure as a cause of discipline problems and saw academic improvement as a possible cure. However, very few of the teachers paid much attention to the fact that the obvious difference in the average level of academic performance of the black and white children was a source of racial friction, as will be discussed in detail in the next chapter.

The teachers' inclination to stress academic achievement and to ignore the impact of their teaching methods on most aspects of peer relations was reinforced by numerous factors. Hence those teachers who were interested in adopting practices that led to more interracial interaction were often pressured to focus exclusively on achievement and to avoid unfamiliar teaching methods. Nontraditional classroom procedures such as cooperative work groups were resisted because they were perceived as undermining academic progress for the sake of social goals. Not too surprisingly, teachers were generally unaware of the large body of research that has accumulated in the last decade suggesting that, when carefully structured, such groups can improve the achievement of slower students without impeding that of their more advanced peers (Sharan 1980; Slavin 1980). Pressures that reinforced the almost exclusive emphasis on academics and the failure to see links between the social environment of the classroom and children's ability and willingness to learn came from parents, from the students themselves, and from certain structural features of the school.

Parents, especially white parents, reacted vociferously when they heard of practices they believed were not conducive to the absolute maximization of their children's immediate academic achievement. For example, Ms. Partridge, a black teacher of mathematics who was more concerned about relations between black and white students than were most, set up learning stations where students who were done with their regular work could undertake unusual extra math-related projects. She said of these projects:

> I thought they were nice little extra credit things . . . like making graphs and counting things. . . . It was a way the kids could socialize. These projects don't really have the pressure of word problems. . . . It was a way of doing things related to math, and the kids could get to know each other because some of the slower children could work on some of these things along with the faster ones.

These projects were clearly designed to promote cooperative inter-action on a relatively equal status basis between students with different achievement levels. For example, one project on elementary probability theory required finding out each other's birthdays. However, some parents strongly objected to such projects.

> *Ms. Partridge* (black): I had several parents call the principal and say, "What does this have to do with math?" They felt . . . that . . . an extra credit assignment should deal with the basics or with getting a child prepared for algebra. Especially with the brighter students, the parents were concerned with getting them into the accelerated program next year. . . . There is a pressure there. . . . Last year I was really amazed that students who got a B+ were highly upset. They said, "My parents will kill me. . . ." I felt that if some of the parents felt so strongly about the [learning] stations I should discontinue them.
> *Interviewer*: Could you identify this pressure [as coming] from the parents of one race more than the other, or . . .

Ms. Partridge: Definitely. It seems to be more the white parents. . . . I don't know whether our black parents don't really understand what's going on here or do not put so much emphasis on A's or B's. . . . I think so many of our black parents feel that their children are coming from inferior schools . . . they don't do as much pushing.

The children, too, were quick to react when they felt that their individual academic progress was being sacrificed to promote another's achievement or social goals. An incident from Mr. Jamison's class illustrates this clearly. Mr. Jamison organized most of his social studies classes in a traditional manner. However, he occasionally set up racially and sexually mixed committees to perform joint projects such as making maps. Students often resisted his efforts in this direction both because it made it difficult for them to sit with their friends and because some students felt it impeded their academic progress.

The tables are set up for committee work today. At one table sit David, Howard, and Keith, the only white boys in the class today. Five of the six black boys present are sitting together at another table. . . . Two white girls and two black girls are seated at the only racially mixed table. Another table seats five black girls. . . . Mr. Jamison announces a committee consisting of Eric (black), Fred (black), Howard (white), Stacey (black), and Leona (black). Howard says, "I don't get along with any of them. . . ." There are continued complaints from numerous children about the committee assignments. Mr. Jamison says, "What's involved in a committee assignment? Am I asking you to hold hands? You don't even have to work together except to stand up and give a report." Howard and David object to being split up. The teacher replies, "You two have always been together." They answer, "And, we've done good work too." Mr. Jamison replies, "I'm not arguing with that. I need you separate this time." When class is dismissed Howard is the last one out. . . . As he leaves he says in a disgruntled tone, "I came here for my own education, not for somebody else's."

Wexler's principal, Mr. Reuben, often stressed the importance of intergroup relations in his dealings with the teachers, as previously mentioned. However, there were strong structural forces at work that reinforced the teachers' tendency to emphasize academics to the exclusion of all other goals. The most obvious of these were the standardized tests in reading and mathematics given at the beginning and the end of each school year. The Board of Education routinely published statistics from these tests on each school by grade level.

When Mr. Reuben discussed the administration of tests with the teachers at a faculty meeting he assured them that individual teachers would not be judged by the gains their students made. One teacher sitting behind an observer murmured, "Yea, yea. Who's going to believe that?" Wexler, like most other schools, had no equivalent test to measure the development of interracial attitudes or interaction patterns over the course of the year.

The role definitions of teachers, counselors, and vice-principals as prescribed by middle school practice in Waterford and as implemented at Wexler were also conducive to teachers' ignoring nonacademic matters. Specifically, teachers were instructed to refer students who were having difficulty adjusting to the school or to each other to the counselors. Furthermore, the vice-principals, not the teachers, decided when an offense was serious enough to warrant suspension. In fact, Vice-principal Kent told the sixth grade faculty that it was inappropriate for them even to make recommendations about suspensions. In a faculty meeting two months after Wexler opened, she stated emphatically, "It is the vice-principal's prerogative to decide who gets suspended and who does not." Further emphasizing the fact that teachers were of little importance in the process, she said that she would post suspensions in her office when she had made her decisions. This meant, of course, that she did not personally let the teachers know the outcomes of cases referred to her and that teachers had to go out of their way to find out promptly about her decisions. So, although the teachers were often exhorted to be concerned about the students' personal and social development, real responsibility for many such aspects of the students' lives was taken from them. Finally, many of the teachers who had come from positions in elementary schools felt swamped by the sheer number of children they had to deal with in a day. They tended to believe that it was impossible to get to know the roughly 125 students on their team well enough to do anything above and beyond their most basic and important job, that of teaching their subject matter.

Given the personal inclination of most teachers to devote all their attention strictly to academic matters, the very real pressures in that direction from students and their parents, the widely shared failure to see linkages between achievement and the social environment of the classroom, and the structural arrangements within the school, it is hardly surprising that teachers emphasized academics to the virtual exclusion of other goals. However, the extent of this emphasis is a bit surprising in light of the school's highly publicized commitment to fostering positive intergroup relations. In fact, teachers not infrequently broke the school's rules or ignored the spirit if not the letter of its policies in their attempts to do all they could to achieve conditions that they saw as conducive to maximizing the students' academic advancement. For example, Mr. Reuben decided that, in accordance with the emphasis on noncompetitiveness and individualized instruction, academic honor rolls should not be posted. Nonetheless, some teams created honor rolls. In addition, individual teachers sometimes posted classroom honor rolls. Although setting up monthly honor rolls for "citizenship" was discussed at meetings of a student advisory committee funded with money provided through an Emergency School Assistance Act grant, this group did not implement the idea.

Teachers often objected to Mr. Reuben's insistence that classes be racially heterogeneous. Since there were major differences in black and white students' backgrounds and in their average levels of academic performance, meeting this requirement meant, in practice, that most classes would have at least a moderate degree of academic heterogeneity. Informal rearranging of classes by teachers to make them more academically homogeneous occurred on numerous occasions, in spite of the fact that this practice fostered resegregation. Also, teachers occasionally came up with classroom rosters which, while racially mixed, virtually guaranteed that the major purpose behind the mixing, the improvement of intergroup relations, would not be achieved. For example, in some cases the children with the lowest reading levels were grouped with those with the highest. This formed classes that met the administrators' demands for racial heterogeneity. Also, there was a clear academic rationale for such arrangements. Teachers argued that the top students needed little supervision and the slowest students needed the most help. Hence, by putting these groups together teachers would be able to free more time to work with the slower students than would have been possible otherwise. However, in considering whether or not to adopt this strategy, faculty members were rarely if ever observed to wonder about the impact of such great academic disparity on either intergroup relations or the academic motivation of the slower students.

The rare teachers who did seriously consider these aspects of the situation almost without exception decided that practices designed to maximize academic achievement were warranted and were likely to succeed in spite of the potential personal and social problems they might entail. One team of teachers planned to regroup their students in February of the school's first year on the basis of reading test scores. They decided to have large classes for the highest achievers and smaller classes for the slower children so that these students could get more individual attention. The "slowest" class of eighteen had only two white students in it. Mr. Little commented on the plan in the following way:

> I have mixed emotions. I can see where it has drawbacks. . . . I guess we are saying that if we want to be teachers we have to try to give them the best academic life we can. . . . There are a lot of drawbacks socially and there is going to be a stigma attached. I found that it hurts the [lower-achieving] kids for a while. After a while it doesn't if you sit down and tell them why it is done. They know they can't read. They know they are slow. Most kids will admit it and I just hope the other kids are compassionate enough not to really get on them. . . .

THE NATURAL PROGRESSION ASSUMPTION

The foregoing was not meant to imply that teachers actively attempted to subvert the basically integrationist goals of the school. Rather, the maximization of academic achievement was so vitally important in their thinking that other goals tended to be ignored or to fall by the wayside. In fact, many teachers participated willingly, even enthusiastically, in special programs designed to foster contact between black and white students, although there was some feeling on the part of a number of them that too much time was devoted to these activities. Important settings for social contact included a summer day camp program as well as the in-school and after-school clubs. Extra pay for supervising the summer program and the after-school clubs undoubtedly was a major inducement for teachers. Yet many of them also enjoyed the informal atmosphere in these nonacademic settings and the opportunity to build strong personal ties with some of their students. In supervising these programs, though, as well as in running their classes, the large majority of the teachers made what I shall call the natural progression assumption, tending to believe that mere contact, in and of itself, would bring about improved intergroup relations. Hence they saw little need to set about structuring the contact in a way designed to promote positive relations. Ms. Nobel, a math teacher, stated this point of view clearly.

> *Interviewer*: Do you think that the relations between black and white children will improve naturally as they spend more time together or do you think that specific things have to be done to push them together or to make them get along better?
>
> *Ms. Nobel* (white): I don't know if you can do anything to make them [get together]. . . . I don't think it's something you can force. . . . I think it will come in due time. . . . Nobody can be forced. . . . If they are they will be negative. . . . So I think forcing them into a situation is not good. I think it has to be free and I've already seen some that the blacks and whites have gotten together . . . they are doing things together on their own now. They didn't know each other in the beginning of the school year. So that was done very naturally. . . . There isn't going to be a race problem.

It is interesting that two of the three teachers who disagreed at all with the majority view typified by Ms. Nobel were black women, Ms. Hopkins and Ms. Partridge.

> *Interviewer*: Do you think that relations between black and white kids naturally become more positive as they spend time together or do specific things have to be done to encourage them? . . .
>
> *Ms. Partridge*: I think they do need some planning. Some of these things will normally happen but if more things were planned to bring the races closer I think we'd get there quicker, because with some of the students you'll never even get them together unless things are planned to force them together.

In addition to making the assumption of natural progression, many teachers hesitated to try actively to encourage more intergroup interaction for other reasons. For instance, a number of them argued that strenuous efforts to promote new friendships generally involved the disruption of old friendships. They felt that the students would not tolerate this and that any vigorous efforts to promote intergroup interaction would backfire by creating what Ms. Nobel referred to above as a "negative attitude." In essence, this is a "backlash" hypothesis. The desire of students to preserve autonomy in their choice of seating and working partners was obvious in the excerpt from field notes on Mr. Jamison's class presented earlier in this chapter. An even more striking example follows.

> Mr. Elliot (white) changed the seating pattern in his class because there was too much noise and problem behavior. The previous seating pattern was based on the children's own choices and was largely segregated. The new seating pattern was much more integrated. The students were unhappy with the new situation and decided to [protest]. They attended class but wouldn't answer when Mr. Elliot would ask a question or call on someone. Children who had been called on would stall or in most cases say they didn't know the answer. . . . There was a lot of nudging, elbowing, and giggling. It became apparent quickly to Mr. Elliot that something was going on. He asked what was the matter and the students told him they wanted to sit in their old seats. Mr. Elliot decided to let them return to their old seats if they would keep the noise and problem behavior down.

The few teachers who did consciously try to increase intergroup interaction in their classrooms felt forced to find subtle ways of doing so that would not create resistance or outright revolt.

> *Mr. Little* (white): I don't think you can push kids to socialize [when] they don't want to. I think it is going to cause problems. . . . I try to do it in different ways, but I don't think the kids know it is happening. I think you can pull some tricks on them. . . . It is just basically a matter of moving tables around so to do their work . . . they have to sit there and talk. . . . Some of the social studies book is so difficult that they have to work together. They have to depend on each other. . . . That's the key, you don't want the children to know what you're doing. . . .
> *Interviewer*: I'm interested in why that is. Do you think they would act negatively if they saw your real reason?
> *Mr. Little*: I wouldn't say they'd act negatively but I think they'd know the reason. . . . They might start thinking about it. It might not be a lasting type of relationship.

Although most teachers believed that increasingly positive relations would gradually evolve between black and white students, they also understood that the academic gap between the average white child in the school and the average black child posed a major impediment to this process. Indeed, when asked to think in detail about their ideas on natural progression most teachers tended to qualify their initial position that blacks and whites would interact more positively over time. Rather, they took the position that positive relations would naturally develop between black and white children from roughly similar home backgrounds and with roughly similar personalities or levels of academic performance. In light of the major social class differences between the whites and the blacks at Wexler, this sort of natural progression implies a very different overall outcome from interracial schooling than a natural progression, which operates in spite of class and school performance level barriers. Interestingly, a number of teachers seemed to feel it was inappropriate for them to try to foster strong positive relations between children who were very different.

> *Ms. Winters* (white): I don't like the ideas of having a power to influence people to the point where they would become friends. . . . I mean, [it's OK to] point out people that have common interests or similar personalities. . . . But I really . . . just wouldn't want to be the person to fix up a friendship. . . . You could say, "You collect stamps and so and so does too" or something like that. But beyond that I wouldn't feel comfortable.

Others like Ms. O'Hara believed that efforts to foster positive relations between very different types of children were sure to fail and were also inappropriate.

> *Ms. O'Hara* (white): Kids, no matter how you plan [aren't] going to [get together] because you say so. . . . Therefore, let things run their natural course and kids will get along. The kids that are good will loaf with those that are good, kids that are mischievous and rotten will loaf together too. To mix them up would be defeating the purpose of life.

THE COLORBLIND PERSPECTIVE

Wexler's faculty tended to subscribe to what Rist (1974) has called a colorblind view of interracial schooling. This perspective sees interracial education as an opportunity for class assimilation, the purpose of schooling being to give all children a fair chance to learn the skills necessary for success in a basically middle-class society. Black staff members at Wexler generally appeared to share this view with their white colleagues, as the following excerpt from an interview with one of the black vice-principals shows.

> *Vice-principal Kent*: I really don't address myself to group differences
> when I am dealing with youngsters. . . . I try to treat youngsters . . . as
> youngsters and not as black, white, green, or yellow. . . . Children
> are children and they're trying to adjust to a situation and sometimes
> they don't know how to. . . . Many of the black youngsters who have
> difficulty are the ones who . . . have come from communities where
> they had to put up certain defenses, and these defenses are the anti-
> thesis of the normal situation . . . like they find in school. It is therefore
> [difficult] getting them to become aware that they have to follow these
> rules because [they] are here . . . not over there in their community.
> . . . I think that many of the youngsters [from the] larger community
> have a more normal set of values that people generally want to see, and
> therefore do not have [as] much difficulty in coping with their school
> situation as do our black youngsters. . . . [The black children] do have
> difficulty in adjusting because they are just not used to it. Until we can
> adjustively counsel them into the right types of behavior . . . I think
> we're going to continue to have these types of problems. . . .

Mr. Dunne, a white language arts teacher, commented in a somewhat
similar vein:

> I think everyone needs to read, to speak, and to try to write correctly.
> You can talk Polish at home, or ghetto language in the street . . . but
> when you are out there in the world you have to be able to read and
> write what everyone else does, the majority. That happens to be English
> and that happens to be . . . spoken by the majority, which is white.
> . . . That's just the way it is. . . .

From the colorblind perspective it is unfair or at least inappropriate to bring up race, since it is essentially irrelevant to one's needs
and the opportunities that should be provided. Even taking note of
race is seen as an indication of possible prejudice.

> When I was arranging the student interviews I mentioned to Mr. Little
> (white) that I thought there was only one white girl in one of his
> classes. I asked if I was right about this and he said, "Well, just a
> minute. Let me check." After looking through the class roster in his
> roll book he said, "You know, you're right. I never noticed that. . . . I
> guess that's a good thing."

Our data suggest that teachers denied that they noticed children's race not only when the researchers were present but also among themselves. For example, when Mr. Jamison was complying with our request to mark down the race of his students on a class roster to enable the research team to learn students' names more quickly, he remarked, "Did you ever notice those teachers who say, 'I never notice what they are'?"

Both black and white faculty members generally agreed that race should not be used as a sorting or selection criterion even if it was only one of the various criteria used. For example, as mentioned briefly in Chapter 1, some white faculty members complained rather bitterly that a black colleague's race had played a part in the decision to appoint this person as a team leader, asserting that the black teacher was qualified but no more so than whites who had been passed over. Similarly, a black faculty member, Mr. Williams, had a continuing battle with Ms. Fowler, the white social worker in charge of the in-school clubs and the after-school activities, because his highly visible and well-regarded media crew consisted virtually entirely of white boys, even though a wide variety of students had applied for membership. Ms. Fowler argued that even if other types of students required more training they should be included. Mr. Williams, the media crew advisor, vehemently argued that he needed the best qualified group and that these students happened to be white boys. He gave in only after Ms. Fowler, who controlled the funds for the extracurricular and summer activities, said he had to choose between changing the media crew membership and losing financial support for his special projects.

In general, the administrators at Wexler, especially Mr. Reuben, seemed much more likely to consider race a valid consideration in planning and decision making than did the faculty. Perhaps one reason for this is that one of the administrators' major areas of responsibility and concern was the school's relations with the external world. For example, Mr. Reuben needed statistics to show that the school was treating blacks and whites fairly, and he needed a school that to the casual visitor looked racially balanced. The teachers, on the other hand, were more exclusively concerned with how effectively they could produce excellence in academic or other pursuits. So, for them, race seemed like a totally irrelevant criterion. Furthermore, many teachers believed that the students shared their viewpoint. Thus, they argued, bringing up race or considering it would only create problems by raising a potentially volatile issue that was not otherwise a real factor.

> *Ms. Monroe* (black): You know, I hear the things the students usually fight about. As I said before, it's stupid things like someone taking a pencil. It's not because [the other person] is black or white. . . . At this age level . . . I don't think it's black or white. . . . They just go about their daily things and don't — I don't think they think about it really. . . . I see them interacting with one another on an adult basis. . . . They are not really aware of color . . . or race or whatever.
> *Interviewer*: You really don't see that as a factor . . . in their relationships?
> *Ms. Monroe*: No.

Our data suggest that, contrary to the teachers' view, race was indeed very salient to Wexler's students. This issue will be discussed more fully later in this chapter when the impact of the teachers' ideology on peer relations is discussed.

THE CLASSROOM AS A WORLD IN ITSELF

The teachers at Wexler were, with very few exceptions, quite professional and enthusiastic about their work. However, an outsider could hardly help but notice their almost exclusive concentration on what happened in their particular classrooms, as opposed to in the school more generally. Lortie (1975) reports a similar concentration on classroom life in his study of teachers in Florida, suggesting that Wexler's teachers were not unusual in this respect. The strong emphasis on classrooms by teachers is hardly surprising since the classroom is the setting in which their responsibility and authority are maximized. However, the lack of interest in and feeling of responsibility for what happened outside the classroom was striking. For example, one of the guidance counselors complained that even though she and the principal had made strong efforts to get teachers to stand in the doorways of their classrooms to serve as monitors as children changed classes, they were largely unsuccessful. In fact, she said that just one or two of the nearly twenty academic teachers for her grade routinely did so. Similarly, after seemingly endless and basically unsuccessful efforts to have teachers monitor the lunchroom, one administrator finally started publishing a weekly schedule that assigned teachers to specific stations in the cafeteria. Undoubtedly this mechanism made it easier to see which teachers were failing to take their lunch duty as well as insuring that adults were in all areas of the cafeteria.

Interestingly, teachers often suggested that students rather than they themselves should have greater responsibility for monitoring the halls and the lunchrooms. In the course of the school's first two years there were several efforts to organize student patrols. However, these efforts generally came to nothing since the school staff was afraid that the patrols might cause as many problems as they solved. For a while a group of parent volunteers organized themselves to patrol the school's corridors. However, this program did not last very long. Eventually the school was assigned some security guards, who roamed the hallways to help keep order.

Not surprisingly given the lack of attention they paid to settings such as the hallways or stairways, many teachers felt they knew little about what happened there. Ms. Monroe's words capture well this sense of the hallways as a mysterious, vaguely threatening part of the school.

> You can never tell in the hallways what's happening exactly. You don't know what's going on. . . . When there are 600 students out there walking around going from one place to another, it's hard to tell exactly what they think.

Compounding this sense of not knowing what was happening outside the classrooms was an awareness that things could easily slip out of control in nonclassroom settings even when teachers were present. However, that lack of control was not seen as too important as long as it did not affect the classroom negatively. Indeed, sometimes teachers used problems in these areas as object lessons in how not to behave in the classroom as the following interview with a white science teacher suggests.

> I think we definitely need [doors to close off the classrooms from the hallways]. It's reached the point now where I have to stop my class many times and say, "Let's wait" [until it quiets down in the halls]. I use it as a learning experience. I say, "See that never happens here or I'll kill you." Kids look out and see others running around. You use this for a positive effect saying, "We can't do that. . . ." I'd rather have doors here and that way I can just shut it out. . . .

Even more surprisingly, teachers sometimes saw problems in other areas of the school as having a positive effect on their feelings of effectiveness.

> *Mr. Little* (white): When those kids come to my class they expect some type of security. . . . There [is] something that goes on in the common facilities area that creates problems. . . . I have no idea what. . . . I find it very pleasing, and I think it's my best year yet because the kids find security when they come to my room.
> *Interviewer*: Do you think they feel any real fear outside the classrooms?
> *Mr. Little*: I think a lot of my kids are afraid on certain occasions to go to gym [or] to walk down the ramps. . . . I remember at the beginning of the year the teachers sitting down and saying how immature these kids are. . . . But that's proved advantageous to us. . . . I enjoy kids looking to me for security. I think of that as part of teaching.

Teachers tended to see the classroom as a special world with rules all its own. Things that were tolerated outside the classroom were not tolerated inside. Thus the task for teachers was not so much to mold children's characters as to control their in-class behavior.

> *Interviewer*: Where there is a case when a white kid . . . says things that might be insulting to a black, what do you do?
> *Mr. Dunne* (white): I really don't go into it. If it's really a problem I talk to them separately or pull them aside after class. I just . . . say, "End it right here!" I tell them, "That's a thing you do out in the street, not here." I say the same when they talk loud.

Within certain limits, each teacher was seen as having the right to decide what particular rules applied within his or her room. For example, one teacher had a poster with a list of fourteen rules for classroom behavior prominently displayed in her classroom. Some of the rules were similar to those laid down in most classrooms. Rule one was, "Students will arrive at class on time." However, some required behavior quite different from that in other classrooms. For example, rule six forbade students to use the pencil sharpener or the water fountain after the first five minutes of class. Other teachers on the same team placed no similar restrictions on the students' behavior. The responsibility for acting in accordance with these rules fell on the students. When a rule was broken, the behavior of the student rather than the necessity of the rule was questioned. Although teachers recognized that students came from homes and prior schools that varied in the extent to which their rules coincided with those at Wexler, they made relatively few allowances for this in judging children's behavior, as illustrated by Vice-principal Kent's and Mr. Dunne's comments quoted earlier in this chapter.

THE TABOO

The four factors discussed above, the academics first, last, and only orientation, the natural progression assumption, the colorblind perspective, and the view of the classroom as a world in itself with its own set of rules, all contributed to the development of a fascinating phenomenon that appeared to have a major impact on the way social relations between black and white students at Wexler developed. This was the development of a norm, strong enough to be called a taboo, that discouraged Wexler's students and staff from making direct reference to, let alone discussing, the fact that blacks and whites exist in this country as relatively distinct social groups. Since this norm appeared to be quite important in affecting relationships within the school, I shall devote the rest of this chapter to: (1) presenting the evidence for the taboo's existence, (2) analyzing why and how it developed and was adopted by teachers and students alike, and (3) exploring the consequences of the taboo's development for intergroup relations.

It is truly astonishing how rarely Wexler's administrators and faculty referred to race when they interacted with each other. For example, during the school's first year, over 30 hours of teacher-teacher and teacher-administrator interaction were observed. In that entire time, school personnel spontaneously made fewer than 10 direct references to race. Any use of the words *black* and *white* in a context referring to an individual or group was classified as a reference to race. So, for example, the statements, "Fifty percent of this school's students are black" or "Jane plays mainly with other white kids," were considered references to race. Racial epithets, as well as words used almost exclusively within one group to refer to fellow members (for example, "Hey, Brother") were also considered references to race. The only major exception to this reluctance of school personnel to even refer to race appeared to be when the principal or other school administrators were discussing Wexler in public situations. In such situations, like the school dedication described in Chapter 1, strong emphasis was often placed on Wexler's attempt to provide a model of integrated education.

The extremely infrequent reference to race was all the more surprising when one considers that our observations included a wide variety of formal and informal faculty meetings and discussions as well as a summer preservice training program designed to prepare the teachers to function effectively at Wexler. Even more striking is the fact that reference to race was literally never once made in either the workshop on affective education classes, the purpose of which was to help students come to know and appreciate others, or in a workshop on classroom management funded by the Emergency School Assistance Act, federal legislation that provides funds to help schools handle special problems that may arise as a result of desegregation.

Similarly, mention of race was extraordinarily infrequent in teacher-student and administrator-student interaction. In over 150 hours of classroom observation during the study's first year, we witnessed only 4 staff-initiated references to race. One of these was an announcement made over the public address system by the vice-principal for the sixth grade, Ms. Kent, on the morning of the very first day of school.

> There are many different people in this school: black, white, oriental, Spanish-speaking, and some with handicaps. There is no rhyme or reason why any of you should bother others because they are different. If you can't act right, there are lots of other kids who want to come to this school. . . . Enough said!

This announcement typifies the attitude of teachers and administrators to racial issues in two important ways. First, the statement made it quite clear that students were expected to get along with others who might be different. Differences in background were not seen as legitimate reasons for negative behavior. The vice-principal let it be known that she expected students to get down to the business of learning without further ado over the fact that interracial education was a new and sometimes frightening experience for many of them. Second, the black/white distinction was placed in the context of other racial and ethnic divisions in spite of the fact that the other groups mentioned were virtually nonexistent at Wexler. In all our observations at Wexler, we encountered only two oriental children and one Spanish-surnamed child, who, as it happened, spoke English fluently without the slightest trace of an accent.

The teachers certainly followed the vice-principal's lead in rarely mentioning race. Some even seemed to avoid issues that might remind students of race or of the history of relations between blacks and whites in this country. For example, in discussing at some length the various classes of people in Roman society, one white social studies teacher mentioned the nobles and plebians but omitted all reference to the slaves. Ms. O'Hara, another white sixth grade teacher, made it clear that she felt reference to race was, at least under some circumstances, completely inappropriate.

> *Interviewer*: Do you feel it's best to openly deal with the fact that some black and white kids aren't used to each other and that they may have fears about each other, or is it better to let things run their natural course without bringing up the fact that race is a factor?
> *Ms. O'Hara* (white): Leaving it run its natural course, period! No other comment on that!

The strength of the teachers' resistance to confronting the issue of race directly is well illustrated by some events that occurred in the spring of the school's first year. A local foundation sponsored two clinical psychologists, one white and one black, who were available for consultation with teachers. The foundation was particularly concerned with racism and felt that the consultants could assist teachers both by encouraging them to handle problems between children and by helping them to analyze the effects of their own practices on the students. The consultants spent the fall term advising teachers who came to them about children who posed behavior problems. In the spring, the consultants proposed a mini-course for teachers to explore issues raised by the interracial nature of the student body. The teachers were generally very unenthusiastic about the course, but Mr. Reuben felt it had the potential for being useful. So he decided that teachers would be required to attend six sessions of about one hour each run by the consultants. The sessions were held during the time in the school day that teachers normally had free for grading papers and planning. Separate sessions of the course were held for each team, although occasionally the vice-principals or the counselors joined in. The teachers' resistance to discussing racial issues is apparent in the field notes below. In this early session of the minicourse, the group leader was trying to administer an attitude questionnaire that he hoped to give again at the end of the course to see if any change had occurred. The questionnaire concerned racial attitudes.

> One of the questions which stirs much comment reads as follows, "You're walking down a street alone and must pass a corner where five young men are loitering." [Some forms of the questionnaires say, "five young black men," others don't specify race, etc.] Teachers are supposed to check various answers to indicate how they would feel in this situation. Ms. Nobel (white) reading one pair of answer options, says, "Feel whiter, feel blacker? That is ridiculous! . . ." The teacher's aide (black) says, "How can anyone feel whiter or blacker? I'm black and I am as black as I can be. And you," she says, pointing to Mr. Handlin, the clinical psychologist, "are as white as you can be. How can anyone feel blacker or whiter?" Mr. Elliot (white) makes a little joke saying, "Maybe you could dip someone in white paint." Nobody laughs much. Ms. Clausen (black) cuts in angrily, "I think this is just plain ridiculous. How could it make you feel whiter? . . . This questionnaire tells me a lot about the person who made it up. . . . The person who made it up is sick!" The teachers chorus rather loudly, "Yeah, sick!"

One could argue that the teachers' resistance to the questionnaires was an outgrowth of their rather natural resentment of an "outside expert" who was asking questions in a sensitive area. After all, the administration of the questionnaire did imply that Mr. Handlin expected to find different reactions to situations depending on the race of the individuals involved. However, the resistance to discussing race continued in later sessions when the element of personal insult or threat was not so clearly present. For example, in one session of the course designed to explore children's reactions to differences between peers, the teachers discussed at some length students' reactions to both overweight children and handicapped children. However, they did not discuss white and black students' reactions to each other, in spite of Mr. Handlin's valiant efforts to steer them in that direction. The resistance is also apparent in field notes from yet another session, which was filled with long, tense silences whenever issues even verging on race were introduced.

> Mr. Handlin, the white clinical psychologist, starts the session by writing on the board, "Wexler is a model of *integration* and *education*."

He then . . . says, "A lot of people, at least people on the outside of Wexler, see the school as a model of integration and education. . . . What sorts of things do you need to meet these goals?" [After a lengthy discussion of the need for fairness, "the upper hand," good curriculum materials, parental support, and small class size], Mr. Handlin says, "Well, now I notice that almost everything you've mentioned so far has been concerned with Wexler as a model for education. But what about the school as a model for integration?" Ms. Winters (white) says, "It's really unrealistic to see Wexler as a model of integration because of its open enrollment. . . . That changes everything." Mr. Handlin . . . asks, "What else would be important?" There is a silence longer than the other silences in the meeting so far. None of the teachers looks ready to respond. Vice-principal Kent (black) breaks the silence saying, "One big problem that we have is the different school backgrounds the kids come from." [She and Mr. Handlin discuss the problems with the educational programs in ghetto schools at some length. No one else participates.]

In the sixth grade, teachers' resentment about the minicourse was so great that the vice-principal for that grade felt compelled to set up a committee to evaluate it.

Mr. Handlin said that Vice-principal Kent met with him and with five building representatives [an elected group of teachers who carry their constituents' concerns to administrators]. The vice-principal had five pages of questions that she wanted answered and really grilled him. Ms. Kent had taken a survey with questions on it like, "Did you find he pushed you into saying things you didn't want to? . . ." [I should note I did not attend the meeting and have not seen a copy of the survey so I do not have independent confirmation of Handlin's view of the situation, although I do know from other sources that a review committee did meet and that many teachers were very angry about the course.]

Students, as well as teachers and administrators, made racial references quite rarely. In fact, in more than 150 hours of classroom observation during Wexler's first year, students were observed making references to race fewer than 20 times. The obvious question that arises is whether race was truly an almost taboo subject or whether we somehow failed to pick up references that were made. Teachers certainly agreed with our perception that race was very rarely mentioned by students.

Interviewer: How often in a week do you hear kids making a reference to race?

Ms. Winters (white): You know, in other schools I heard it, but not here. . . . I was really listening for it. . . . I don't think I heard it in a [typical] week. I think maybe once or twice a month.

Interviewer: When you heard these references, were they usually positive or negative?

Ms. Winters: Usually it was positive. I hear black kids [mentioning] it . . . but I never heard the white kids say anything.

Ms. Monroe, who is black, agreed with Ms. Winters's assessment of the situation.

I haven't heard any name calling as far as racial lines go. There's only three kids that I can think of that do that. . . . Otherwise, they just go about their daily things. . . . Last year [at another school] kids were more conscious of color. . . . They would fight a white person just because it was a white person and I haven't seen that here.

Ms. Richards, a white teacher who was unusually concerned with relations between black and white children, encountered real difficulties with students when she tried to deal with such issues as advisor to a student group set up with Emergency School Assistance Act funds.

Interviewer: Do you think the kids . . . understood that they were there as a group to improve race relations?

Ms. Richards: Initially they did . . . and there was resistance on their part . . . like non-verbal resistance. They just thought it was hopeless . . . kids were really rather passive and afraid. . . .

Interviewer: Did the kids even get into a discussion on what attitudes whites and blacks hold toward each other here and that sort of thing?

Ms. Richards: They were very reluctant to bring that out. . . . When I would bring it up, they would cut me off. . . . The more I did [this], the more they resisted the whole thing.

Students' awareness of the taboo is shown clearly in the following field notes, which recount a conversation with Ms. Fowler, a white social worker, who was one of the few adults at the school to spontaneously mention race with any frequency. It is significant that she was not a regular school employee. Rather, her position was funded by a local foundation that was concerned with race relations.

Ms. Fowler said that a short while ago she had heard from Martin (black) that another child had done something wrong. The offense was serious enough so that she wanted to track down this individual. She asked Martin to describe the child who had committed the offense. Martin said, "He has black hair and he's fairly tall." He didn't give the race of the other person even though he went on to give a fairly complete description otherwise. Finally, Ms. Fowler asked, "Is he black or white?" Martin replied, "Is it all right for me to say?" Ms. Fowler said that it was all right. . . . Martin then said, "Well, the boy was white."

Students themselves also maintained that actual references to race were rare, especially when teachers were around.

Interviewer: You know the other day I was walking around the school and heard a sixth grade student describing a student from the seventh grade house to a teacher who needed to find this student in order to return something she had lost. The sixth grader said the seventh grader was tall and thin. She described what the girl had been wearing and said her hair was dark, but she didn't say whether the girl was black or white. . . . Why do you think she didn't mention that?

Sylvia (black): The teacher might have got mad if she said whether she was white or black.

Interviewer: Do some teachers get mad about things like that?

Sylvia: Some do . . . they holler. . . .

Interviewer: Now when you talk to kids who are black, do you ever mention that someone is white or black?

Sylvia: No.

Interviewer: What about when you're talking with kids who are white?

Sylvia: Nope.

Interviewer: You never mention race? Why not?

Sylvia: They might think I'm prejudiced.

Interviewer: You said that sometimes black kids might not like someone mentioning group membership by saying things like black and white. Have you actually seen cases like this . . . where black kids have been angry about it, or — ?

Sue (white): Yeah, I've seen that. It's, I don't like — I don't know why, but I never say black or white.

Interviewer: [A situation like that in Sylvia's interview above in which race was not mentioned is described.] Why do you think he didn't mention whether the student was black or white?

Dan (black): 'Cause he didn't want to get beat up, probably. 'Cause if you talk color, probably they beat you up.

Interviewer: Who will beat you up?

Dan: Anybody. . . . If it was a white teacher and you said the kid was white, he [the teacher] would probably be embarrassed himself. . . . It would probably embarrass the kids [too].

Interviewer: Why do you think that's so?

Dan: Well, it happens sometimes in my class.

Interviewer: Now when you talk with kids who are black, do you ever mention that someone is black or white?

Dan: No. . . .

Interviewer: What about when you are talking with kids who are white? Do you ever mention whether someone is black or white to them?

Dan: No. . . . I don't like talking about other races. . . .

References to race remained quite rare in the study's second year, although there did appear to be some easing of the taboo. For example, we noted more than twice as many references to race per hour of observation in the study's second year as in its first. Unfortunately, it is difficult to know whether this apparent change was one that occurred throughout the school or whether it was due to the fact that different teachers were observed in the study's two years. For example, two of the teachers who did cover topics related to race in their classes, Ms. Hopkins, who assigned a project based on the book *Roots*, and Mr. Jamison, who discussed apartheid in South Africa, were not observed in the study's first year because they taught seventh grade. There were some indications, however, that the taboo did actually lessen somewhat over time.

Interviewer: Do you think a fight between a black and white should be handled any differently than one between two kids of the same race?

Mr. Little (white): Hopefully not. . . . I probably wouldn't have said anything about being black or white. . . . You know, there is a thing . . . when we were talking in class about a person who was black . . . I was sort of hesitant, wondering what reaction it would bring. . . .

Interviewer: Now, let me make sure I understand what you were saying. . . . If you were talking about someone like George Washington Carver, would you say, "He's a well-known scientist who is black."

Mr. Little: *In the beginning I wouldn't have.* I don't know why, but I never kind of — I had a fear when I came here of what was going to happen. *Now it doesn't bother me.* . . . Before I was at an all black school, which was much easier. You just came out and discussed things like prejudice, why there is hatred between blacks and whites when they don't know each other. It hasn't come out here yet. . . . Maybe I haven't — maybe I've made sure to keep it down. I really don't want to hear it, you know. (Emphasis added.)

Field notes from a meeting during Wexler's second year also suggest a weakening of the taboo over time.

I asked the social worker Ms. Fowler (white) what impressions she had about the way things were going this year, being careful not to preface my questions with any remarks which might direct her thoughts to any specific type of change. The first response she made was, "I think people are more comfortable with being in an interracial environment this year. . . ." Ms. Fowler went on to say that last week she had overheard a student trying to tell a teacher something about another teacher. The student couldn't remember the teacher's name so he described him, saying, "He teaches social studies on team B, I think. . . ." The first teacher still wasn't sure whom the student was referring to, and she said very casually to the child, "Is he white or black?" The child replied, "White." Ms. Fowler said, "I was so amazed when I heard that. That's something that I never would have heard last year."

Although the strength of the taboo appeared to moderate slightly in Wexler's second year, references to race were still quite unusual. For example, in the approximately 250 hours of classroom observation during that year, only about 40 such references were witnessed. Given that race had a strong impact on interaction patterns at Wexler, as will be discussed at length in the coming chapters, the question as to why verbal reference to race was so infrequent arises.

Origins of the Taboo

The earlier discussion of the teachers' ideology suggests a number of reasons why Wexler's faculty might have adopted a strategy of verbally ignoring race. First, since academics had such overwhelming priority in the teachers' minds, most of them rarely thought seriously about social relations between black and white students. When they did think about such relations, they tended to focus almost exclusively on behavior that disrupted learning or challenged their authority. Since overt in-class racial problems were extremely rare, black/white relations did not become a focus of their concern. Secondly, the colorblind perspective meant that the teachers tended to think it was inappropriate to notice or respond to children's racial group membership. Thus problems that arose were treated as if race were not a factor unless there was unmistakable evidence to the contrary. Third, the natural progression assumption tended to make teachers hesitant to do anything specific with reference to race that might upset the assumed natural evolution of positive relationships between children. Finally, the image of the classroom as a world of its own, functioning according to rules and regulations quite different from those of the outside world, also contributed to the development of the taboo by leading teachers to be comfortable with discouraging all reference to race in spite of its obvious importance in many nonclassroom situations.

Strongly reinforcing the tendency to avoid racial reference that flowed from the teachers' ideology was the fact that many teachers felt unprepared to handle the dynamics of discussing race-related issues in an interracial situation.

> *Ms. Sharp* (white): I have an AE [Affective Education] period, but I don't run AE. I have no training in it. You need training in it. I think you can do more damage than you can do good. . . . If you are expected to run an AE and guidelines are set down, then I think there is some obligation that a person be trained. I feel no more competency in group process than I do in aerodynamics and engineering. You wouldn't expect me to build an airplane without giving me some training in it. And I really feel that I could confuse group process more than I could enhance it, quite frankly.
> *Interviewer*: How do you use that AE period then?
> *Ms. Sharp*: It is generally a directed study period.

Like Mr. Little, who was quoted earlier, Ms. Winters said that she had discussed race-related matters with her students when she taught in a black school. However, she did not do so at Wexler.

> *Ms. Winters* (white): One discussion we had in a sixth grade class at Hoover [an all black school] was about why white shop owners are very suspicious when a group of black kids come in. And you know someone said, "Why are all white people like that?" and someone said, "Well, Ms. Winter's white." Then the other one replied, "Yea, well she's a teacher. . . ." I wasn't in the category of black or white, I was in the

category of teacher. . . . I haven't had the occasion to get into discussions like that [at Wexler].

Later Ms. Winters explained her reasons for not discussing race at Wexler.

> *Interviewer*: Do you think at a place like Wexler it is best to . . . deal openly with the fact that black and white kids may not be used to each other . . . or is it best to . . . just treat them like they are here and there is nothing too special about the school?
> *Ms. Winters*: I don't know. I guess I sort of prefer the second approach. . . . I don't know how I would handle the first approach . . . is probably what I am saying. . . . I would get too bogged down in it.

As the above quotations suggest, race-related issues not only had low priority for teachers; they also were threatening because teachers felt unprepared to handle them. Hence it was not surprising that a norm forbidding reference to race evolved. This norm allowed teachers to concentrate on the achievement of their highest priority goal while protecting them from situations about which they felt uncertain. The potential dangers of using race-related words seemed clear to all, and students' reactions on some of the rare occasions on which race was mentioned, or believed to be mentioned, suggested that the teachers' fears of getting "bogged down" were not without some basis.

> [Today in Mr. Handlin's minicourse] Ms. Nobel (white) said she agreed with Mr. Little (white) that you really shouldn't go and make an issue of [group] differences. Ms. Winters (white) said, "Yes, I think that's true. For example, today Ms. Harper (a black teacher's aide) was . . . giving a spelling test. One of the words on the test was *knight* . . . and she gave the word and then used it in a sentence, 'The black knight rode out of the castle.' One of the kids said, 'She is prejudiced. Look at that; she is prejudiced!' Ms. Harper defended herself by explaining that the black knight was just a character in a story and she didn't pick him out because they were both black."

In addition to minimizing the probability of unpleasant scenes like this, the taboo allowed teachers to live comfortably with facts and actions that might have been open to serious question if full discussion of their implications were encouraged or allowed. The taboo increased the teachers' freedom of action as well as simplifying their decisions since fewer considerations had to be weighed in judging each act. Some examples may clarify these points. Recall the case of the white teacher mentioned in Chapter 1 who purposely miscounted votes in an election so that a "responsible" white boy represented her homeroom rather than an "unstable" black girl. The teacher, as far as I could tell, did not consciously consider the race of the children in making her decision. She looked at the two children as individuals and decided that one was a more desirable student representative than the other. In reflecting on her action, she worried a bit about her subversion of the democratic process. However, she apparently did not consider the fact that she had changed the racial composition of the student council. Hence, the existence of the taboo let the teacher do what she wanted without fear that someone might call her action racist as well as undemocratic. The taboo also helped insure that those teachers who noticed worrisome facts would not raise potentially disruptive questions. For example, although, to our knowledge, roughly 80 percent of all students suspended at Wexler were black, the question of why this was so and whether anything could or should be done about it never arose.

Recall that although teachers generally avoided mentioning race, Wexler's administrators did not show this tendency in formal public situations. Two factors may help to explain this difference in behavior. First, given all the publicity that surrounded Wexler's opening as a model integrated school, completely ignoring this aspect of the school in public remarks might well have been a more risky and provocative strategy than acknowledging it. This was especially true in public settings such as hearings about the school before the Board of Education. As will become apparent in Chapter 7, much of the testimony about Wexler there on the part of parents and other concerned citizens dealt explicitly with its status as an interracial school. Second, many of the public situations in which administrators discussed the school, like the school dedication and graduation ceremonies, were relatively formal and highly structured, so that challenges or replies from those in the audience were most unlikely.

Glaser and Strauss's (1964) work on awareness contexts is useful in illuminating what occurred at Wexler and how it is similar to what occurs in social life elsewhere. By the term *awareness context*, Glaser and Strauss refer to "the total combination of what each interactant knows about the identity of the other and his own identity in the eyes of the other" (p. 670). The term identity refers here to important aspects of a person, such as race, that are relevant to an interaction. Glaser and Strauss delineate several types of awareness contexts. For example, in the open awareness context each person knows the other's true identity as well as his or her own identity in the eyes of the other. Glaser and Strauss developed their typology of awareness contexts in studying a hospital ward. There, doctors and nurses, like the staff at Wexler, were often faced with facts that were threatening to themselves and their clients. Not knowing how to discuss a threatening subject, like the approaching death of a patient, they, like the teachers at Wexler, tried to structure the situation so this subject need not be faced. However, there is one major difference between the hospital situation and Wexler. Hospital personnel, being "expert" on the subject of death, often are able to create a closed awareness context in which they, but not the patient, know important facts about the patient's identity, such as the fact that death is not far off. At Wexler, a closed awareness context was not possible since the threatening part of each individual's identity, his or her racial group membership, was clear to all. Rather, people at Wexler generally seemed to operate within what Glaser and Strauss have termed a pretense awareness context, that is a context in which interactants know each other's identities and each other's views of their own identities but pretend to be aware of neither. More specifically, people were clearly aware of their own race, of the race of others, and of the fact that others knew their race, but they often pretended that they were not. Since maintaining a pretense context requires the cooperation of all parties involved in an interaction, one might expect that school personnel would have had a difficult time imposing an awareness context that ignored race unless there was reason for the students to enter into collusion with them. Hence this chapter will next address the question of why the students generally appeared to accept the pretense awareness context although their actions toward each other were clearly influenced by racial group membership. (See Chapters 3-6.)

Student Acceptance of the Taboo

Students were very unsure of themselves when they entered Wexler. The sixth graders, most of whom came from small elementary schools, were faced with a large school of over 1,400 students. Most children were bused to Wexler from their local communities, so they lost the security of a neighborhood school close to their homes. In addition, because of the open enrollment policy combined with Wexler's policy of putting students from different elementary schools together in teams, most students knew few if any of the other children in their classes. The school nurse reported that the students' anxiety and uncertainty were evidenced in an unusually high number of minor psychosomatic complaints, especially among white students. Almost one-third of the children interviewed about their first reactions to Wexler mentioned spontaneously that they had been scared. Also, several children mentioned feeling lost or overwhelmed because of the school's size.

> *Interviewer*: OK — Now think back to the very first day of school here . . . how did you feel about the idea of coming here?
> *Tom* (white): Scared.
> *Interviewer*: Scared. A lot of people have said that. Why was that?
> *Tom*: Oh, 'cause I wouldn't know a lot of the people here. . . . I may be put in a class where I know somebody who hates my guts.

> *Interviewer*: OK, now I want you to tell me about your first day at Wexler. . . .
> *Peggy* (black): Well, it was all right. I came in late and I looked like a big drag, you know. My hair wasn't fixed right at all; I wasn't dressed right, and I was real scared. . . .

Sherif's (1935) work clearly shows that when faced with an ambiguous situation people are especially open to influence from those around them. The students at Wexler faced just such a situation. They were on unfamiliar territory, and, even more importantly, a great many of them were encountering an interracial school for the first time. Without established peer groups to guide them, the students were in a position to be maximally influenced by their teachers. Hence they may have been influenced to adopt the teachers' norms about reference to racial matters because they were in need of a way of orienting to the situation and had no one else to depend upon. One teacher remarked in mid-September of the school's first year about the unusual degree of reliance on teachers he felt the students were showing:

Mr. Little (white) told me today that the kids seem to rally around the teachers to an unusual degree. "Perhaps," he remarked, "it's the only thing they have in common."

The norm the teachers modeled, that of avoidance of racial reference, was obviously a "safe" solution for students. Its adoption greatly reduced the risk of inadvertently offending each other and precipitating unexpected and undesired confrontations. Similarly, the practice of mentioning a wide variety of racial and ethnic groups when any mention of blacks and whites was made even though these other groups were not represented in significant numbers at Wexler also was a safe strategy since it provided a context in which blacks and whites were in some ways similar to each other (for example, both being at Wexler in contrast to Indians and Chinese) rather than one in which black and white were starkly contrasting opposites.

Table 2 suggests a number of interesting patterns that support the contention that students made racial references mainly in situations where the risk was minimized. Although the numbers in the table cannot be interpreted as in any way giving precise frequency estimates, the patterns are so strong that some general conclusions seem warranted. First, it is clear that students tended to break the taboo primarily in interactions with students of their own racial group. So, for example, nearly 80 percent of the references to race made by black children to other individual students were directed to other blacks. This tendency to discuss race only within one's group was vividly illustrated in an incident that one of the sixth grade teachers mentioned in Mr. Handlin's minicourse described earlier.

Ms. Rather (white) said that she had tried an exercise in her Affective Education class which was interesting. She had pairs of students get together and list out all the differences and similarities between them . . . they could think of. She said that in most of the pairs which were composed of two black or two white children race was listed as a similarity. However, not a single mixed-race pair listed race as a difference.

Making reference to race within one's own group is less likely to result in offense than making such reference to an out-group member for a variety of reasons. Positive reference to one's own race in the in-group situation affirms friendship and solidarity, whereas such reference made in the presence of an out-group member

TABLE 2
Racial References during Wexler's First Two Years

Directed To	Student black			Student white			Staff black			Staff white		
	−	0	+*	−	0	+	−	0	+	−	0	+
Students												
Black	11	4	4	2				1				
Small mixed group		3										
White	4	1				1					2	
Staff												
Black	2	1				1	2					
Small mixed group									1	1		
White											4	1
Oneself	2	2										
Entire Class or School	3		2			1		5			3	

Note: Only references to race actually witnessed by project staff were coded. Hence a number of references about which various informants spoke are omitted from the table. This conservative strategy was adopted since project staff made a point of noting all references that occurred in their presence. School staff were probably much more likely to selectively note or report various types of reference. Racial references made by students or staff in conversation with members of the research team are not included in this table.

*References to race were coded as negative if they were meant to be derogatory or to tease or hurt others. Purely descriptive references were coded as neutral. References were coded as positive when they appeared to affirm or assert group membership and were accompanied by signs of pride in it or at least acceptance of it.

Source: Compiled by author.

might seem like an invidious comparison. Negative references, too, are somewhat safer within groups since the person making the negative comment shares that group membership. Hence whatever is said about the other's group membership applies to the initiator of the comment as well. This is quite different from the situation in which the insult does not apply at some level to oneself as well as to the butt of the comment.

It is also clear from Table 2 that black children were more likely to make racial references than white children. In fact, in the first two years at the school, we observed only three instances in which white students made any racial reference. White students tended to be very leary of mentioning race, even in a very neutral way, because they were afraid black students would respond negatively, in spite of the fact that no negative implication was intended.

> *Interviewer*: Think of the times that you . . . mentioned, when black kids were unhappy or angry because someone used the word *black* or *white*. . . . Were the words used in a nasty way or in a factual descriptive way?
> *Sue* (white): Just the fact [way].

White children clearly avoided negative racial references at least partly out of fear of the consequences.

> *Interviewer*: How often do kids make fun of the way others look or talk?
> *Mark* (white): Pretty often.
> *Interviewer*: What sorts of things . . . would they be . . . likely to make fun of?
> *Mark*: [Being] white or black. . . . Well, none of the white kids would say anything about the black kids, but the black kids usually say something about white kids . . . stuff like honky and white cracker. . . .
> *Interviewer*: And white kids don't do that back to the black kids?
> *Mark*: No, 'cause if you called them nigger . . . all of them would be on you at once.

Keith, another white boy, agreed that whites were unlikely to use racial epithets.

> *Interviewer*: Well, when kids make fun of each other . . . do they often use words like honky or nigger?
> *Keith*: Yeah. . . . White kids don't call black kids niggers, but black kids call black kids niggers. Black kids call a lot of white people honkys. . . .

This pattern of more frequent reference to race by black children is also compatible with the argument that racial references were avoided because children wanted to play it safe. As will be discussed in Chapter 4, the black students at Wexler behaved in a somewhat more physically assertive way than the whites, so the white children had to be a bit more careful about not offending out-group members than blacks did if they wanted to avoid a physical confrontation. Secondly, our society's history is such that calling others white is not likely to have the potential to injure or distress them that calling them black has often had. The traditionally powerful position of whites relative to blacks and long-held beliefs about white superiority mean that relatively few white children are very sensitive about being white and some may even feel at an advantage. On the other hand, reminding a child that he or she is black makes salient membership in a group that has traditionally been subordinate in this country. Hence black children may feel somewhat freer to try to insult whites by using racial epithets than vice versa because the insult is less likely to hurt deeply and is thus less likely to evoke a strong reaction.

One other finding, not shown in Table 2, is also compatible with the contention that students avoided mentioning race because they were concerned about others' responses rather than because they did not notice or think about it. In one series of interviews, students were asked how likely they were to mention the race of other students in a variety of situations. Whereas most students indicated that they tended to avoid making such references in the company of peers, especially peers of another race, they also said that they were very likely to mention race in conversations with their parents about Wexler. Thus, in the relatively accepting and unthreatening atmosphere of a family setting, students' reported behavior was very different from that observed in school. Such reports were consistent with informal data gathered from parents who said that references to race were common in their children's everyday comments on events in school.

For many students, the strategy of avoiding racial reference was adopted out of an active desire to get along well with out-group members in addition to a desire to avoid confrontation. The school's open enrollment policy meant that children at Wexler were likely to be relatively accepting of interracial contact. Few students chose Wexler primarily because of its interracial nature. However, a number did give direct or indirect indication of relatively positive attitudes toward interracial schooling, as the following excerpts from two interviews show. Talking in their first interviews about why they chose to attend Wexler, students said:

Linda (black): Instead of meeting all black people you can meet some white, and some Chinese. . . .

Alice (white): I could have gone to a private school. I tried out for it and made the test, but I told my mother I didn't want to go there.

I told her that it seems to me that's where people who grow up to be snobs go.

The tendency to avoid making reference to race undoubtedly did minimize the occurrence of some types of misunderstandings between students. Yet this tendency may have had some largely unappreciated negative consequences as well. First and most obviously, the children by and large lost the opportunity to educate each other about issues relating to their race in the casual give and take of the classroom atmosphere. The need for such education, especially on the part of some white children, was apparent. For example, one white sixth grader who could discuss aspects of ancient Greek civilization with confidence was surprised to learn from a black classmate that Africa was not a part of the United States. Another white boy who was interviewed during our research expressed astonishment when the interviewer mentioned that Martin Luther King was black, saying, "I always thought he was white!" To the extent that natural interchange and discussion were hampered by the students' careful avoidance of racial reference, their education was clearly impeded. Furthermore, as will be discussed in the next chapter, misunderstandings between black and white children that related to differences in their socioeconomic and cultural background were not infrequent. The ability to discuss the meaning of such differences might well have prevented some of these misunderstandings or at least have lessened the likelihood of their recurrence.

3

SEPARATE AND UNEQUAL

Strong efforts were made by Wexler's administrators to prevent the resegregation of Wexler's sixth and seventh grade students into all-black or all-white classes. Yet, such efforts could do little to insure that, once in racially mixed classes, black and white children actually had much direct contact with each other. Within each classroom the teacher's policies and the students' own preferences had an impact on the amount of racial contact that far outweighed that of school administrators. Overall, especially in the first year or so, such contact was surprisingly infrequent, as will be discussed below. Although there were many factors that contributed to the generally low level of classroom contact between whites and blacks, one of the most important of these was the difference in the average achievement level of the black and white students. Since this achievement gap played such an important role in influencing the amount and type of black/white contact that occurred at Wexler, I will first discuss its extent. Then I will demonstrate the ways in which the instructional practices adopted by many of the teachers and the social processes set in motion among the students by the achievement gap led to curtailment of or strain in contact between black and white students.

THE ACHIEVEMENT GAP

As mentioned in Chapter 1, on the average black and white students at Wexler came from very different home backgrounds and exhibited markedly different levels of academic performance. Specifically, the scores of black students on standardized tests of ability and achievement were on the average roughly one standard deviation below those of whites. This difference was clearly reflected in the students' grades. For example, on one fairly typical math test in a class we routinely observed, almost 50 percent of the white students received A's, compared with about 7 percent of the black students. When asked by their math teacher on a questionnaire what their final math grade *should* be, only 15 percent of the black students on one seventh grade team said they deserved A's compared to 48 percent of the white students. Only one of the over 50 white students who filled out the questionnaire assigned himself a C compared to almost half of the 43 black students.

Similarly, year-end academic honors went disproportionately to whites. Sixty of the 68 sixth grade children who received awards for maintaining an A average during Wexler's first year were white. The next year when this same group of children graduated from seventh grade, over 85 percent of the children who received certificates for academic merit were white, although the student body was just over 50 percent black. As these students moved into the eighth grade, in which they were separated into the academically accelerated and the regular classes, approximately 80 percent of the students in the former track were white whereas about 80 percent of the students in the regular track were black.

The difference in the average academic performance of black and white children was clearly reflected in differential participation rates in classroom activities.

> Mr. Little asks for another example of the way in which geographic factors influence people. Billy (black) raises his hand and, when called on, says that desert people wear white clothes to keep the heat off them. Although the teacher has asked numerous questions today, this is the first time a black child has raised his or her hand. . . . Typically, four or five white children have had their hands in the air, with two or three of them waving their hands with enthusiasm and making little noises like "Ooh, ooh" to signify how much they want to be called on. . . . In response to the next question, eight white children and one black child, Billy again, raise their hands.

Perhaps black children participated less often than whites because they were less sure of their answers and hence more likely to be embarrassed by being wrong.

The teacher says to his sixth grade class, "Use the term *agricultural surplus* in a sentence. . . ." He then calls on Alice (white), who says, "Because man invented the plow he developed an agricultural surplus which let people turn into specialists which helped lead to urbanization." Looking somewhat surprised, perhaps by the length and conceptual complexity of this sentence, the teacher says, "Yes, that's right. That's a good use of *agricultural surplus*." Next he asks the students to use *dynasty* in a sentence. Eight or ten students, most of whom are white, raise their hands. The teacher calls on Laura, a black student whose hand is raised. Laura says in a soft hesitant voice, "Well, I had a good one, but I forgot it."

CLASSROOM POLICIES AND RESEGREGATION BY ACHIEVEMENT LEVEL

Instruction at Wexler was generally organized in one of three basic ways. Most teachers spent the majority of their classroom hours using the one method they liked best. However, they also frequently used one or more of the other methods or some combination of methods as these seemed appropriate to the material being covered. The three teaching methods — traditional, individualized, and group-oriented — had varying effects on interracial contact.

The traditional method was, of course, built around lectures and one-to-one teacher-student interaction, to which all students were supposed to listen. Teachers in traditional classes lectured, led class discussions in which they called on students in turn, and posed questions for individual students to answer in front of the class.

In individualized classrooms, each child was allowed to proceed at his or her own pace. Teachers made use of contracts, in which the child agreed to perform a certain amount of work in a given period of time. The work assigned varied according to the student's performance level. For example, Ms. Winters assigned five new spelling words a week to some students and ten or fifteen words to others. Since the students were working on different material, the teachers did not instruct the entire class simultaneously. Rather, they circulated from child to child, making comments and providing assistance. Although there was much teacher-student interaction, it was usually quite private.

Group-oriented methods varied widely. By far the most common was homogeneous ability grouping within classes. Typically, two or three groups were created on the basis of grades or test scores and were given different amounts and types of work designed to be suitable for them. Although children in a group were seated near each other, they were generally expected to work by themselves and were graded as individuals. In sharp contrast to such classrooms were those in which students were put into academically hetero-geneous groups. Although such grouping was relatively rare, there were two distinct variations on this procedure. First, and more commonly, each student was seated in a heterogeneous group but worked and was graded as an individual. Much less frequently, each child was assigned to a heterogeneous group to carry out some joint project for which the group received a grade. Not one of the academic classrooms observed employed this technique with any consistency. In fact, during three years of observation in academic classrooms at Wexler, we encountered fewer than 15 instances of such group projects involving more than two students.

The instructional techniques described above had very different implications for the development of black/white relations and, more particularly, for the extent to which the achievement gap between black and white children was highlighted. Yet it should come as no great surprise, in light of the strength of the academics first, last, and only orientation and the colorblind perspective, that teachers rarely reported considering such issues in making decisions about which instructional techniques to use.

Traditional teaching methods made the academic differences between blacks and whites very obvious. Children's successes and failures were apparent to the entire class, as were their rates of participation. Black and white students generally agreed that aca-demic performance could be a route to peer status. Thus, the very public nature of academic performance in traditional classrooms helped to create unequal status between blacks and whites and often confirmed racial stereotypes.

Differences in academic performance were not so obvious in completely individualized classes for two reasons. First, students tended to interact privately with the teacher rather than publicly. Second, teachers using individualized instruction often graded some-what differently from those using traditional methods. Competitive reward structures were common in traditional classes, with students' grades depending not only on how well they did but also on how well others did. In the individualized classes, grades were based more, although not exclusively, on how well the students did the particular tasks assigned to them. Children who learned five new spelling words could get an A if that was their task even if other students had learned two or three times as many. Although individualized techniques downplayed competition by setting up an individualized reward structure, it was clear that they did not come close to eliminating awareness of the achievement gap between blacks and whites. The children in individualized classrooms often actively sought out information on how their peers were doing, wandering around the classroom asking others where they were in the course of study or comparing the volume and difficulty of their assignments. The overall level of peer interaction seemed markedly higher in individualized than in traditional classrooms, in which such interaction was generally discouraged because it was perceived as distracting students from attending to the teacher. Nonetheless, the interaction that occurred in individualized classrooms was primarily within race. Part of the reason for this was that children of the same race were more likely to be working on similar material and thus were more likely to be of assistance to each other on academic tasks. However, both racial fears and friendship patterns also played an important role in determining whom children talked with as they wandered around their classrooms.

Like traditional teaching methods, homogeneous ability grouping within classes made group differences quite salient, although just how salient depended on the particular grouping strategy used and the achievement levels of the black and white children in the class. Illustrative of one extreme was the classroom of a black teacher, Mr. Hughes, who divided his classes into a fast group, Group 1, and a slow group, Group 2. In the class we observed, Group 1 was entirely white and Group 2 was entirely black with the exception of one white boy.

Interviewer: You mentioned that when you group by ability level you get mainly whites in your upper group. I know that's the way it works out in the one class I have observed. . . . Do you have . . . black [children] . . . in the upper groups in some of your other classes?
Mr. Hughes: Yes, I believe I have one.

Mr. Hughes organized his classes into fast and slow groups to facilitate academic instruction, but the social result was enforced racial segregation that prevented black and white children from interacting in any extended way.

> Class hasn't started yet and Steve (black), who is in Group 2, is standing near Sally, a white girl in Group 1. He has a sweatshirt draped over his shoulders and a pick in his hair. Mr. Hughes says to Steve, "I'm going to tell you something. I don't want to see you over here again." Steve walks back into the Group 2 area. As soon as Mr. Hughes turns his back, Steve returns to Sally. They struggle, slapping at each other. Kitty, a white friend of Sally's, calls out, "Mr. Hughes." The teacher says, "Steve, get back over here." Steve returns to the Group 2 area, saying, "She's got my pencil." The aide says, "We'll get another one."

In fact, about the only time that black and white children were allowed to mingle in this class was when Mr. Hughes moved students from their assigned seats as a form of punishment. Under these circumstances, interracial contact was rarely either extensive or positive in nature.

In addition to preventing direct interaction and physical proximity, homogeneous grouping also emphasized the achievement gap between white and black students in a number of ways. First, as in Mr. Hughes's class, the labels assigned to different groups, like Group 1 and Group 2, often made the status order very clear. This was reinforced by frequent references to the differences in their work.

> Steve and Brad, both black, occasionally do Group 1 work, although they are in Group 2. Today at the beginning of class Mr. Hughes says to them, "I want you to work in Group 2 today. They are doing hard work in Group 1. . . ." Mr. Hughes explains the Group 2 problems to the class, saying, "This is very easy to do. I expect you to do it in about 5 minutes." Brad says, "Mr. Hughes, can we do the other problems?" referring to the Group 1 problems. Mr. Hughes replies, "You are going to find them frustrating." It's hard to pick up a clear yes or no in his answer. Brad and Steve watch as he explains the Group 1 problems. Later Mr. Hughes says, "OK, how many people don't know how to do the problems? . . ." Brad raises his hand. Mr. Hughes says to him, "I'm going to have to put you in the other group. These are too hard for you." He goes over to Brad and Steve to get them to work on Group 2 problems. Steve protests, saying, "I'm on number three."

The clearly different work for children in the different groups also prevented most types of task-oriented interracial cooperation since black and white students were generally performing different tasks.

Much more common than Mr. Hughes's division of students into two groups was division into three groups. Mr. Cousins, a white teacher, divided most of his classes into three academically homogeneous groups. In the class observed, Group A, the highest achieving group, was all white and Group C, the lowest achieving group, was black except for one white boy. The visual effect was muted somewhat by the presence of a racially balanced middle group, Group B. The social learning opportunities within Mr. Cousins's Group B, when considered in isolation from the rest of the class, seemed ideal. Black and white students in close physical proximity, working on the same material at the same time and at the same general skill level, had an excellent opportunity not only to observe each other but also to interact over considerable periods of time on an equal-status, reciprocal, and sometimes cooperative basis. But, considering the class as a whole, the social cost of this grouping pattern was high. The higher-achieving black students surely noticed that they had been paired with those in the lower half of the white distribution. And students in the racially homogeneous upper and lower groups scarcely had any more opportunity for interaction with peers of the other race than those in the more completely resegregated classes. Furthermore, the structural message of these racially unbalanced groups was still that the school considered white students as brighter than black ones.

A few teachers grouped children heterogeneously, believing that such grouping was conducive to academic development because the students within such a group could help each other.

> *Interviewer*: Have you ever used ability grouping?
> *Ms. Winters* (white): No . . . because if all the haves are on one side and the have nots are on the other, they aren't going to be able to share anything. So [when I group] I always group so that there are a variety of abilities in a group, so if one person doesn't have the ability. . . . Sharing information isn't cheating. Pure learning is very important. There were times when I couldn't get something across but a student could . . . explain it in one sentence.

Such grouping practices were clearly conducive to interracial interaction, although even children within these groups tended to interact more with those of their own race and sex than with out-group members.

> As was the case last week when they were initially assigned to [academically heterogeneous] groups, the students sat around five tables, each of which has six chairs around it. At four of these five tables there was a remarkably clear arrangement of students by both sex and race. For example, the white boys invariably sat next to the black boys, who sat sandwiched between them and the black girls. The black girls were bordered on the other side by white girls, who sat between them and the white boys, thus completing the circle. . . . In spite of the fact that the children tended as far as possible to sit next to those of the same race and sex, the new seating arrangement seemed to lead to a great deal of interaction across racial and gender boundaries. The children talked with considerable freedom to the others at their tables. For example, today I've noticed white girls and black boys talking several times. White boys and black girls seemed to speak with each other less frequently.

The contrast between the almost total lack of cross-race interaction in Mr. Hughes's class, where children were grouped homogeneously, and the very frequent interaction in classes where they were grouped heterogeneously is made clear from the following relatively typical excerpt from field notes taken in a class in which children were often in academically heterogeneous groups:

> Mr. Little says, "I'll be right back. Finish your work alone." Daneen (black) and Susan (white) are working together. . . . Chuck (black) joins their conversation by making a comment about the assignment.

The teachers' decisions about how to group their students appeared to influence not only the frequency with which black and white students interacted but also the way they felt about each other.

> *Interviewer*: Are there some times when black and white kids get along better than others? . . .
> *Becky* (white): For me there are. Like in reading [blacks] stay on one side of the room and the whites stay on the other. . . . Now in language arts, [the teacher] puts us together. So it's more like we talk in language arts and we hate each other in reading.

Although there was a considerable amount of cross-race interaction in academically heterogeneous groups, the achievement gap still tended to encourage children to work with others of their own race, as will be discussed in the next section of this chapter.

As indicated earlier, children were rarely organized into groups, be they homogeneous or heterogeneous, for academic projects for which they as a cooperating group were given a grade. Perhaps one reason for this was the students' resistance to such projects when they were not allowed to choose their work partners themselves. Such resistance had many sources. Children objected to being separated from friends and sometimes literally refused to be the only boy or girl in their group. Academic considerations also played an important role in the resistance, especially when the groups were academically heterogeneous, as illustrated in Chapter 2 by the complaint of the high-achieving white boy who refused to work on a project in a predominately black group saying, "I came here for my own education, not for somebody else's."

In summary, the two most commonly used instructional techniques, traditional methods emphasizing lectures and public teacher-student interaction and homogeneous ability grouping, generally made the difference in the average level of achievement of Wexler's black and white students very salient. In the former case the difference in the participation rates of blacks and whites was obvious as was the fact that whites tended to answer more rapidly and to be able to handle more advanced material than their black peers. Furthermore, the competitive reward structure used in traditional classes encouraged quick and simple comparison between any two students. In the latter case, many children were physically separated into segregated or nearly segregated subgroups within their classes. Since knowledge about the relative achievement level of the different groups was commonplace, traditional stereotypes about the intellectual superiority of whites could hardly help but be reinforced. In spite of this fact, the middle groups in ability-grouped classrooms were often very successful in promoting relaxed, friendly, and relatively equal-status interaction between students.

Individualized instruction, which was less common than the methods discussed immediately above, was much less likely to make the achievement gap obvious for several reasons. First, academic performance in individualized classes was rarely public. Second, students generally understood that their grades on papers and tests depended on improvement or performance relative to some varying baseline. Thus grades did not serve to place students in a clear-cut academic hierarchy, as they did in classrooms using more conventional grading practices. Nonetheless, it must be noted that most children knew at least roughly how their work compared to that of others and that when they did not, they often initiated activity designed to produce this information. Although the salience of the achievement gap was mitigated somewhat in individualized classrooms and a relatively large amount of peer interaction occurred there, the amount of cross-race interaction was fairly low. Students in individualized classrooms were generally free to choose those with whom they interacted, and for the most part they chose others like themselves in both sex and race.

Instructional methods like heterogeneous ability grouping that brought black and white children into close contact were relatively rare. Although such techniques were clearly more conducive to cross-group interaction than the others, the existence of the achievement gap posed some problems that were not easily overcome. These will be discussed in some detail in the next section of this chapter.

THE IMPACT OF THE ACHIEVEMENT GAP
ON ACADEMIC COOPERATION

As an institution intended to serve as a model of integration as well as of academic excellence, Wexler was committed in principle to fostering positive interracial contact. Planning for the school's extracurricular activities clearly recognized cooperation as one means of encouraging positive interracial contact, and black and white children cooperated quite smoothly in these programs literally every day. Although the academic achievement gap did not seriously impede cooperation in many types of activities, it often did so in academic classrooms. First, as discussed previously, the primary teaching methods employed in academic settings were not conducive to cooperation, and especially not to cooperation between children at different achievement levels. For example, black and white children kept physically separate in ability-grouped classes had little opportunity to cooperate with each other. However, the relative lack of academic cooperation between black and white children cannot be attributed solely to such factors, for the students evolved complex webs of cooperative relations that were important even in situations in which cooperation was explicitly forbidden. These networks generally consisted of children similar to each other in race and sex.

The purpose of this section is to explore some of the ways in which the achievement gap operated to reinforce the children's tendency to seek out others of their own race to cooperate with on their work. Before proceeding with this task, it is important to consider the nature of cooperation in an ongoing social situation such as a classroom. For purposes of this chapter, cooperation will be defined as working with others for mutual benefit. Note that this definition of cooperation does not require joint efforts toward a *shared goal*. It applies to such behavior, but also to situations such as those discussed by Amir (1976) in which individuals coordinate their activities so that each is able to reach his or her own separate goal more easily than would otherwise be the case.

Analyzing cooperative behavior in an ongoing social situation raises an interesting and difficult conceptual problem that is not apparent in laboratory studies of cooperation. In a social organization like Wexler, individuals recognize that they will most likely be in contact over a long time period. Thus someone who accepts assistance today may help his or her benefactor tomorrow. A perspective that sees these two acts as separate instances of helping rather than as parts of a continuing cooperative relationship has ignored an important social reality. To illustrate this point, consider the following classroom incident:

Tony (black) goes to the pencil sharpener which is located in the front of the room. The sharpener isn't fastened down so Tony asks Paul (white), who is sitting nearby, to hold it steady. Paul immediately jumps up and holds the pencil sharpener in place. When Tony's pencil is sharp both boys return to their seats.

The incident as it stands seems to describe an instance of helping rather than cooperation as defined above, since Paul derived no apparent benefit from the interaction. If anything, he gave up something since he took time out from his work. On the other hand, if one knew that yesterday Paul requested and received Tony's assistance in sharpening his pencil or in some other task, one might see this instance of helping as one small link in a chain of behavior that builds a long-term cooperative relationship between the two boys.

I have chosen to raise this issue here because the fine, rather ambiguous, but very important line between helping and cooperation is important in understanding the behavior of children in interracial schools, as will become apparent later on in this chapter.

Perhaps the least problematic form of voluntary academic cooperation observed at Wexler was sharing and caring for the various materials necessary for the completion of academic tasks. When black and white children sat next to each other, either because they were assigned to adjacent seats or, less frequently, because they chose to sit together, they appeared to have little trouble engaging in this sort of cooperation.

> Today the students are working on vocabulary lists. They are picking out words they don't know which appear in their textbook and looking these words up in a dictionary. Amy (white), Sarah (white), Stacy (black), and Eleanor (black), who are sitting around a small table, take turns using the dictionary and occasionally talk with each other quietly.

However, the situation was quite different with regard to the sharing of information. Indeed, even in nontest situations in which cooperating was clearly legitimate, information was shared mainly by children who belonged to the same racial group unless the teacher specifically required cooperation between out-group members. One reason for this was undoubtedly that the children tended to like to work with their friends, and their friends were generally of their own race and sex. In addition to this, the students generally made a sharp distinction between giving information away — that is, helping — and cooperating — that is, trading information or assistance. This distinction is illustrated by two incidents that occurred in a class right after the teacher had specifically stated that the students could work individually or with others on a workbook assignment. Under such conditions, the students clearly did not want to give information away to out-group members although they were willing to trade it and to work jointly with friends to obtain it.

> At Table B a small conflict has arisen. Alice (white) and Mary (white), who are friends, have been working together closely while Mark (black) and John (white) have been working by themselves. The girls start complaining loudly that Mark is copying their answers. Alice puts a book up in front of her paper to block Mark's view, saying to him angrily, "Will you quit it!" She calls the teacher over saying, "Keep

Mark away from my paper! Look at him copying!" Mr. Little asks Mark
if he's been copying. Mark looks at John, who's been working by himself the whole time, and says, "Didn't we work one out by ourselves,
John?" When John doesn't reply, Mr. Little warns Mark not to copy.

Mark's attempt to gain information by copying was treated very
negatively by the girls at his table. Such a reaction was quite usual
when a child who was not a friend tried to copy answers. Yet straight
copying of answers was frequent among friends and generally occasioned little comment. Two factors help to explain these rather
different reactions to copying by friends and others. First, helping
a friend is different from helping someone else because of the
ongoing nature of friendship. Children clearly expected their friends
to reciprocate academic favors, so the helping could be seen as part
of an extended cooperative relationship even if the reciprocation was
not immediate. There is generally no history of mutual assistance
with strangers or mere acquaintances that would lead one to expect
later reciprocity. Second, the children at Wexler seemed by and large
to have friends who were roughly similar to themselves in their level
of academic achievement. To the extent that this was the case, a
child could realistically expect a friend to be able to repay academic
assistance at some later point in time if not immediately. However,
there was no reason to assume that a stranger would be able to do so.

Although children often resisted attempts by those who were not
friends to copy their work, they were eager to trade information.
Students tended to seek out their friends for such trades first.
However, it was not uncommon to see children wandering around
the classroom in search of anyone who had the information they
needed. Those with information were likely to part with it readily
if they could get needed information in return.

At Table A, Silvia (black) is talking to Susan (white) from Table C.
Susan has come over to swap answers. She says, "If you give me 4, I'll
give you 11. . . .

Later, another girl from Table A joins in the bartering, trading Susan
another answer.

In essence, the students acted as if they were very aware that
information was a valuable commodity. Although one might give
information to a friend, in general those who had information

exchanged it. Those without it were not in a strong position, as suggested by the following incident involving a black student and a white classmate whose level of academic achievement was markedly higher:

> Tim (black) lightly hits John (white) on the arm to get his attention. He then asks, "How do you spell *grain*?" John makes no response whatever, not even acknowledging that Tim has touched him. [Later] Tim turns to John and says, "How do you spell *syllables*?" . . . John makes no . . . response.

Even if a relatively low-achieving child had information he or she was willing to exchange, it often was of little interest or value to the higher-achieving children, who were able to get the easier answers themselves without much effort. As an interview with a black child who generally did solid B work suggested, those who were at the top of the academic pecking order were in big demand as work partners.

> *Interviewer*: Are there certain boys at Wexler that others are especially likely to want to work with in class?
> *Chuck*: Yeah. Bruce (white) and Mike (white).
> *Interviewer*: Why does everybody want to work with them?
> *Chuck*: 'Cause they are smart!

This same child explicitly recognized the extent to which continued access to the high achievers as work partners and information sources depended on the ability to reciprocate.

> *Interviewer*: Do you find it hard to get someone [like Bruce or Mike] to help you, or − ?
> *Chuck*: Usually it's easy, 'cause you can pay them back later.

Chuck, though, was in a very different position from many black children who had little realistic hope of being able to set up an on-going reciprocal trading of information and assistance with the children who were most likely to be able to help them.

Some low-achieving children, recognizing that they could not set up a cooperative relation on the basis of exchange of academic favors, did not even try to do so. Rather, they, in essence, became the protector of higher-achieving children, who were not infrequently a target for hostility from some of their lower-achieving peers.

Interviewer: Are there some kids who are more likely to be picked on than others?
Micki (white): Yeah. People who are real smart or who they just don't like.

Thus some black children provided protection, which the white high achievers were especially likely to feel they needed, in return for academic help. One eighth grader explained:

Sally (white): You get exposed to a lot of black people who are trying to act tough. . . . You have to know a lot of people. You have to get yourself a black friend.
Interviewer: How do you do that?
Sally: You just have to be nice and show you care a lot. Also, you have to take your time to help them.

As Sally's remarks suggested, high-achieving children, who were often white, sometimes gave assistance to lower-achieving black children as part of a conscious strategy designed to forge a link between themselves and a child who they felt could provide effective assistance should they be harassed by other students, black or white.

A number of teachers believed that academic assistance was not always given with a clear quid pro quo in mind and that some children helped others who were weak academically out of purely altruistic motives. However, the results of such efforts were not always as positive as expected.

Ms. Shore (white): A few [of the brightest white children] are exceptionally kind. . . . I mean that in the true sense of being kind. . . . They are understanding and oftentimes they will say, "I'm done with my work. Would you mind if I go over and help him?" That's never done with a sense of superiority or ridicule or anything. . . .
Interviewer: How do the kids who are offered help receive it?
Ms. Shore: Sometimes they are receptive to it. Some children will not respond. . . . They don't like people seeing the level of work they are doing. . . .

No matter what the motivation of the helper, it is easy to see why the child who is offered such help might feel anger or shame. Taking help from an academically advanced peer is not like getting assistance from a teacher, whose formal role is that of helper and whose superior knowledge poses no threat to one's self-esteem. Nor is it comparable to accepting help from a peer whose academic performance is similar to one's own. In this case, the child who needs assistance is not likely to be shamed by his or her inability to do a particular problem. Also, it is reasonable to expect that some-time before long the debt incurred by accepting help can be repaid. So the help can be seen as one incident in an ongoing cooperative relationship. Quite on the contrary, if one student is far more advanced academically than the other, accepting assistance means exposing one's relative weakness to the helper and incurring a debt one is unlikely to be able to pay back.

Social psychological theory and research suggest that such imbalanced relationships are often unstable as well as uncomfortable for the person who has received assistance (Blau 1964; Greenberg 1980; Homans 1961; Walster, Berscheid, and Walster 1973). Spe-cifically, this research suggests that individuals often see requests for help as indicative of their own incompetence and that accepting help from someone who is relatively similar, such as another student, can threaten self-esteem (DePaulo and Fisher 1980; Fisher and Nadler 1974). People seem especially unwilling to accept help from similar others when the chances of being able to repay such help are slim (Clark, Gotay, and Mills 1974; Greenberg and Shapiro 1971). The reactions of children who were offered seemingly altru-istic assistance were consistent with these conclusions. Rather than always accepting help with gratitude, they often rejected it, being unwilling to accept help that felt like charity and not cooperation for the mutual benefit of the individuals involved.

> *Interviewer*: Are there any things the white kids do that annoy the black kids?
> *Vice-principal Cooper* (black): Some of the better white students . . . want to be teachers. . . . They offer advice and help where it is not wanted. Not necessarily not *needed*, but not *wanted*. That stimulated a lot of problems. The first year I was here . . . the majority of the problems that came to me [were of that type].

The imbalance in academic achievement created not only situ-ations in which the children who did less well were angered or humiliated by offers of help; it also created situations in which the higher achievers were annoyed by the attempts of lower-achieving children to get help when the higher achievers did not care to give it. For example, in test situations, where the felt need for collaboration on the part of the lower-achieving students was often quite strong, the higher-achieving students were rather unlikely to be willing to share information with them. Many higher-achieving children obviously resented attempts to copy in test situations, especially if those attempting to copy were not friends. Often they took measures to prevent copying even when no clear efforts to copy were being made.

> The words *Literature Test* are on the blackboard in Ms. Hopkins' (black) class today, and the students almost without exception are bent over their mimeographed sheets, apparently working very hard. They are very quiet. . . . One of the first things I notice is the striking difference in the test taking behavior of the white and the black children. [In general, the white students in this class get markedly better grades than the black students.] Every single one of the white children has his or her book on end in front of his or her test paper, apparently to protect the paper from the eyes of other students. However, only one black child has done this. . . . [Ten minutes later] Miriam, who is white, gets up and goes to the pencil sharpener. When she leaves her desk she moves her book from its standing position, placing it so that it now covers her paper completely. When she returns . . . she puts the book back up on end.

Blacks who were especially high achievers also adopted such tactics.

> Stu (black) has built a fort around his test paper with three books standing on end. He has given the fort a little roof using a piece of paper.

Thus such protective behavior was not associated exclusively with whites. Rather, it was most apparent in the high achievers, the large majority of whom were white.

Overt friction about copying was apparent in the surprisingly large number of situations in which the teachers did not make it absolutely clear whether cooperation between students was acceptable, although there was some strong reason to believe that it was not officially allowed. In cases such as this, the students who knew the answers tended to guard them, because they had relatively little incentive to share them and they would rather not take a chance on incurring the teacher's wrath. The children who needed the answers, on the other hand, wanted help and tended to see getting this help as desirable, even if it was not completely legitimate.

> Kids are taking final tests today. The seats are arranged in traditional rows. Sharon (black) and Susan (white) talk briefly. Then Sharon starts copying off of Susan's paper. At first, Susan holds her paper so Sharon can see it. Then Susan glances towards the teacher several times and moves her paper back into normal working position. Sharon whispers and motions for Susan to move the paper back where it was. Susan keeps glancing at the teacher and keeps her paper in its new position where it is shielded from Sharon's eyes.

Although the above excerpt suggests that blacks and whites did sometimes share information under test circumstances, very often the black children, especially those who were relatively low-achieving, were not included in the cooperating networks with white children. Attempts to join these networks frequently met with overt rejection.

> Two white girls are working together on a quiz. Patty (black) pulls her chair up behind one of them, Laura, who says sharply, "No!" Patty says, "I just wanted to see the questions." Laura points to the wall where the questions are displayed and says, "They're up there." Patty moves back to her original place. . . . Four of the five black girls in this class, including Patty, have moved close together to complete the test.

Sometimes the lower-achieving children did not actively try to join in a cooperating group of higher achievers but instead tried to find other ways to profit from that cooperation.

> James (white) is consulting Harry (white) about the correct answer to one of the test questions. Mark (black) watches them eagerly. He is straining forward, listening to them with his eyes wide open and his pencil poised over his paper.

Occasionally, no attempt was made to keep an onlooker like Mark from profiting from the collaboration of his neighbors. Quite frequently, though, cooperating students took conscious steps, such as whispering or covering their papers, to prevent such onlookers from benefiting from the results of their cooperation.

THE ACHIEVEMENT GAP AND RACIAL STEREOTYPES

The achievement gap not only impeded both legitimate and illegitimate academic cooperation between blacks and whites but, on occasion, also led to misunderstandings between children. Furthermore, it helped to foster the belief that whites are brighter and more interested in learning than blacks.

> *Interviewer*: Do you think that being in a school like Wexler has changed white kids' ideas about blacks?
> *Mary* (white): It changed mine. It made me prejudiced really. . . . You know, it is just so obvious that the whites are smarter than blacks. My mother keeps telling me it's socioeconomic background, that the blacks in Avon [an affluent integrated section of the city] are nice people. But, I keep thinking every time I see a black person, "Stay away from me." The blacks are the ones who come down the halls with rubber bands and shoot them at you.

Black students at Wexler as well as whites tended to see academic effort and achievement as characteristically white.

> *Sylvia* (black): Blacks are badder than whites. . . . I ain't never seen a white person in the seventh grade cut class. When you look around you see the black kids walking the halls. . . . I guess they [blacks] don't care about learning. The white kids, when it's time to get their education, they can't wait.

The strong association in students' minds between racial group membership and academic performance is not unique to Wexler. A number of other studies of children in desegregated schools suggest that these students often perceive whites as more intelligent and/or more academically motivated than blacks. It should come as little surprise to learn that this perception is sometimes found among the whites in a school but is not shared by their black peers (Brigham 1974). Yet other schools resemble Wexler more fully, with blacks sharing the view that whites are brighter, more hard-working, or both (Collins and Noblit 1977; Green and Gerard 1974; Ogbu 1974; Patchen, Hofmann, and Davidson 1976). A few fairly sophisticated students at Wexler seemed quite conscious of the role that social class played in the superior academic performance of white students. The large majority, however, tended to think exclusively in terms of racial group membership, which is, after all, much more visible than social class background.

The children were sensitive to the fact that, in most classrooms, doing well meant doing *better* than others. Thus the whites' generally high level of academic performance became a potential source of friction between blacks and whites. Interviews with students suggested that black children were more likely than whites to believe that students worked for good grades primarily in order to look better than their peers. Thus, lacking disconfirming information, black children often perceived white students' performance as an arrogant display designed to impress or humiliate others. White students' behavior sometimes clearly supported this impression.

> *Ms. Fowler* (white): A white parent called [me], concerned about . . . her child. A black child was picking on her. I got the two kids together and we talked about it. . . . The black kid had perceived the white kid as being a goody-goody and making fun of her because she always had her hand up and knew the answers and she always did exactly what the teacher told her to do. It had nothing to do with the black kid . . . but the black kid was perceiving this because of her feelings about herself. . . . [Also] the white kid would do some facial . . . expressions that made the black kid feel badly. . . . An expression like, "Why are you asking such a dumb question?" . . . or "Why are you taking . . . the teacher's time?" Or the white kid might turn her chair to have her back to the black kid.

Occasionally academic performance did seem to be used as a display to impress peers. Much more frequently, calling attention to one's academic prowess seemed meant to gratify the self or to please the teacher rather than to hurt lower-achieving peers. Yet such displays put children who could not get the answers, or who could not get them quickly, in an unpleasant position.

> The teacher says, "Who knows the answer to question four?" and calls on Lilly (black) who starts to answer incorrectly. While she talks, children all around her wave their hands in the air, straining in the teacher's direction. Some call out, "I know," or "Call on me!" The teacher calls on Cecelia (white), who gives the correct answer.

Many black students came to feel that white children were arrogant and conceited. They saw this conceit as closely linked to racial prejudice since it implied that whites were better than blacks.

Theresa (black): Some white kids act conceited. They don't want to talk to you. . . . You be talking to them and they'll talk to you for about a minute or so, and then they'll go over to their other friends and act like they don't know you.

Interviewer: Do you ever wish there were more black kids at Wexler?
Carolyn (black): Yes. 'Cause I don't like the white ones. They think they're better than black kids.

Many white students at Wexler had a big stake in believing they were not prejudiced. Research by both Dutton (1976) and Gaertner (1976) suggests that such feelings are not unusual. These students recognized that they often avoided blacks and felt superior to them. But these feelings of dislike and superiority were, in their minds, based on evidence and not prejudice.

Laura (white): I sound prejudiced, but I don't mean to. . . . I have a friend who is colored. Don't get me wrong. How can I explain this? White people – er – OK, take Jewish first. . . . [Laura is Jewish.] Jewish parents always want their children to go to college. That's a real big thing. . . . I think it's the same with most white people. . . . But some black parents just don't care. . . .

Thus, although there was agreement that whites generally out-performed blacks at Wexler, there was no agreement on the issue of whether whites were prejudiced. Most whites argued that they were not conceited or prejudiced. Yet many blacks felt they could discern clear evidence of prejudice and conceit in the behavior of whites. This finding parallels the conclusion of Patchen, Hofmann, and Davidson (1976) that black students see whites as much more likely than blacks to be stuck-up or to expect special privileges for them-selves. Like the white children at Wexler, the whites in the study by Patchen and his colleagues did not share this view of the situation. Indeed, they saw blacks as somewhat more stuck-up and likely to expect privileges than whites.

In addition to believing that whites were more intelligent than blacks, children at Wexler also saw whites as more rule-abiding, as suggested by the excerpts from the interviews with Mary and Sylvia presented a few pages ago. The sentence-completion responses of a white sixth grader also illustrate the image of blacks as rule breakers.

Martin (white): A lot of people think that black kids are *mean or vandalize*. A lot of people think that white kids are *hard workers*.

Whites, in contrast to blacks, were seen as being good both academically and otherwise, sometimes even too good for other children's tastes.

Harry (white): A lot of people think that white kids are *goody goody two-shoes*.

Daryl (black): A lot of people think that white kids are *smart*.

The belief that whites were more rule-abiding than blacks was also evident in the responses of students to a questionnaire given by a seventh grade teacher who asked all of his students to assign themselves citizenship grades and to indicate why they had rated their behavior as outstanding, satisfactory, or unsatisfactory. The teacher reserved the right to change self-assigned grades if he thought they were very unrealistic but rarely exercised this option. White students were as likely to grade their own behavior as outstanding as they were to grade it satisfactory. In sharp contrast, the large majority of black students considered their behavior satisfactory, with fewer than one-quarter of them rating themselves as outstanding. (Self-assigned unsatisfactory grades were very rare in both groups, although proportionately somewhat more frequent among blacks.) The students' comments explaining their citizenship grades suggested that many considered academic achievement relevant. However, the second consideration clear in many of their comments was in-class deportment. Consistent with higher self-assigned grades in citizenship, whites tended to claim exemplary behavior more often than blacks.

Jim (white): I should get an outstanding because I'm in class early, I talk little, I'm consistent. Also, I'm smart and I do my work.

Stan (black): I should get a satisfactory because I'm bad one day and good the next.

Sonia (white): I should get a satisfactory because I've tried to work quietly, I've never disrupted class, and I'm always on time. I might have talked a little.

The image of blacks as rule breakers was strongly reinforced by the fact that over 80 percent of the children suspended at Wexler were black even in the school's first year, when blacks were only 50 percent of the student body. Students were well aware of this disparity in suspension rates, although they underestimated its magnitude slightly. When asked in interviews to estimate suspension rates for various groups of children, both black and white students saw blacks as at least twice as likely to be suspended as whites.

In summary, at Wexler whiteness became associated with success in the most fundamental role of children in the school situation — that of the student. White children accepted readily being part of a group that performed well in the student role. But the more whites worked at achieving academically and obeying school rules, the more they tended to appropriate for themselves success in the role of student and to leave blacks the choice of accepting that role but admitting failure in it or rejecting it and condemning themselves to conflict with the demands of the school.

4

GENDER: THE GREAT DIVIDE

With few exceptions, classes in Wexler's sixth and seventh grades tended to have roughly equal numbers of blacks and whites as well as of boys and girls. Such balance within the classrooms did not, however, guarantee that black and white students would have intense, prolonged, and direct contact with each other. Chapter 3, for example, discussed the ways in which some teaching methods led to virtual resegregation within classrooms. Furthermore, even when teachers encouraged interaction between black and white children through practices such as seating them near each other, the achievement gap, combined with other factors such as prior friendships, led students to prefer to work with those of their own race.

One pattern that emerged in situation after situation at Wexler was that the tendency to cluster in racially homogeneous groups was stronger among girls than among boys. This finding is not at all unique to Wexler but has appeared in other studies of desegregated schools (Hall and Gentry 1969; Jansen and Gallagher 1966; Schofield and Sagar 1977; Ziomek, Wilson, and Ebmeier 1980). Yet rarely have researchers attempted to explain this increasingly well-documented phenomenon. The purpose of this chapter is to explore the nature of social relations in male and female student groups at Wexler in order to shed some light on why black and white boys interacted considerably more frequently than black and white girls. I will examine the way in which gender-linked differences in behavior patterns interacted with differences in the behavioral styles of black

99

and white children with regard to rough-and-tumble play to create quite different patterns of black/white relations among boys and girls. To set the context for this discussion, I will briefly describe the extent to which boys and girls interacted across racial lines. Then an analysis will be presented of differences in the ways boys and girls formed friendship groups and in the activities they engaged in with their peers, so that the implications of these differences for the evolution of black/white relations in male and female peer groups can be explored.

RACIAL ISOLATION

Previous studies of desegregated schools have reported marked or even extreme degrees of resegregation. Sometimes this resegregation is imposed by the school. Often, however, at least some of it is undertaken on the students' own initiative. Such voluntary resegregation seems to be especially marked outside the classroom. For example, Cusick and Ayling (1973) found it impossible to talk with black and white students during the lunch hour in one school because blacks always sat at one set of tables and whites at another, and the students were unwilling to deviate from this pattern.

Resegregation initiated by the students was less extreme at Wexler than that reported in previous studies (Gerard, Jackson, and Conolley 1975; Scherer and Slawski 1979; Silverman and Shaw 1973). Nonetheless, it was a fact of daily life that was striking to even a casual observer. The pervasiveness and extent of the voluntary resegregation is perhaps best illustrated by discussion of the seating patterns in the school cafeteria. These patterns were mapped roughly once a week for two years. On a typical day, when the seating positions of the approximately 250 students in the cafeteria during any particular lunch were recorded, fewer than 15 of them sat next to someone of the other race. The large majority of the students doing so were boys. In fact, it was not unusual for fewer than 5 of the approximately 125 girls to be sitting next to someone of the other race (Schofield and Sagar 1977). The same strong tendency toward racial isolation was also evident in the hallways as classes changed and during other activities for which students could choose their own partners.

I spent the entire seventh grade lunch period today out in the play-ground. [Students are free to use the playground when they have finished lunch.] There was very little racial mixing. . . . A group of black boys played football for nearly the entire period while a small group of white girls stood and talked near the back wall of the school. One black girl joined this group briefly. . . . There were two games of tag going on at separate basketball courts. One group consisted solely of white boys, although a black boy joined the game for a few minutes. All the boys in the other tag group, except one, were black. . . . One group of white girls began running races on the sidewalk along the one side of the school. [This is one of the few examples of spontane-ously organized active play that I have seen among girls here either this year or last.] At one point several black boys lined up with the white girls at the starting line as if preparing to run a race. . . . There were a succession of false starts due to the boys beginning to run before the girl who was serving as the "starter" said "Go." . . . Finally the boys drifted away. . . . The girls then ran their race.

As indicated in Chapter 3, the amount of interracial interaction within each classroom was heavily influenced by the teacher's decisions about such matters as whether or not to group children into academically homogeneous work groups. However, even in classrooms that encouraged interracial interaction, the children still showed a tendency to interact primarily with those of their own race and sex. In academic classrooms, as in the cafeteria and on the play-ground, this tendency was stronger among girls than among boys (Schofield and Francis 1982; Schofield and Sagar 1980). Wexler's staff were quite aware of this difference in the boys' and girls' behavior.

Interviewer: Do you see any differences between boys and girls in the way they react in the interracial situation?
Ms. Engle (white): I think the boys react better than the girls. Girls can be very catty and they want to have their own friends and that's it. . . . The girls seem to stick to themselves [within each racial group] more.

Interviewer: Do you see any difference between boys and girls in their reaction to being in an interracial situation?
Ms. Partridge (black): Girls are more clannish than boys and they tend

to hold onto their own little groups. . . . It's kind of hard to break into a circle that's been going on for a year [or more] . . . . Boys . . . discuss sports and they tend to have more to talk about [cross-racially] than we [females] do. . . .

INTERACTION PATTERNS IN MALE AND FEMALE PEER GROUPS

The vast majority of peer interaction at Wexler took place among students of the same gender. Indeed, as will be discussed in more detail in Chapter 5, students often went to considerable lengths to avoid certain types of contact with peers of the other sex. Thus, to a large extent, children's direct interracial experiences were with students of the same gender. For this reason, an analysis of differences in interaction patterns in male and female peer groups becomes crucial to understanding the development of black/white relations.

There were striking differences in the structure of peer inter-actions in male and female groups at Wexler. Girls tended to interact in small groups of just two or three. The membership in these dyads and triads was relatively stable from day to day. In contrast, when the situation in which they found themselves allowed it, boys tended to interact in markedly larger groups. This difference is consistent with that found in previous studies that have examined the size of the groups in which boys and girls interact with peers of their own sex (Laosa and Brophy 1972; Lever 1976; Mitchell 1981; Waldrop and Halverson 1975). Boys, like girls, clearly had friends whose company they consistently sought. However, such pairs of friends often formed the nuclei of larger groups whose membership varied substantially from day to day and from activity to activity.

One of the primary reasons for this difference in boys' and girls' friendship patterns seemed to be differences in the activities in which boys and girls engaged when free to decide how to spend their time. Girls rarely played formal games that required large numbers of participants or even the various sorts of informal games that occupied a great deal of the boys' time. Rather, they spent much of their free time talking with each other.

Interviewer: What [type of person] would you prefer to be friends with?

Sally (white): The ones that like to talk, about anything. . . . My girl-
friends . . . tell me the things they did yesterday. . . . One gets high.
The other goes out all the time. The other one rides around in a car
[with boys]. . . . I feel comfortable.
Interviewer: What's it mean to be friends?
Sally: Trusting, loyalty, patience. Trusting is the most [important].

The few games girls did play generally did not require either marked
physical activity or teams of people.

In sharp contrast, the boys spent much of their free time playing
games, many of which, like basketball and football, required teams
of individuals to compete against each other. The contrast between
the social behavior of boys and girls is apparent in the field notes
excerpted earlier in this chapter that report that the foot races
witnessed during a lunch period were one of the few examples of
spontaneously organized, formal play involving physical activity
among girls witnessed by an observer in over a year at Wexler. Even
this game involved individual rather than team competition. Boys,
on the other hand, were constantly getting groups together for
pickup games requiring teamwork between individuals.

The emphasis that boys placed on games requiring physical skill
was but one sign of a major difference between boys and girls at
Wexler that had an important influence on the development of
black/white relations. Boys, in clear contrast to girls, placed a high
premium on athletic prowess, physical strength, and toughness
more generally, as evidenced by the following excerpt from field
notes taken in a seventh grade class:

John (white) says, "Did you see Iron Man? Man, he can do anything!
He's so strong!" Harry (white) replies, "Aw, he's nothing. Spider Man's
the one. . . ." A discussion of the relative strength of Iron Man, Spider
Man, and Tarzan continues as the boys try to decide which one to
draw as the emblem on their notebooks.

The boys' emphasis on physical prowess also spilled over daily into
their classroom behavior, as evidenced by the following notes taken
in a science class:

Bill (white) resumes arm wrestling with Chuck (black). Then James
(black) wrestles with Keith (white), beating him easily. Bill says to
James, "You were straining." When James accuses Bill of having strained

too [when he was wrestling], Bill replies heatedly, "I wasn't! You can't laugh [as I was doing] if you are straining."

Indeed, a great deal of the boys' interaction seemed directed toward proving and displaying athletic skill and physical strength. Informal arm wrestling tournaments were legion, as were a variety of behaviors such as playful shoving, tussling, mock boxing matches, wrestling, and "fun" fights. Occasionally, boys reenacted particularly dramatic fights with great gusto. This behavior was never observed among girls.

Athletics and the other forms of physical play described above were more than just play. Boys used such interactions to compete with each other for highly valued places at the top of a male dominance hierarchy, which they rather systematically set about constructing. A sixth grade guidance counselor told of an incident that occurred in the "time out" room to which children were sent if they became unruly in class.

> John (white) and Greg (black) started talking . . . about who could "take" whom in a fight. They went through a whole list of names saying, "Well, Joe (black) can take Henry (black)." . . . "Henry can take Jack (white)." . . . "Bill (black) can take Martin (white)," until they came to two kids who could beat a lot of others, but who hadn't yet tested each other. One of these kids, William (black) was in the "time out" room. So, John, Greg, and William tried to leave the room to find the other kid for a showdown.

Girls were much less frequently observed engaging in such efforts to establish a dominance hierarchy based on physical prowess or, for that matter, in ostentatious displays of physical strength or toughness.

> *Interviewer*: You're saying that girls and white kids get suspended less than boys and black kids. Why do girls get suspended less than boys?
> *Ellen* (white): They [girls] are not as much interested in all the power and everything. Boys are always interested in who's the strongest . . . . Around here, girls don't care if they're the strongest one in the whole school and they can beat everybody up. . . .

Omark, Omark, and Edelman's (1975) cross-cultural research with somewhat younger children suggests that this difference between boys and girls is not unique to Wexler, nor indeed to children in this country.

Whereas girls, especially white girls, placed much less emphasis on athletic prowess and toughness than boys, they placed more emphasis on being attractive to the opposite sex. In fact, even in the sixth grade, a great deal of the social interaction among girls revolved around grooming themselves and each other and discussing relations with the other sex. The girls' interest in attractiveness was evident in the grooming behavior, which occurred frequently, even in academic classes.

> Sonya (black) goes over to a table of six white girls and starts combing the hair of one of them. I've frequently seen black girls combing each other's hair. This is the first time in the two months I've been observing here that I've seen one of them comb a white girl's hair.

Discussions of hair, clothes, and other aspects of physical appearance were frequent among girls who were friends, and girls who flouted the dress norms at Wexler were often teased and taunted. The teasing of girls about their physical apperance was by no means the province of girls alone.

> *Sally* (white): Girls, . . . I guess they're a little bit afraid. They just don't like to hear the things [boys say] about them . . . like "Your feet are too long," "Your shoes look funny," "Your dress is crooked," "You need to iron your pants," stuff like that.

Much of the girls' concern over apperance and dress stemmed from a desire to be attractive to boys as well as to avoid censure. Indeed, relations with the other sex were one of the major causes of girls' fights.

> *Interviewer*: What do [girls] fight about?
> *Vice-principal Cooper* (black): Oh, the girls fight about boyfriends. . . .
> *Interviewer*: And what about the boys?
> *Vice-principal Cooper*: The fellows fight as a result of horseplay that gets out of hand, bumping and wrestling, and so forth.

Relations with boys were so important for girls that popularity with other girls was influenced by their popularity with boys.

Interviewer: Are there certain students who are more popular than others with the girls?
Ellen (white): Yes, for example, Lois (white).
Interviewer: Why is she so popular?
Ellen: The boys always bother her. . . . They push her and just a couple of days ago one kissed her in the hall.

In contrast, boys interviewed in the sixth and seventh grades never indicated that their places in their peer groups depended on relations with girls.

The differences in boys' and girls' social behavior described above led quite directly to greater interracial mixing among boys than among girls. Girls, who tended to spend their free time talking with just one or two friends, sought out individuals to whom they could feel very close. The emotional tone of the relationship was important to them, since they often shared secrets and what one eighth grader referred to as "deep conversations." The nature of the girls' favorite social activity, talking about experiences including those like illicit behavior and relations with boys, which were quite personal, militated against the development of interracial friendships. It is quite clear from social psychological theory as well as from experimental research on the topic at Wexler that individuals are less likely to choose to be with those of the other race in most relatively intimate social situations than they are in more formal, impersonal situations (Schofield and Snyder 1980; Triandis and Davis 1965; Triandis, Loh, and Levin 1966). A study by Moe, Nacoste, and Insko (1981) supports the preceding analysis by finding that girls tend to see interracial friendship as a more intimate relation than boys do. This finding is consistent with the emphasis on intimacy that is apparent in girls' thinking about friendship in general (Lever 1976; Mitchell 1981; Rubin 1980).

A number of other factors were also conducive to the choice of same-race girls as friends. First, many of Wexler's students came from segregated schools and already had at least a few friends from those schools with whom they maintained a close relationship. Similarly, neighborhood-based friendships, which tended to be between children of one race because of residential segregation, were also frequently maintained. Since the girls did not seek out large numbers of others to play or talk with, friendship groups based on prior experiences often did not expand to include many others. When this was the case, there was relatively little opportunity for interracial friendships to develop.

Compounding the factors discussed above that inhibited interracial interaction among girls was their emphasis on attractiveness to boys. This focus did little to encourage positive interaction between black and white girls since attracting boys was not dependent on a student's relations with other girls. Hence, girls were able to go about their business with little incentive to get to know girls of the other race. As will be described in Chapter 5, girls often plotted with their close friends to advance their romantic interests. However, letting others know one's romantic desires was risky since such desires were often not reciprocated. Thus, romantic schemes were generally constructed with close friends, who tended to be of the same race. The competition for boys occasionally led to negative interactions between girls, as indicated earlier in Vice-principal Cooper's comments. Although such competition was a major source of fights among girls, these fights were generally between girls of the same race since most, though not all, children tended to focus their romantic desires on others of their own race.

Just as many factors contributed to the relatively low rates of interaction between black and white girls, a number of factors combined to encourage both positive and negative interracial interaction among boys. First, as discussed previously, although many boys had bosom pals of the same race with whom they spent a great deal of time, the boys enjoyed many athletic activities that required relatively large numbers of people. Although it was far from unusual to see completely segregated groups playing basketball or touch football at Wexler, the sheer need for a large number of people for many of the boys' favorite free time activities increased the probability that they would end up spending some of their time in racially mixed groups. But it was more than the fact that a certain number of players were necessary to make a good game that encouraged interracial interaction among boys during their free time. The rule-bound nature of most games gave some structure to the boys' interaction, which undoubtedly eased the strain of dealing with individuals with whom they might be uncomfortable. Thus roles were reasonably well delineated, and the students knew how to behave and what to expect from each other. In addition, although many games and team sports require the type of cooperative activity that Sherif (1967) argues is conducive to improved intergroup relations, athletic contests are not particularly intimate situations. One need not reveal much to other participants that is not available as public information to anyone who happens to be watching. Thus children who were anxious about interacting with members of the other race were not in a particularly threatening situation. Finally, many whites had a real incentive to seek out blacks as teammates in certain types of games since many black boys at Wexler excelled in athletics.

The black boys' relatively greater physical prowess served as an incentive for white boys to seek to interact with them in certain situations. However, sometimes it combined with an important difference in behavioral style between blacks and whites and with the boys' emphasis on toughness and physical strength to produce considerable tension between black and white boys. Thus, before discussing further the nature and amount of interracial interaction among boys at Wexler, it is important to explore this difference in some detail.

ROUGHNESS, TOUGHNESS, AND RACE

There is no doubt that both black and white students at Wexler saw blacks as physically tougher than whites and as inclined to use this toughness to defend themselves and to dominate others. This finding is mirrored in studies of other desegregated situations. For example, Patchen, Hofmann, and Davidson's (1976) study of nearly 4,000 black and white students in desegregated high schools found that both groups of students rated blacks as tougher than whites. Similarly, Green and Gerard (1974) found that elementary and junior high school students, black, Mexican-American, and white, saw blacks as stronger than whites or Mexican-Americans.

The strength of the association at Wexler between being black and being tough is well illustrated by the responses of 80 sixth grade boys, 40 black and 40 white, to a sentence-completion task. Embedded in a wide variety of other sentence fragments about life at Wexler were phrases like "Most of the black kids in the school . . ." and "A lot of people think that white kids. . . ." Over one-half of both the black and white boys completed these questions in a way that emphasized the physical toughness and aggressiveness of blacks (Sagar 1979). A typical response appears below.

Tom (white): A lot of people think that black kids *fight too much.* . . .
A lot of people think that white kids *aren't strong enough.*

The association between toughness and blacks was strong among the girls too, although perhaps not as marked as among boys.

> *Donna* (black): The white girls are scared of the black girls.
> *Interviewer*: Why do you think that is?
> *Donna*: They [black girls] just like to bully.
> *Interviewer*: Do they bully other black girls?
> *Donna*: Those who let them. . . . Most of the time white girls . . . can't defend themselves as well as a black girl can.

Given the clear link between social class and emphasis on physical toughness for both whites and blacks, such differences are not too surprising (Folb 1973; Miller 1968). Yet, as in the case of academic achievement, students tended to see race, rather than social class, as the causal variable.

The most innocuous way in which such differences manifested themselves was in differences in play style. Black children, especially black boys, were much more frequently observed engaging in various sorts of rough-and-tumble play than were whites. Some of this play seemed designed mainly to develop or exhibit physical skill.

> Ms. Bays (white) turns to draw a Venn diagram on the blackboard. Kenneth (black), who has been playing with a wooden dowel with some yarn attached to it, gets out of his seat, walks about five feet toward the front of the room, jumps in the air while rotating his body in a nearly full circle and then walks back to his seat.

Often this play involved simulated fights conducted in a way that produced some of the motion and excitement of a real fight without the physical danger. Examples of this type of play included shadow boxing and "fun fights" in which punches were intentionally pulled so that no contact or only light contact was made. Reenactments of real fights served the same purpose.

> [Two black boys, Tom and Chuck, have just been taken to the vice-principal's office for fighting in class.] As soon as the teacher leaves the room with Tom and Chuck, Bob and Greg (both black), who watched the fight with great interest, jump out of their seats and run to the spot where it started. . . . Greg says, "They went down three times," and the two boys do a blow-by-blow recounting and reenactment of the fight, except that they pull their punches and just go over near the wall rather than crashing into it as Tom and Chuck did.

The reenactment and discussion of the fight lasted for two to three minutes. . . . It is interesting that two white boys who were within five feet of both the initial rather dramatic fight and the reenactment took hardly any overt notice of either. One . . . worked studiously on a cartoon drawing the whole time and the other started drawing a pyramid-like structure on a blank sheet of paper, carefully filling in hundreds of bricks, one at a time.

The wide variety of rough-and-tumble play that occurred at Wexler is illustrated by the following excerpt from notes taken during the first thirty minutes of a science class.

Richard (black) says to me (a white male observer), "I just won a fight. . . . I didn't even know him." I ask, "What were you fighting about?" He replies, "Oh, we just started wrestling around. . . . I had him [Andy, who is white] in a full nelson and it was a choice of snapping his neck or running when the teacher came. So I ran." Bobby (black) and Mark (black), who are wrestling by the light switch, fall on the floor and roll out into the hall. . . . Joe (black) and Stan (black) have a "fun" fight at the drinking fountain while Jerry (white) and Steve (white) wrestle on the other side of the room. Then Stan heads over and joins this fracas.

These notes were taken in an unusually rowdy class, yet they are typical in four important ways. First, the girls neither joined in the boys' physical play nor exhibited such behavior in interaction with other girls. This is, of course, quite consistent with traditional sex roles and with previous studies of children's social behavior (Maccoby and Jacklin 1974). Second, the black boys, who were essentially equal in number to the white boys in this class, accounted for a disproportionate amount of the rough-and-tumble play. Third, although the majority of the physical play was within racial groups, there was some involving both white and black boys. Finally, if we can believe Richard's report, in this case, as in the majority of interracial physical contests, the black child emerged victorious.

Black children, especially boys, appeared not only to engage in more physical display and rough-and-tumble play than whites, but also were widely perceived to be more likely to "hassle" others, both black and white. Research in other desegregated schools suggests that a similar pattern is quite widespread. For example, when Scherer and Slawski (1978) compared the patterns of peer interaction found in five ethnographic studies of desegregated schools, they found that hassling of white students by black students was common. These authors define *hassle* as "to purposely annoy or provoke the other" (p. 24) and illustrate the concept by referring to an incident in which several students purposely walked between a boy and a girl who were talking as they strolled down a hallway. Even though most instances of hassling seem trivial in many respects, it is clear that white students did not perceive them as such. The pervasiveness and symbolic importance of such encounters led many white students to feel both annoyed and afraid.

> *Annie* (white): Most of the black kids are really bad. . . . There are little things I can't even remember, like lots of times they just come in and pick on you. You can't really go tell the counselor because it's too small, but if you're here all year and those little things keep happening it seems a lot bigger.

Closely related to but more serious than hassling was intimidation, that is, engaging in behaviors designed to make others afraid. Sometimes the evocation of fear seemed to be the only goal of intimidation. Frequently, though, intimidation was used in an attempt to get something, such as compliance with a request.

At Wexler, many black as well as white students believed that blacks were, by and large, more likely to intimidate others than were whites. For example, when asked, "Do you think that white or black kids are more likely to intimidate others, or is it about equal?" roughly half of the black students and three-quarters of the white students interviewed replied "blacks." In sharp contrast, not a single one of the over 40 children interviewed maintained that whites were more likely to intimidate others. Blacks were, however, more likely than whites to differentiate between "regular" and "bad" blacks.

> *Bobbi* (black): Some blacks is friendly. . . . The friendly blacks get along with whites. But the black people think they're bad. They just don't like people that much. . . . They pick fights with whites and then with blacks. They fight with everybody.

A great many of the black children shared the white children's negative reactions to aggressiveness in peer relations.

Interviewer: Do you ever wish there were more blacks in this school?
Kathy (black): No, more whites 'cause they ain't as rowdy!

Interviewer: If you could change one thing about the students [here] what would that be?
Joe (black): That there would be no fighting and all that.

A significant number, however, saw no problem with it. For these children, the problem lay in the white children's lack of willingness or ability to stand up for themselves.

Interviewer: Do you think white children have any trouble learning how to act toward black kids?
Donna (black): Yes . . . They just can't take it. They don't know how to fight.
Interviewer:Do you think black children have any trouble knowing how to act towards whites?
Donna: No.

Although the frequency with which black and white children engaged in intimidation was one factor of importance to the evolution of intergroup relations, the type of individual who was typically the object of each group's intimidation was also crucial. Both observation and the student interviews suggested that whites tended to direct virtually all of their intimidation toward other whites. Indeed, when asked whom white children intimidated when they engaged in such behavior, not a single one of the students interviewed said that whites generally intimidated blacks, and relatively few even said that whites intimidated children of both races.

Interviewer: So, you think there's a lot of intimidation. . . . Do certain students bully certain others . . . or does everybody in general do it?
Don (black): The black students bully the white students most of the time.
Interviewer: Do white students ever bully the black students?
Don: Not that I know of.

Patchen's (1982) study of interaction patterns in several desegregated high schools, one of the few other studies that have carefully looked at negative interracial behavior, found patterns remarkably similar to those outlined above. Specifically, his study found (1) somewhat higher rates of physically expressed hostility on the part of blacks than on the part of whites and (2) a tendency for whites to avoid directing their hostility toward blacks.

Patchen (1982) also found a tendency for blacks to direct their hostile or aggressive acts more or less equally to both whites and blacks. The findings at Wexler in this regard were similar but not identical to Patchen's. In sharp contrast to whites, who avoided physical intimidation of other-race peers, and consistent with Patchen's work, blacks at Wexler directed their intimidation toward both black and white students. That is, whites were neither exclusively picked out as the objects of intimidation nor carefully avoided by intimidators. Contrary to Patchen's findings, however, there was some evidence that whites received a slightly disproportionate amount of intimidation from black students.

> *Interviewer*: Do you think black or white kids are more likely to intimidate others?
> *Marc* (white): Black kids.
> *Interviewer*: And who do black kids intimidate, mainly whites or blacks?
> *Marc*: Whites.

There were a number of factors that appeared to contribute to whites being somewhat disproportionately the objects of intimidation by blacks at Wexler. Jealousy, especially jealousy over whites' academic success, appeared to be one factor that motivated some black children.

> *Maurice* (black): Black kids be getting on them white people.
> *Interviewer*: They do?
> *Maurice*: Yeah, because they be jealous of what they be having.

> *Interviewer*: Do you think black or white kids are more likely to intimidate others or is it about equal?
> *Joe* (black): The blacks. . . . They always be picking at the white kids. . . . They be pushing them around, hitting them in their head and all that. . . .
> *Interviewer*: Why do you think that is?
> *Joe*: I don't know. I think they're jealous . . . 'cause probably they [whites] work harder than them [blacks] . . . .
> *Interviewer*: Who do black people intimidate mainly?

Joe: White people.
Interviewer: Hum, who do white people intimidate mainly?
Joe: They don't intimidate nobody.

The tendency to intimidate physically those who displayed unusually high levels of academic achievement is not surprising when one recognizes that such achievement can be used aggressively for self-aggrandizement. Making salient this possibility was a hand-lettered sign conspicuously posted one year near a classroom door: "Don't knock your competitors. Just beat their brains out by being so superior that anyone can tell." The fact that whites were widely believed to be conceited and to feel generally superior to blacks made some black children quick to take offense and to feel the need to defend themselves, even though offense or attack may not have been intended.

Although jealousy and anger at perceived feelings of superiority appeared to be behind some of the intimidation of whites, another even more important factor was the white children's reaction to intimidation. The white students were much more likely than blacks to let themselves be taken advantage of. Often they yielded when just a little resistance would most probably have saved them from yielding and established a very different precedent for the future. The children, both black and white, recognized an easy target when they saw one.

Interviewer: Are there certain kids who are more likely to get picked on than others?
Barb (white): I think the kids that are scared to stand up to people get picked on. My friend [is an example]. She's scared of people just walking past her that look strange to her. . . . She's scared of mostly everything I could name.
Interviewer: And because she's scared all the time, kids are more likely to pick on her?
Barb: Right!

Interviewer: Do you think black children have any trouble knowing how to act toward white kids? . . .
Wendy (black): Yes, 'cause black children at Wexler always hit on white people's heads and [are] always pushing and shoving on them. They know they can run over them.

Mr. Hughes, himself black, noticed the clear difference in the behavior of black and white children who were threatened or annoyed.

> I think . . . that usually the white kids . . . take more. They walk away from a fight. If a black youngster hits a white youngster, many times the white youngster walks on away. . . . If a white kid steps on a black kid's toes . . . the black usually retaliates.

The rather mild behavior that whites perceived as intimidation and their reaction to it is well illustrated by an excerpt from an interview with Ann, a white girl who frequently had trouble in her dealings with black children.

> *Interviewer*: How much intimidation is there here at Wexler?
> *Ann*: It happens all the time.
> *Interviewer*: Can you describe the last time you felt intimidated by something?
> *Ann*: It was in art class one day. . . . Me and my girl friend Jane (white) had a wax thumb because we were doing batik and otherwise you get green dye all over your hands. . . . Then this girl, this black girl, Leslie . . . wanted to see it. So Jane gave it to her. What could Jane say? If Jane said no, Jane'd get beat up. So, she gave it to her and said, "Please don't dig out the thumbnail." Leslie said she wouldn't. But she kept drawing on it harder and harder and finally the nail came out. [Ann describes at some length how she and Jane asked Leslie to return the now damaged wax thumb cover.] This other girl, a friend of Leslie's, was around too. She started tearing it up . . . and then she said, "Here Jane, you can keep it now." And they twisted it into balls and threw it at us. . . . So we got angry. . . . They kept hitting us and we kept on telling them to stop. . . . Finally, we just left. The teacher didn't even notice. We went up to Vice-principal Kent. . . . Leslie got suspended 'cause she always bothers me.

Sometimes teachers recognized that being very sensitive or afraid could be a problem that children needed to learn to deal with.

> At today's planning meeting for Team A, Mr. Little (white) said, "Next we have to make a listing of the children with social or emotional problems, from the most to the least abusive." There was no explanation of the purpose of the listing given. Ms. Nobel (white) went through her record book, and every time she saw the name of a child

whom she felt should be considered, she read the name out loud. [Fifteen minutes of notes omitted.] Ms. Winters (white) said, "What about Ann?" One of the other teachers said, "No, she hasn't any problem." Mr. Little disagreed, "But she can't even take someone saying to her, 'I'm going to kick your butt.' She needs to be able to take that. She has a social problem." Another teacher queried, "What about Leslie? She's the one who dishes it out." Mr. Little replied, "No, she is OK. She can take it too." Both Ann (white) and Leslie (black) were added to the list.

More often the unusually active or aggressive child ended up in trouble while the unusually timid child received support and sympathy.

The white children were clearly more afraid for themselves physically than the black children. Indeed, in a survey of over one thousand of Wexler's students conducted by the school, one-third of the white students indicated that they often felt afraid in the hallways. In sharp contrast, only about 10 percent of the black children reported such fear. White children were also more likely to report specific kinds of victimization than were blacks. For example, whites were one and a half times as likely as blacks to report having been forced to give money to another student (16 percent vs. 10 percent). Similar or even more pronounced differences in reported victimization by someone of the other race are also evident in Patchen's (1982) study of interracial high schools.

One important factor in the whites' sense of being threatened was their own propensity to interpret even apparently playful acts as attacks, especially when the perpetrator of the act was black. The symbolic interactionist perspective is useful in illuminating what appeared to be occurring at Wexler. This perspective argues that the meaning of acts is not necessarily inherent in them. Even knowledge of the external context in which an act occurs does not let one predict with certainty the meaning it will have. Rather, the interpretation of a piece of behavior is highly dependent on the perspective and the expectations of the perceiver (Shibutani 1961). Black children, especially boys, did appear to initiate considerably more mildly aggressive physical activity than whites. However, this difference in and of itself did not seem enough to account fully for the sense of threat felt by many white children. Rather, to understand the origin of the white students' feelings, it is crucial to examine the children's perceptions about what their various interactions signified.

Black and white children differed noticeably in the ways they interpreted various levels of physical contact. Compared to black children, whites appeared predisposed to see ambiguous physical contact situations as dangerous or as motivated by an intent to annoy or intimidate (Sagar and Schofield 1980). Vice-principal Kent's comments supported this observation.

> I noticed [that in the fall] a lot of black youngsters used to touch white youngsters' hair and just feel it. Probably the little white girls would become angry and start crying. . . . [They] didn't know how to take this. Now some of them do.

Ms. Fowler, a social worker at Wexler, told of a somewhat similar situation in which a white boy experienced physical contact in the hall as intimidation even though in her judgment it was not intended as such.

> Ms. Fowler (white) said that one concerned white mother called her up to talk about the school, saying, "My son says that a good day at Wexler is a day when there is no intimidation!" The mother was shocked and upset by the statement. Her son said the intimidation was mainly pushing and shoving and sometimes hitting out in the halls, and that black children were almost always the initiators of such behavior. . . . The mother said that, from her son's description of the incidents, she was unable to tell whether they were really meant as intimidation or not. Ms. Fowler [who spends much of her day in the hallways] felt that much of the pushing or hitting was not meant as intimidation, but that some children just wanted the others out of their way and would barge through without meaning to scare anyone. . . . I myself was once almost literally knocked over by a rather heavy black child who was pursuing another black boy up the ramp. I'm sure the child gave no thought to the fact that he bumped into me. He was intensely occupied with catching up with his companion. However, the bump rather hurt. If one were anxious or fearful, it easily might have been interpreted as an instance of intimidation.

The fear that many white children at Wexler had of blacks was apparent in their reactions to blacks' relatively mild and playful dominance behavior. This is well illustrated in the following field notes on an encounter between Greg, a large black boy, and Saul, who was white. Saul, slender and very quiet, wore glasses and was one of the most intellectually oriented children in Ms. Monroe's science class.

> Greg drops a small piece of wool which has come from Lydia's shawl on Saul's head. Saul ignores [this] and continues reading even when Greg and Martin [a heavy black like Greg] take it off and put it on a couple of times. Martin then wanders over to Len, a white boy who is sitting alone as Saul was. He puts the piece of wool on Len's head. Len puts his head down on the desk, ignoring Greg . . . so studiously that it doesn't seem natural. . . . [A few minutes later] Saul stops reading and busily spends several minutes constructing a fort out of five empty tables and nine chairs. He fits the tables together so that they form a solid circular wall around him and leave just enough room for him inside the circle. Then, making it even more impenetrable, he brings up nine chairs, [arranging them in a manner which blocks] off the only way you can enter the center part, which is, of course, by crawling underneath the tables. He then goes and just sits inside of this fortress very quietly. No one reacts immediately. However, before too many minutes have passed Martin comes and sits at one of the chairs facing Saul at the center of the table. Then Dick, a white boy, comes over and sits in another of the chairs. These two kids start to dismantle the fort, saying, "Hey, let's make some other arrangement." Saul acquiesces without protest and leaves the place where he had been sitting.

The very fear and uncertainty that predisposed white children to interpret ambiguous events as threatening or mildly threatening events as serious intimidation also fed the spread of rumors about intimidation.

> The four white boys then went on to talk with Ms. Fowler (white) about how black kids beat white kids up. Ms. Fowler asked if any of them had been beaten up or threatened. They said, "No." But they all said they had heard through friends of friends or some other tenuous connection about instances of intimidation or actual fights.

The white children initially adopted one of three major strategies in dealing with the threat they perceived from black children. One strategy employed by many children was submission. They failed to protect themselves or to call on others to do so. Many of these children were afraid to report problems to teachers because they were convinced that retribution would follow. Hence they saw no way out of their predicament. They were afraid not to submit and afraid to ask others to intervene on their behalf. Again, there are striking similarities between the conclusions of this study and Patchen's (1982) research. Patchen reports, for example, that whites were twice as likely as blacks (40 percent vs. 20 percent) to report that they had been pushed or hit by other-race students but had decided not to push back.

Another widely used strategy was withdrawal from the situation. The child did not object. He or she did not overtly refuse to do what was requested but just disappeared.

> One of Tony's sneakers was on the floor when I entered the classroom today. Tony (black) says to Dave, who's white, "Pick it up." There is no response from Dave. Tony starts toward Dave repeating the command. Dave retreats to another part of the room. Pursuit is difficult because the tables are very close together. Tony . . . picks up the sneaker himself and sits down next to Ted (black).

White children sometimes took flight at the approach of black children, even if the latter approached in a very ordinary and nonthreatening manner.

> Today the class is viewing the movie, *Conrack*, on the closed-circuit television. . . . Two white girls, Linda and Margie, have been seated on a shelf inside a cabinet-type piece of furniture all period so far [about 25 minutes]. This cabinet is near the door, as far from the TV screen as possible. It has no doors, so the shelf can serve as a seat and the sides of the cabinet come out around the seats to make a rather private and protected cubby hole. Linda and Margie have been playing little hand games or just talking quietly. . . . Rob (a large black child) wanders over to the cabinet and takes a seat. The girls *immediately* vacate their places and move to the floor nearby although there was room for three children in the cabinet if they had been willing to sit close to each other. . . . [After about three minutes] two other black boys . . . join Rob in the cabinet and another is standing nearby talking to them. The girls have moved again. One has gone to a table at which several white girls and one black girl are seated. The other, Margie, has taken a very unusual position . . . sitting on the floor in a corner space which is about two feet square. The corner is protected on three sides. [Two sides consist of the classroom's walls as they meet in a corner. The supply cabinet, which juts out into the room about two feet, forms the third wall.] I can't help but wonder how Margie feels. She certainly looks very isolated. Her earlier perch was . . . considerably more

comfortable and clearly had a better view of both the TV and the classroom.

In addition to submitting and withdrawing, white children frequently just ignored behavior by blacks that they found annoying. They acted as if nothing at all had happened. In fact, they acted as if the black child did not exist. Ralph Ellison's (1952) thesis that blacks are treated as "invisible" by whites was amply borne out by the behavior of many white children at Wexler.

> Jim, the new white student, walks past Richard's (black) seat on his way to his table. Richard says with reference to Jim, "He's working for once." Then Richard goes over to where Jim is now sitting. He feigns a couple of punches to Jim's cheek. He may actually have made contact, but not hard. Jim makes no noticeable reaction.

> Martin, who is black, gets up and crosses the room to the pencil sharpener. He passes behind Tim, who is also black, and makes an X on the back of Tim's shirt with his pencil. Tim turns, frowns and checks his shirt to see if the other fellow has actually written on it. He looks slightly angry. As Martin continues towards the pencil sharpener, he passes behind Rex, a white boy, and does the same thing to him that he just finished doing to Tim. Rex doesn't even turn his head. He continues sitting in his rather slouched position and ignores Tim, who clearly wants to get a little bit of mischief going.

Many white children tended to ignore blacks as much as they could even when the behavior of the blacks was not perceived as threatening. Some children felt this made sense because blacks and whites had little in common. Others hesitated to approach or respond to blacks, even when there was no obvious reason not to, because they feared a negative reaction.

> *Laura* (white): The black kids and the white kids don't really associate with each other. . . . Like I try to ignore the blacks.
> *Interviewer*: Why do you do that?
> *Laura*: Well, they ignore me too. . . . We don't really associate. . . . There's nothing really we have in common. . . . The black kids are talking about their own things.

> *Margie* (white): The black kids really have to like you before you can like them, 'cause he'd be the one who'd want to beat you up or something

if you tried to be friends and he didn't like you. But all the kids in our classroom are really nice. They're even nice to their enemies . . . but they just have a feel for fighting, so they fight.

Submitting, withdrawing, and ignoring all appeared on one level to be "safe" strategies for handling perceived threat because they minimized the chance of overt confrontations. Yet, like the taboo against racial reference, these safe strategies were in some ways dysfunctional. Adopting them, especially the strategy of submitting, appeared to encourage dominant behavior on the part of the more active children. The child who routinely submitted even when the threat was minimal only reinforced the dominant behavior of the other children, who learned that they could get what they wanted with little or no effort. The strategy of ignoring, in addition to encouraging the more dominant children to do whatever they wished, sometimes seemed actually to provoke more intense efforts to annoy in order to gain at least some response. Indeed, black children often interpreted white children's withdrawing from them or ignoring them as signs of conceit and feelings of superiority. When this interpretation was drawn, behavior that started as an attempt to engage another in rough-and-tumble play sometimes turned into an attempt to intimidate a reluctant playmate. Thus in some cases a vicious circle was set in motion that was difficult to break. Whites ignored or withdrew from blacks because of fear of their rough-and-tumble style. Blacks interpreted whites' behavior as motivated by prejudice or conceit and, being angered by such treatment, engaged in more clearly aggressive behavior, which frightened whites even more.

THE WHITE BOYS' DILEMMA

The first section of this chapter discussed a variety of differences between the social interaction patterns of boys and girls. The second section explored some differences in the behavioral styles of black and white children that led to tension between them and to some fear on the part of white students. This third section will explore the ways in which certain of these differences between boys' and girls' peer interaction patterns interacted with black/white differences in behavioral style to create a rather uncomfortable and threatened position for the white boys. As discussed previously, the boys at Wexler had considerable contact with boys of the other race because of their interest in sports and the emphasis in male peer groups on proving one's physical prowess in contests with others. Yet, on the average, the black boys had the edge in such competition. Thus the white boys were on the defensive. Seriously exacerbating the problem for the white boys was the fear that many of them felt of blacks, which led them to perceive ambiguously aggressive behaviors performed by blacks as more threatening than identical behaviors performed by whites (Sagar and Schofield 1980). Thus, what might have been enjoyable rough-and-tumble play between two whites took on an element of threat when a black and a white were involved. Since the boys engaged in a great deal more rough play than the girls, the black/white differences in behavioral style relating to such play were more salient for the boys than the girls. Even if the white boys did not initiate rough-and-tumble inter- actions themselves, they were likely to be directly challenged to compete. Although many of the white boys felt afraid in such situ- ations, it was harder for them than for white girls to use strategies such as submitting, ignoring, or withdrawing since to do so brought their masculinity into question. Whereas the white girls often bunched into small groups that avoided blacks, the white boys had to find a way to deal directly with them.

By the spring of their first year at Wexler, the white boys evolved a strategy for dealing with the threat they felt they faced. Some of them began to coalesce into a group with a special group name and modes of behavior. Signs of the group's activities were manifold. For example, large block-letter graffiti reading, "Mouse Power," appeared in chalk on the outside of the school building near the playground. Some students even wore T-shirts emblazoned with their club's name.

> *Vice-principal Kent*: I see the youngsters getting together in groups . . . that some people outside might characterize as gangs. . . . One of the groups, called the Mice, has about thirty or forty members. . . . An- other group that has emerged [is] called the Dogs, and I am surmising . . . there are about fifteen or twenty youngsters [there] . . . . I think one group may have an initiation process; the other may not. . . . I don't think that the groups themselves have come into conflict with each other. . . . This . . . is something I don't like to see started.

Interviewer: And you say the groups are integrated?
Vice-principal Kent: Yes, some of them.
Interviewer: Are they sort of fifty/fifty?
Vice-principal Kent: Oh, no! They are very lightly integrated as far as I know. The Mice [most of whom are white] are very lightly integrated. The Dogs are not integrated, come to think of it. [They are black.]
Interviewer: Are these groups only male?
Vice-principal Kent: Yes.

Although the vice-principal believed that the Mice were "lightly integrated," other sources, both students and teachers, claimed it was an all-white group just as the Dogs was a black group.

A number of facts about these clubs suggest that the initial impetus for them was the difficult position of white boys at Wexler. Although information about the clubs was hard to obtain since the school made its disapproval of them very clear quite rapidly, it appears quite certain that the white group, the Mice, became active first. The contention that the club membership was an attempt on the part of individual white boys, who felt insecure in their physical competition with the blacks, to band together to gain strength in numbers was supported by several facts. First, many of the members of the Mice were academically strong students, the very students who many felt were the most likely to be intimidated. Second, the white boys on our interview panel all spontaneously characterized these clubs as either fighting or protection clubs. In sharp contrast, only one black boy perceived the clubs in this way. The others all categorized them as athletic or social in nature. Finally, the associations of the club names seem most suggestive. One thinks of mice as scampering around only when it is safe to emerge from their small holes. They are hardly the powerful or ferocious beasts after which adolescent boys often name their groups. Also, if this is not too fanciful, mice are quite clearly associated with the word *white*. The name of the black club, the Dogs, gives rise to a somewhat more imposing image than the name the Mice. However, even this name falls considerably short of inspiring terror. As a matter of fact, it was quite consistent with the black boys' physically active rough-and-tumble behavior.

Excerpts from the interviews illustrate the very different way these clubs were perceived by black and white boys.

Interviewer: And what sort of things did the Mice do?

Mac (white): They didn't do much, except when somebody beat up one of the Mice [the whole group] went after that kid and beat him up.

Interviewer: Do you remember where the club name came from?

Mac: No, well, Matthew . . . was going to be Matthew Mouse and I was MacMouse. . . . I don't know. It sounds better than Rat. . . . It was just made up. It's original. I've not heard about that many mouse gangs.

Interviewer: We were talking about the Mice and the Dogs. What sort of clubs are they?

Don (black): [They] play games and everything. . . .

Interviewer: What kind of games?

Don: Soccer, football, baseball.

Interviewer: What else do they do?

Don: That's all. . . . They have parties too. . . .

Interviewer: Why do you think these groups started?

Don: Maybe 'cause people wanted to be with their friends or something.

Although Vice-principal Kent referred to the existence of other groups, the Mice and the Dogs were clearly the two major ones operating. Most teachers were unaware of any other groups, although a few students talked vaguely of the Cats and Rats or even the Foreign Legion. No real evidence of the existence of the other groups was found, and students who gave these other club names were generally unable to say what type of student belonged to them.

Obviously, the existence of two fairly strong boys' clubs or gangs, one black and the other white, posed considerable potential danger to the tolerably smooth relationships that had evolved over the course of Wexler's first year. The school was sufficiently concerned about the potential for problems to hold a meeting at which one of the white counselors, Mr. Foley, and the principal, Mr. Reuben, spoke with the boys. The adults stressed the fact that clubs could turn into fighting gangs and that the school was concerned about them. The counselor volunteered to serve as an advisor to the clubs if they wanted to do things like raise money for field trips. Then students who were group members were asked to identify themselves by standing. Most apparently did so. The school took the further step of notifying the parents of group members about the clubs. Vice-principal Kent said that the school did not feel it could require parents to discourage the clubs. However, school staff hoped to undermine the clubs by persuading the parents of the potential dangers associated with them.

The school's efforts to break up the clubs were successful. In interviews during the school's second year, students unanimously agreed that the clubs had ceased to function.

> *Interviewer*: One thing we discussed last year was the clubs like the Mice and the Dogs. Are these clubs still active?
> *Norman* (black): No, there's no clubs like that [this year].
> *Interviewer*: Do people ever talk about them?
> *Norman*: Not since Mr. Reuben told them not to.
> *Interviewer*: Oh, so that is why they fell apart?
> *Norman*: Yeah, I guess so.
> *Interviewer*: What did he say? Do you remember?
> *Norman*: He said if you had a gang you might end up having fights and stuff like that. . . . They went along with him because there's no clubs now.

Wexler averted a potentially serious hazard by undermining the clubs. However, without realizing it, the school also destroyed one mechanism that the white boys had developed to help them handle what they perceived to be a very real threat. Operating in an environment that virtually assumed positive intergroup relations, that almost outlawed discussion of problems perceived by the children as racial in nature, and that tended to ignore students' experiences in places outside of the classroom, in which much of the rough-and-tumble play and intimidation occurred, some of the white boys turned inward to their peers for support. Denied the comfort of a group identity and the strength that numbers bring, some of the physically weaker or more timid white boys had difficulty finding an effective way to handle the sense of threat they felt.

5

THE FOURTH R: READING, 'RITING, 'RITHMETIC, AND ROMANCE

As indicated in the preceding chapters, there were numerous factors operating at Wexler that led students to interact primarily with others of their own race in spite of the school's basic commitment to fostering positive relations between black and white students. Even stronger than the students' tendency to spend their time with others of their own race was their tendency to cluster into single-sex peer groups. Yet ironically, although the students actively avoided those of the other sex in many situations, they were keenly aware of each other as the objects of romantic and sexual interest. An analysis of interaction patterns between boys and girls of middle school age is of considerable interest in and of itself, since it is during this early adolescent period that children must begin to grapple with what it will mean to be an emotionally and sexually mature adult. This analysis takes on added importance, however, when one realizes that the burgeoning of sexual awareness and romantic interest that occurs in early adolescence further complicates relations between blacks and whites.

This chapter will first explore the extent to which segregation on the basis of gender occurred at Wexler as well as the students' reactions to and explanations for this segregation. This analysis is a necessary backdrop to understanding the ways in which the students expressed their romantic and sexual interests. Since students develop so rapidly during early adolescence, I will examine the evolution of relations between the sexes from sixth to eighth grade, sketching out the major changes that occurred during that time period. Finally, I will discuss the ways in which the burgeoning of romantic interests, as well as the existence of some of the differences in behavioral style discussed in the previous chapter, influenced the development of intergroup relations at Wexler.

GENDER SEGREGATION

When students at Wexler were free to choose others with whom to play or work, they overwhelmingly selected those of their own sex. Indeed, voluntary resegregation on the basis of gender was markedly stronger than such resegregation on the basis of race. The analysis of seating patterns in the school cafeteria, referred to in Chapter 4, showed this phenomenon clearly (Schofield and Sagar 1977). Indeed, frequently no more than half a dozen children out of more than two hundred in a given lunch period sat next to someone of the opposite sex, compared to a dozen or more sitting next to someone of the other race. The overriding importance of gender was made clear when children had to choose between interacting with someone of their own race or sex. Virtually without fail, children in such situations interacted with a classmate from the other racial group. The resistance to joining a group of students of the other sex was so strong that students occasionally accepted punishment rather than do so.

> Mr. Little instructs the students to form groups of *three* for a science experiment. None of the groups formed are sexually integrated. . . . The teacher notices a group of four boys and instructs one of its members, Juan (black), "Go over and work with Diane." [Diane's group has two black girls in it.] Shaking his head, Juan says, "No, I don't want to!" Mr. Little says quietly but with an obvious edge in his voice, "Then take off your lab apron and go back to the regular class." Juan stands absolutely still and doesn't reply. After a long, heavy silence, Mr. Little says, "OK. I'll do it for you." He unties Juan's apron and sends him out of the room.

Students not only sat near those of their own gender but also exerted noticeable pressure on mavericks who, through carelessness or preference, tried to break out of the segregated pattern.

The chairs in Mr. Hudson's (white) room are arranged in the shape of a wide, shallow U. As the first few kids come into the room, Harry (white) says to John (white), who is starting to sit down in an empty section of the room along one side of the U, "Don't sit there, that's where all the girls sit." Harry and John sit elsewhere. . . .

Virtually every study that has compared the impact of gender and race on interaction and friendship patterns in children of junior high school age or younger concludes, as this one does, that sex is a considerably stronger grouping criterion than race. For example, Krenkel (1972) found that when playing and eating, fourth, fifth, and sixth graders in a desegregated school were much more likely to form sexually segregated than racially segregated groups. St. John and Lewis (1975) concluded that gender has a much stronger influence than race on sociometric measures of friendship choice among sixth graders. Singleton and Asher (1977, 1979) assessed both sociometric choices and actual peer interactions in elementary school children. The tendency to in-group choice along gender lines was dramatically stronger than that for in-group choice along racial lines. In fact, in the sociometric data, sex accounted for roughly twenty times as much variance as race. A similar sociometric study in Wexler's sixth grade yielded consistent but less striking results, with sex accounting for about four times as much variance as race (Schofield and Whitley 1982).

The strength of the children's tendency to cluster in groups of their own sex is intriguing since many of the factors that played an important role in leading to voluntary racial resegregation could hardly account for gender segregation. Two of these factors are, of course, differences in socioeconomic status and area of residence. Furthermore, the achievement gap, which led both to resegregation and to friction between blacks and whites, was negligible in the case of boys and girls.

The factors that contributed to pervasive gender segregation were no doubt numerous and complex. Without attempting an exhaustive analysis of all of them, I would like to outline some in order to set off in sharp relief the fundamental differences between the racial and sexual aggregation at Wexler. First, in striking contrast to their general policy of avoiding all mention of race, school personnel, from administrators to teachers, openly mentioned gender and saw it as a legitimate basis for making certain types of distinctions as well as for grouping children. Thus, for example, no one seemed to think twice about the wisdom or necessity of having separate gym and health classes for boys and girls. Furthermore, teachers often found gender a convenient distinction to use in managing their classrooms.

> At the end of class, the teacher (white) says, "OK ladies, let's get ready. Hand in all of your papers." He and Jim (black) stroll toward the door. His hand rests on Jim's shoulder in a friendly fashion. As they near the door where the girls are lining up, Jim halts, saying, "I ain't no lady." The teacher says, "OK gentlemen, push in your chairs. Let's go." Class is dismissed.

Although Wexler's staff fostered single-sex peer groups by many of their practices, it would be incorrect to see their actions as the only or even the major cause of the gender segregation that occurred. The students, especially the boys, clearly preferred single-sex groups for many activities. To some extent, this preference was based on the differences in boys' and girls' interests and skills. For example, as was discussed in Chapter 4, many of the boys were very interested in sports, a topic of considerably less fascination to the majority of girls. This high level of interest led many boys to engage in sports more than girls, which, of course, increased their skill level. However, even those girls who were interested in sports were not attractive teammates for boys. If a girl was not skilled, she was a burden to a team and an unexciting competitor. If she was skilled, she posed a potential threat to the boys' masculine pride, which did not completely offset the contributions she might make as a team member. The following field notes illustrate the way in which boys and girls often acted when required to participate on coeducational sports teams as they occasionally were during affective education periods:

> Today, Ms. Monroe (black) and Ms. Emery (white) have planned kickball as the AE activity. A boy suggests that the boys should form a team and play against the girls, but no one takes him up on it. Three white girls go sit on the playground to work on their homework as the others form teams. Later, the ball lands a few feet from them, but they ignore it, working industriously. . . . A small, slender white girl, Amanda, makes a foul, then a strike. The pitcher, Gerald (black), gets

very angry with her as she lets six or seven of his reasonably good pitches go by. Finally, she kicks the ball. Gerald catches it easily. He then throws it at her with unusual force as she runs to first base. She is out. James (black), one of Amanda's teammates, mutters in a disgusted tone, "You girls!"

The differences in boys' and girls' interests stood out clearly in enrollment figures for the in-school clubs and after-school activities. Although some of these activities appealed to both sexes, a great number appealed exclusively or primarily to one group. So, for example, the advanced sewing club was the girls' territory, whereas boys predominated in the model rocket and bodybuilding clubs. In interviews, students again and again asserted that their preference for same-sex friendship groups stemmed from these differences in interests.

Interviewer: In your class, do the boys mix more with the boys or the girls?
Harry (white): The boys!
Interviewer: Why?
Harry: Well, there's boy talk and girl talk.

Interviewer: I've noticed in the lunchroom that very often boys sit together and girls sit together. Why do you think that is?
Bob (white): So they can talk. The boys talk about football and sports, and the girls talk about whatever they talk about.

Note that Bob knows what boys talk about. He maintains he does not know what girls discuss, but he assumes it is different.

Although different interests and skills accounted for some of the gender segregation at Wexler, a number of more subtle factors related to the students' particular developmental stage – early adolescence – were also conducive to that outcome. Students at Wexler were at a point in their lives at which both the physical changes accompanying puberty and the changes in social expectations relating to their developing sexuality made their gender identity quite salient. Many of Wexler's students, like the sixth grader, Jim, quoted earlier in this chapter, who asserted, "I ain't no lady," seemed bound and determined to be perceived, to use a phrase that was employed constantly by one group of children, as "real men" or "real women." This assertion of gender identity took a form that ironically led to isolation between boys and girls. Specifically, some children demonstrated their maleness or femaleness by emphasizing the differences between themselves and the other group. Especially, but not exclusively, among boys this emphasis on the difference between boys and girls was sometimes accompanied by denigration of the out-group.

> Sarah (black) came up to me in class today and asked if I was married and had children. After answering her, I asked if she wanted children someday. She said, "Yes, yes!" going on to explain that she wanted a girl but not a boy saying, "Boys are too icky." She discussed boys' deficiencies at length, ending her catalogue of their faults by saying, "Boys have to get their butts kicked!"

> The children are signing up for the in-school clubs. . . . Three white boys up in the front of the classroom are making fun of the clubs involving traditionally feminine activities. . . . John says sarcastically, "Sewing. . . . Wow!" Harry chimes in, using the same falsetto tone, "Oh my, quilting. . . . " At the end of class, the teacher (white) says, "Okay, line up — ladies first." When Mike (white) heads toward the door, the teacher says, "Oh, I see. Mike is a lady. . . . " Meanwhile, Harold (black) has been bothering Dede (black), who says to him in an annoyed tone, "Why don't you quit, boy?" Harold (black) shouts back, "Shut up, girl," putting great contempt in his tone as he says *girl*.

As discussed above, one way of demonstrating masculinity or femininity is to stay apart from and to emphasize the differences between oneself and the other sex. It is, of course, also true that success in sexual or romantic relations with the other sex is generally seen as a mark of masculinity or femininity. Indeed, although Wexler's students generally maintained that boys and girls did not often become friends, they were very aware of members of the other sex as potential romantic or sexual partners. In fact, they assumed that virtually any personal relation between a boy and girl would be romantic or sexual in nature. Questions about children getting to know members of the other sex were virtually always interpreted as questions about romantic or sexual relations by teachers and students alike.

Interviewer: How do boys and girls get to know each other?

Jennifer (black): The boy just says he likes you, and he starts calling you, and after that you go steady.

Interviewer: What kinds of interactions are there between boys and girls at Wexler?
Ms. Berner (white): Mostly it's caveman stuff. . . . There's probably only about six to eight sexually active girls in my classes. . . . There is also the goofy stage, quietly breathing at each other.

The assumption that virtually all relations between boys and girls are romantic is not unique to Wexler. Clement et al. (1977) report that the fifth and sixth graders in a Southern school, like the students at Wexler, assumed that boys and girls who spent time together or showed interest in each other were romantically involved. This assumption often leads children to avoid the types of interactions that might lead to friendship. For example, Fine (1981) argues that preadolescent friends spend a great deal of time in activities designed to socialize them into adolescent or adult roles. One example of such activities would be working together on class projects. Yet boys and girls at Wexler tended to avoid contact with each other during this sort of task at least partly because of the possibility that working together might suggest romantic involvement.

Interviewer: Do boys and girls mix much in your class while they are working?
Stacey (black): No, because people like to work with their friends. . . .
When you're working on a project . . . your friend has to call and come over to your house. If it's a boy, it can be complicated.

Indeed, some children avoided even casual conversation with those of the opposite sex out of concern that it would be interpreted as a sign of romantic interest.

Sally (white): If you talk with boys, they [other girls] say that you're almost going with him.
Interviewer: What does the boy think?
Sally: I don't know. I can't tell what a boy thinks. It's hard.
Interviewer: You mentioned you have deep conversations with your girlfriends. Do you ever have conversations like that with boys?
Sally: Never. I mean, it never crossed my mind.

Rather ironically, then, the development of friendship between boys and girls was impeded because the children were aware that they were approaching the age when they might begin to become deeply involved with each other in a romantic or sexual way.

Although peers tended to discourage most types of cross-sex interaction, much of the interaction within same-sex peer groups revolved around preparation for future relations with the other sex. The boys, especially those in the seventh and eighth grades, often quite openly discussed sexuality. Girls, from the early sixth grade on, devoted many of their conversations with friends to romantic intrigues. Both groups of children showed a strong awareness of the future intertwining of the male and female roles.

> Looking up from his book, Vincent (black) says to Stan (black), "I want an education. Then, I'll get married and have a family."

Thus, although the children believed that they had few interests in common to share as friends with members of the other sex, they had definite romantic interests and expected to form lasting mutual attachments in the future. It is interesting to note that they did not seem concerned about the potential contradiction between their conviction that boys and girls were not sufficiently similar to be friends and their intention to form deep and lasting cross-sex romantic and sexual relationships in the not-too-distant future.

THE DEVELOPMENT OF ROMANTIC AND SEXUAL BEHAVIOR FROM SIXTH TO EIGHTH GRADE

Both students and teachers agreed that the amount of romantic and sexual interest shown by the students at Wexler increased dramatically from sixth to eighth grade. Furthermore, the ways in which these interests were expressed also changed markedly over time. These changes were quite accurately, if briefly, outlined by an eighth grader.

> *James* (white): Back in kindergarten, boys and girls liked each other, and in the first grade, they talked to each other. . . . In third grade, they thought the other [group] was strange and ran around saying, "You got the cooties. . . . " In sixth grade, [it] was the same, but they started to change. . . . When I was in the sixth grade, people would

still pull each other's hair and stuff like that . . . [but] at the end of the year, they were starting to change. . . . . In the seventh grade, it's starting to change, people [are] maturing. In eighth grade, they started having relationships. . . .

Although it is obvious that at any given point in time some children in a particular grade were more openly and actively involved in romantic activities than others, it is possible to sketch a picture of the evolution of the students' romantic behavior from the sixth through the eighth grades. Such a sketch, while not accurately describing the development of each and every child, can point out the general patterns that set the context in which black and white boys and girls interacted with each other.

As the eighth grader James pointed out, the sixth grade was an important transitional year in relations between boys and girls. At the beginning of their sixth grade year, most of Wexler's students showed relatively little overt romantic interest. This was especially true of the boys, who were slower than the girls to show clear signs of such interest. Soon though, many of the girls began to discuss boys with their friends and to plan romantic intrigues. Although some boys became interested in romance toward the end of their sixth grade year, most lagged well behind their female counterparts in showing evidence of such interests. Many appeared basically unconcerned with romance through most of the seventh grade.

Interviewer: When kids are romantically interested in each other, what do they do?

Ms. Winters (white): Smack each other! In teaching sixth grade, you see the same patterns no matter what class you have. . . . The girls start noticing the boys about mid-October, and the boys start noticing the girls about mid-March or the beginning of April. Some of the boys were very open this year, announcing they were going with so and so. "Going with" meant that they called each other a couple of times, and they might have met at the roller-skating rink. . . . It's very friend-oriented, within a group.

Ms. Partridge (black): You hear the . . . girls discussing boys and dates and things. . . . You see whispering about . . . who likes who . . . [but] at this age [seventh grade] . . . most boys are really not interested in girls. . . . There are a few isolated cases. . . . On this team I really can't think of more than five boys that . . . I've heard say that he's in love. . . . They are really serious about it. . . .

Although sixth grade boys and girls occasionally telephoned each other or met for roller-skating or the movies, by far more common were awkward expressions of romantic interest such as hitting, teasing, or bothering, as indicated by Ms. Winters's further comments on romance.

> The cafeteria is a good time to watch it. You'll see a group of girls smacking one of the boys and running away, or pouring chocolate milk down his back. . . .

The earliest indications of romantic interest seemed designed primarily to gain the attention of the object of that interest. As illustrated by Ms. Winters's comments above, these behaviors were often, on the surface at least, quite annoying and contained no obvious indication of romantic intentions. Yet these attempts to gain attention by pushing, taunting, or reporting another to the teacher were generally correctly understood by the children. Recall, for example, how in Chapter 4 a sixth grader reported that girls who were "pushed" or "bothered" by boys gained status within their own peer group. Exemplifying overtly negative but nonetheless romantically intended behavior were the insults that boys and girls often traded about each other's physical appearance. Generally, although not always, these insults were traded in a playful way.

> Warren (black) has his hand and wrist taped up, and one of his . . . classmates, Stacy (black), asks him about it. He says, "I was trying to split a cinder block. I did split a brick." He runs out of the gym calling, "Don't look at me, girls." Cynthia (black) replies scornfully, "Who'd want to look at you?" Warren expands his chest as far as he can and repeats over and over, "This chest is a rock." Janet (white) says, "What chest?"

Toward the end of sixth grade and throughout seventh grade, the awkward attempts to gain others' attention by annoying them one way or another were gradually supplemented by more overtly romantic behaviors. For example, direct declarations of romantic interest became more frequent. Often a same-sex peer served as a messenger who conveyed the initial indication of such interest. A more subtle but equally effective technique involved teasing within a single-sex peer group in a context that virtually assured being overheard by the person who was the object of the group member's desires. In both cases, the person whose romantic inclinations were being discussed typically denied the allegations heatedly. Thus news of the interest was transmitted rather subtly, allowing the person who liked another to gauge the other's reaction without the risk of actually admitting his or her own interest.

Another overt sign of romantic interest, which was rare indeed before the end of the sixth grade but which proliferated after that point, was the sending of love letters. For example, two girls wrote a note to two boys asking them to become their boyfriends. The negative reply, written on a torn scrap of paper, is reproduced here complete with spelling and grammatical errors.

Me and Sam all ready have girl friend. we ain't going to tell you there names cause you might beat them up.

The girls then responded on the back of the boys' reply.

But when you quit them, will you go with us?

The girls also kindly provided two options, "Yes" or "No," so all the boys needed to do was to circle the "right" answer. The boys ungallantly circled "No." Although love letters like these were sometimes sent, anonymous letters delivered by a third party or phony letters meant to tease were more common.

Interviewer: Do black and white kids show romantic interest in the same ways, or — ?
Ms. Monroe (black): Yes, hitting each other, punching, chasing down the hall. . . . They write love letters, anonymously though. . . . They give them to me, and I'm supposed to pass them on. . . . Girls say, "This is a note. Would you please give it to this person?" I say, "OK." I don't want to interfere with their romantic tendencies. . . . I give it to them, and I don't read it either. I should have, probably. . . . Really, I hope it was nothing obscene.

Love letters were sometimes sent in a friend's name. Although this was similar in many ways to the widespread practice of one's friends announcing one's romantic preference, it seemed to embarrass all concerned more, perhaps because the note could be shown around, and its contents sometimes made the alleged sender seem a little silly.

> Billy (white) and three other seventh grade boys at his table suddenly laugh very hard and loud. . . . Billy gives Lana (white) a note. Lana shows it to Barb (black) and the other girls at her table, and they all laugh. Lana says, giggling, "Maybe we should show this to Ms. Carone [their teacher]. . . . " Don (black) says, "Is my name on it?" Lana smiles but doesn't answer. Billy, in response to questions from the girls, is repeating, "I did nothing of the sort," while he laughs uproariously. . . . It turns out that Billy wrote a note to Barb, signing it with Don's name. The note said, "Dear Barb, I like you very much. You look so like the morning dew. Will you please go to the movies with me on Friday night? Circle Yes, No, Maybe. Love, Don Scott."

Toward the end of sixth grade and in seventh grade, Wexler's students, especially the boys, sometimes expressed their attraction to another in such a pronounced or playful way that it could be written off as teasing or fooling around. Such behavior often occurred in the company of peers who provided support and validation of the playful intent.

> Daniel, a black boy, comes running up to Sara (white). . . . He grabs her, putting his arm around her shoulders. She tries to get away, but before she can completely extricate herself, Joe (black), who has run up behind Daniel with a camera, snaps a picture. The two boys run away laughing gleefully. Joe says, "We've got the evidence!" Eric (white) jokes with a wide grin, "He tried to rape her."

The most striking example of the playacting of romantic interest was a mock wedding organized by some sixth graders near the end of the school year. Vice-principal Kent described this event as follows:

> Some girls were teasing another girl about liking a young man and . . . announced there was supposed to be a mock marriage. . . . They said, "We're going to have a marriage ceremony." One student was going to be the Rabbi . . . another the Maid of Honor, another the Best Man. [There was going to be] a catered lunch of cookies and pop. It was really cute, and . . . amazingly enough, it was an integrated group, and I thought that was really novel. . . . The culminating point was that the bride was going to smash a piece of cake into the groom's face. . . . Well,

we discussed it with them and asked . . . [if] the bride and groom [both white] would go through with it. . . . They said, "No," so the whole thing was called off.

The awkward, teasing, and playful expressions of romantic interest just described clearly persisted into the eighth grade, as indicated by the following excerpt from an interview with a white eighth grade girl:

> You always kid around with the boys. . . . All I do is talk a lot, joke and punch, and stuff like that. With girls . . . you don't act so rough. You act like someone were talking with you. . . . With boys, you can't talk to them; they get silly. . . . If somebody hits you . . . you say, "I'm gonna beat you up," and hit him back. . . . You call each other nicknames . . . Mental, Crazy, Hot Temper. . . . They . . . snatch your papers, take your pencil . . . hide your book. . . .

Yet eighth grade was different from sixth grade in that dating had become a real issue, and parties held for boys and girls became much more frequent. The proportion of students who actually went out on dates was not high; yet dating and going to parties at which both boys and girls were present became of great interest and concern.

> *Interviewer*: Is there much dating in the eighth grade?
> *James* (white): Well, Jewish kids have parties. . . . They have lots and lots of parties. . . . Sometimes they talk about it. . . . Kids have told me they've gone on dates with girls, but I'm not friends with anybody who does.
> *Interviewer*: You said that some people talk about it. [What] will they say? . . .
> *James*: They'll boast about it. . . . I think the kids that don't usually get along with girls are shy. . . . They don't get along because of their shyness.

Boys were not the only ones to boast about their exploits with the other sex.

> *Sally* (white): There's this one girl . . . she talks mostly about how she was on the street corner last night on a bench, and a drunk man came up to her and put his arm around her . . . and how she was talking to these cute boys. . . . It's just wild stories. . . . You know they exaggerate.

Interviewer: Well, why do you think they exaggerate?
Sally: To make it look better . . . so *they* look better.

In the eighth grade, romantic relations began to model themselves more closely on adult patterns than previously. First, as described above, dating and attending mixed parties became common enough for students to be well aware of these practices as very real possibilities for themselves, even if they were not directly involved. The expectation of new adult modes of relating between the sexes was symbolized when the school held a dance for eighth graders, whereas nothing of this sort was seriously contemplated for sixth or seventh graders. Second, although the same-sex peer group still played a vital part in romantic activities, the boys and girls who were attracted to each other began for the first time to spend a moderate amount of time together, either by themselves or in small groups. The common patterns of courting behavior in the sixth and early seventh grades were not conducive to the development of deep emotional relationships, at least partly because they rarely allowed any relaxed or extended contact. Typically, contact and communication during these episodes was highly constricted and had virtually no content except for the indication of romantic or sexual interest. Even these constricted contacts were often made by the friends of those involved rather than by the parties themselves. Thus romantic interests were very unstable, and small incidents led to quick transfers of affection from one person to another. This led one seventh grade teacher to remark, "By the end of this year, it was like a soap opera." However, in the eighth grade, although contact was still often strained, it did occur more frequently and more deeply than in the earlier grades.

Related to the changes in romantic relationships between sixth and eighth grade described above was the fact that mutuality became more important in the eighth grade than before. Specifically, in the earlier grades students who were attracted to others often took pains to hide this attraction or to express it in ways that allowed for other interpretations if the attraction was not reciprocated. For example, as discussed previously, touching and "bothering" were recognized as an indication of romantic interest. They could, however, be treated as something quite different, such as an attempt to annoy, since no direct declaration of interest was required. Thus the child initiating the interaction was protected from public humiliation.

If the response to the overture yielded no indication that the other child reciprocated the interest, the reality of its romantic motivation could easily be denied. Furthermore, norms about the expression of romantic interest were such that the children tended to expect some form of overt rejection, even if the other party was actually interested. In the eighth grade, though, when dating and going together were real possibilities, it became crucially important to be able to judge the real feelings of the other. Thus, for example, the practice of considering someone as your boyfriend even though he had no knowledge of this status was much less possible in the eighth grade than in the sixth.

Just as the expression of romantic interest became more frequent, more pronounced, and more adult as the children moved from sixth to eighth grade, so too did their expression of awareness of their own sexuality and their sexual attraction to others. Even in sixth grade, the students were far from unaware of sexuality, but the expression of that awareness, like the expression of romantic interest, was generally either quite covert or very awkward.

> *Ms. Monroe* (black): At the beginning of the year, I didn't notice anything but toward the middle, after they had sex education and health [laughter] . . . the tulips came up. . . . The boys started looking at the girls and whistling if they wore a dress. Toward spring when the girls started wearing halters, the boys started looking even more.

> *Ms. Winters* (white): A couple of the [sixth grade] boys this year were a little open . . . a little sexually aggressive, grabbing girls' chests or grabbing their backsides. I had to issue a few threats there!

By seventh grade, many boys showed an active interest in sex. For instance, one group of seventh grade boys took advantage of a lull in a math class to have an animated discussion of kissing, including the mechanics of French kissing. Comments such as "Look at those legs," or "What an ass," were relatively common. Interestingly, such comments were often made about female teachers, perhaps because, at least in the sixth and seventh grades, many of the female students were not very mature physically. Most of the boys' references to sexuality occurred within their single-sex peer groups rather than being directed toward female classmates, although little attempt was made to keep classmates from overhearing. Often these discussions were focused on obtaining and sharing sexually related information.

> Bob (black) is reading a *National Geographic*. Sam (white) says, "Hey, Bob, are there any naked ladies in that book?" Bob laughs and says, "Yeah, here is a naked pygmy," as he shows the magazine to Sam.

Although the boys emphasized avoidance of girls in many situations and were slower than girls to show signs of romantic interest in the other sex, they clearly saw heterosexuality as the only appropriate sexual orientation. Indeed, one of the most frequent terms of abuse used between boys was the epithet *faggot*, which one boy announced "means a guy who loves other guys."

Although girls showed an interest in romance even earlier than the boys, they were rarely, if ever, observed discussing sexuality in a relatively open manner and were much less likely than boys to use epithets that questioned another's sexual prowess or orientation. Nonetheless, they were far from unaware of their burgeoning sexuality.

> Joan (black), who is remarkably mature physically for a sixth grader, is wearing a very tight fitting sweater and skirt today. While the other students work, she dances down the middle aisle showing off her body effectively, throwing her arms around . . . rotating her hips and thrusting out her breasts. . . .

> One of the new graffiti in the girls' room today says, "I'd like to do it to David because he is so pretty!" Nearby, written in a different hand, are two large heart-shaped graffiti. Each one has ten to fifteen pairs of names inside like, "Jim and Laurie, Janet and Doug, Sally and Bill."

The same sort of overacting of attraction that was used to express romantic interest was also used as a technique for displaying sexual interest, especially by the boys.

> The substitute for Mr. Hudson is a young attractive black woman with unusually large breasts. The boys are really reacting to her presence. Harold and Leon, both black, sit right in front of her in the first row and try to elbow each other out of the way. Harold says, "I was here first," and Leon responds that he needs to sit up front to "check her out." Leon volunteers his name and asks the teacher hers. When she tells him, he says, "That's pretty. . . . " When the teacher gets to Leon in the roll call, she mistakenly calls him Len. He corrects her but then

adds in an obviously phony "love-sick" voice, "but you can call me Len if you want to."

As children matured, the hitting, grabbing, and punching most prevalent in the sixth grade were gradually supplanted by other forms of touching. Most of this touching was not overtly sexual in content, but it did allow the students to begin to explore what physical contact with the opposite sex was like.

> Jeff (black), a seventh grader, who teases Marion (white) a lot, leans over and touches her neck with his hand. The touch is in between a caress and a poke as he walks his fingers across her neck. . . . Marion first smiles at Jeff. Then she frowns slightly, but she doesn't look angry. Jeff looks at her, giggles, and quickly dashes off.

This tentative and ambiguous physical contact developed, in some children at least, into more definitely sexual types of physical contact. Such contact in school was relatively unusual, but far more rare in sixth grade than in the eighth. Furthermore, the context of this contact also changed dramatically as the students matured. For example, in the sixth grade such kisses as there were tended to be stolen, that is, one person, almost always a boy, was the initiator, and the object of his attentions often resisted or fled. Another example of this stolen contact occurred frequently during the seventh grade lunch period when boys would come up behind a girl's back and snap the elastic in her bra. By eighth grade, in addition to this stolen contact, one began to see mutually agreed upon physical contact that served as a symbolic way of publicizing the existence of a romantic relationship.

> *Interviewer*: How can you tell in school who are boyfriends and girlfriends?
> *Sandra* (white): Yeah, they talk to each other.
> *Interviewer*: Do they hold hands?
> *Sandra*: They don't just hold hands. . . . [They] kiss.
> *Interviewer*: When they kiss, what do the other kids do?
> *Sandra*: Nothing. . . . Just walk past, that's all.

Clear expression of sexual impulses was strongly discouraged by most teachers at Wexler, at least partly out of concern about parental reactions. For example, the clinical psychologist who was available to seventh grade teachers for consultation about classroom problems said that teachers' concerns about the sexual interests of their students was one of the major foci of her work. Specific behaviors brought to her attention ranged widely. Some teachers discussed their concern about the occasional use of obscene, sexually oriented words by students. Another was quite upset when a boy made a collage of pictures of nude women in response to an assignment in an affective education class to create a collage "of the things that interest you most." Other school staff consulted her about how to deal with a boy who was found masturbating in the boys' room and who once or twice exposed himself to girls in the hallways.

In contrast to boys, girls' sexual behavior was not so often perceived as a problem, primarily because it was much less overt. However, as indicated earlier, some of the girls who were well developed physically seemed to take pains to show off their bodies with tight clothes. Such behavior and other students' reactions to it deeply concerned many of the teachers.

> Mr. Jamison (white) mentioned today that some of the white children resisted working with blacks in his [seventh grade] social studies class. He said that Susie is one of them. He added that she gets uneasy sometimes, at least partly because she's afraid of the boys and went on to say that some of the black boys had "harassed and pinched her." He continued, "I told her she had to realize she's a little girl in a woman's body, and she can aggravate the problem by wearing those tight clothes." Mr. Jamison said that one day when Susie came to class in a tight sweater, he thought, "There's an accident waiting to happen," and sent her to the counselor's office. When she came back, she was wearing a jacket.

RACE AND ROMANCE: INTERRACIAL ATTRACTION AND ITS IMPACT ON BLACK/WHITE RELATIONS

In contrast to their generally negative view of students' overtly sexual behavior, Wexler's staff was quite tolerant, or even encouraging in an amused way, of romantic intrigues. Recall, for example, that Ms. Monroe willingly responded to requests that she pass on anonymous love notes to their intended recipients. Yet there was one major exception to the generalization that the school did little to discourage romantic involvement between students; that exception was the case of interracial romance. The school's policy of encouraging contact between black and white children clearly did not extend to romantic relationships.

> One of the in-school club activities is the production of a Broadway musical. Ms. Fowler (white) talked with the teachers producing the show and told them that the lead parts had to be more or less evenly divided between blacks and whites. [Ms. Fowler controls the funds for the club program.] One of the teachers (white) pointed out that this might mean having interracial couples since the musical has a romantic plot. After some discussion, Ms. Fowler and the teacher decided that they would avoid casting mixed couples to the extent possible because they were concerned about objections that might be raised to the whole idea of the play otherwise. . . . Ms. Fowler also said that, to date, no dances have been scheduled at Wexler partly because of her feeling that the students are too young and partly because of concern about problems that a racially mixed dance might raise.

Although no one at Wexler seemed inclined to do anything that might encourage interracial romances, attitudes about those that sprang up unaided varied widely. Some teachers' primary reaction was surprise since the idea of interracial romance was quite new to them.

> *Interviewer*: When a child shows signs of romantic interest in someone of the other race, can you remember if their friends have reacted any differently than if it's someone of their own race?
> *Mr. Little* (white): There was no reaction, absolutely none. . . . They never realized there were any problems or anything. . . . I guess, bringing something from my background, I was shocked when I heard it. Not shocked, but I was surprised. . . .
> *Interviewer*: Times have changed a lot, I think.
> *Mr. Little*: Yes, that's the truth!

Occasionally, however, teachers reacted quite negatively to indications of interracial romance. For example, in one case two white girls began to show an interest in two black boys. They cut classes to follow the boys and asked black girls for information about them. A white female teacher telephoned one of the girls at home to say that she was worried about the kinds of friends the student was making. Other teachers, while taking no overt action in this case, discussed at length their fears about where such relationships would lead. The issue was seen as sufficiently "hot" to warrant the involvement of both the principal and one of the clinical psychologists who functioned as a consultant at the school.

Fortunately, from the school's point of view, interracial romances were quite rare. Teachers and students alike reported that the vast majority of students focused their romantic interests on someone of their own race. The comments of Mr. Cousins, a seventh grade teacher, are typical.

Interviewer: What proportion of the time do you think that white boys show an interest in black girls compared to white girls?
Mr. Cousins (white): Very little, [just] occasionally. . . . Kids are starting to become aware of . . . dating and that sort of thing, but we have not advanced to the point where they would actually consider having an interracial relationship. . . . There are rare cases . . . but becoming aware sexually of someone of the other race, I don't think [happens] so much.

Although interracial romances were quite rare, it was clear that when they did occur, they virtually always involved white girls and black boys. As in the example cited above of the white girls who followed two black boys around, the girls were often open about their interest and quite aggressive in pursuing it.

Ms. Richards (white): In the eighth grade, we saw a lot of white girls really interested in black boys. . . . I didn't see the reverse.
Interviewer: When you say the reverse, do you mean black girls interested in white boys or black boys interested in white girls?
Ms. Richards: Either way. . . . There were fights over these boys . . . between white girls. . . . Some of the black girls said that the boys in question were immature, that they would rather have someone older. . . . There were some blatant incidents that the whole eighth grade knew about. . . . Some girls [from the accelerated track who were] interested in some of the regular students would hang out by the doorway [to these students' classroom]. They would use every excuse to go over there. Their grades were falling because they were so interested in all of this.
Interviewer: Do you have any idea why these particular boys had — ?
Ms. Richards: They are very mature-looking . . . and they kind of had this dapper thing about them. . . . Those boys treat all of the girls, black and white, very nicely, and I guess it was impressive.

The imbalance in interracial attraction that favored white girl/ black boy romances was most visually apparent at a dance for eighth graders sponsored by the eighth grade student council during Wexler's second year.

Five white girls start dancing with each other, and a very stylishly dressed black boy comes over and joins the group. At his arrival, the girls, who have been dancing in a semi-circle, change their formation to a straight line so that the boy is dancing facing all of them. After a few minutes, a black girl joins the group. . . . During the next record, four black boys go over and join the five white girls. There are about 50 black girls dancing and only 7 or 8 white girls, but 4 of the 12 black boys who are dancing are with white girls. During the entire dance, I did not see a single white boy dancing with a black girl or a group of black girls. However, there were several instances like that described above in which black boys joined groups of white girls and one in which a black boy and white girl danced as a couple.

These romances between white girls and black boys were of particular concern when, as was often the case, there were very marked social class differences between the students.

Discussing student romances with me today Ms. Mosby (white) said, "One thing that really intrigues me is the way white girls seem to fall for the black guys. . . . " She observed that white girls in the accelerated eighth grade classes who came from "good" homes frequently were quite interested in black boys whom she termed, "real low life." When I asked her to explain this term she said she meant boys, often from poor families, who had been held back a couple of years . . . and who were also rather tough. . . . She said she had taken it upon herself several times to talk with girls, asking why they were interested in these boys and suggesting that they were not really ideal boyfriends.

One of the romances that crossed both racial and social class boundaries created a minor crisis at the school.

Mr. Reuben (white) told me that . . . romantic relationships often developed between white girls from wealthy, socially-prominent families and black boys from economically-deprived backgrounds. He illustrated his point by mentioning two black eighth grade boys who were fifteen years old and "very tough." A romance evolved between the daughter of a wealthy and prominent physician from Hadleytown [an affluent, largely white area of the city] and one of these black students from Rockville [a poor black area]. The girl became so infatuated that she would wander into Rockville on evenings and weekends looking for the boy. Her parents even threatened to hire a security guard to watch their house to make sure she did not leave it when not authorized to do so. Furthermore, her father came to Mr. Reuben and insisted that he and the teachers insure there was no contact in school between his daughter and this boy. Mr. Reuben remarked, "We had to watch her like a hawk." Indeed, teachers were assigned to watch the girl in the lunchroom to make sure she did not talk with this boy. When I asked Mr. Reuben how he felt about involving school staff in preventing a romantic relationship in a case like this he replied that it was a practical necessity saying, "If these relationships develop and the parents get upset . . . it's very bad public relations for us."

An obvious question that arises is why the few interracial romances that emerged so predictably involved black boys and white girls. Studies of interracial high schools (Petroni, Hirsch, and Petroni 1970) and statistics on interracial marriage suggest that this phenomenon is consistent with a larger social pattern. Analysis of peer relations at Wexler suggests some of the factors that account for this phenomenon, at least in Wexler's case.

Just as there were gender differences in the onset of romantic interest in the other sex, with girls showing romantic interest somewhat earlier than boys, so too there were racial differences. Specifically, blacks showed signs of romantic and sexual interest somewhat earlier than their white counterparts. After briefly discussing this assertion, I will show how this situation helped to make romantic relationships between black boys and white girls more frequent than those between black girls and white boys.

Teachers, both black and white, noticed the earlier emergence of overt sexual and romantic interest in black than in white students.

Ms. Partridge (black): Black girls . . . become interested in boys quicker than white girls. . . . They tend to come together to do things . . . because of their interest in boys [more than white girls]. Near the end of the [seventh grade] year, you can hear the white girls discussing boys . . . whereas the black girls do this at the beginning of the school year.

Mr. Cousins (white): The black females are obviously a lot more advanced emotionally [than the white females] and . . . the boy/girl thing with black females and black males is a lot stronger. . . . The white girls . . . are more "little girls."

Students, too, noticed this difference, as indicated by the comments of James, an eighth grader.

Interviewer: You said you sometimes see kids walking down the hall with their arms around a girl. . . .
James (white): Black couples, that's the kids I see walking with their arms around each other. Whites usually talk in the halls.

Much of the difference in the romantic and sexual behavior of Wexler's black and white students may have been due to differences in social class.

Interviewer: What percentage of the kids on your [eighth grade] team have boyfriends or girlfriends?
Ms. Jackson (white): There are about 11 pairs out of 150 kids. . . . [Compared to my "regular" team], the [accelerated students] mix more in small groups, usually two boys and two girls. Streetwise kids jump that puppy love stage. . . . There are . . . sexually active girls on my team; I heard about two couples who "went all the way. . . . " Middle class blacks are more like the accelerated kids though.

Previous research, however, suggests that although social class is related to sexual behavior in early adolescence, race also has some independent impact on it (Broderick 1965; Zelnik, Kantner, and Ford 1981).

Whatever the reason for the blacks' somewhat earlier interest in romantic and sexual relationships, the existence of this difference helped to account for the imbalance of interracial pairs at Wexler. Recall that I indicated earlier that girls showed evidence of romantic interest before boys, a fact that is hardly surprising in light of developmental differences among preadolescent males and females. Thus many sixth or seventh grade girls who were quite interested in boys discovered to their dismay that the boys did not reciprocate their interest very satisfactorily. However, black boys did appear to be somewhat more aware of themselves sexually and more interested in romance than white boys. Thus they were more interesting targets for romantic desires than white boys since they were more likely to respond in appropriate ways. Although the difference in developmental pace favored white girl/black boy relationships, it clearly undermined the possibility of black girl/white boy couples since the black girls were very out of step with the white boys, being characterized by the relatively more mature attitudes of both girls and blacks. It is little wonder then that Ms. Richards, who was quoted earlier in this chapter, found black girls expressing interest in older boys.

Black boys were attractive not only because they displayed somewhat more interest in girls than white boys. They also had several other factors working in their favor. First, as discussed in Chapter 4, black boys, especially the older ones from lower- or working-class homes, tended to fit the traditional masculine stereotype better than their white peers, being perceived in general as tougher and more athletic. The importance of a "masculine" image was vividly illustrated when a black seventh grader who temporarily became a local hero by showing courage and resourcefulness when a school bus caught fire was suddenly besieged by potential girlfriends, black and white.

> *Vice-principal Cooper* (black): I guess the nearest to romance around here was Doug Williams. He was the student that stopped the bus. . . . All of a sudden he had a group of little girls . . . interested in him. . . . He had his pick.

The very thing that enhanced the attractiveness of black boys, the image of blacks as somewhat tougher and stronger than whites, tended to undercut the attractiveness of black girls. To boys at a stage in their development in which they were particularly anxious about appearing masculine, assertive, and occasionally aggressive, girls posed something of a threat.

Although there was always the possibility that awkward attempts at expressing romantic interest, such as hitting or poking, would be misunderstood and would serve to scare rather than attract the object of that interest, this problem was especially severe in the relatively few situations in which black girls evidenced interest in white boys. Because many of these boys felt a bit cowed by blacks, whatever their sex, and aggressive behavior does not fit well with the traditional feminine role, awkward courting behavior directed from black girls to white boys was especially likely to be misinterpreted.

Mrs. Thompson (a white parent) told me that there is a black girl in her son Ed's class who is very precocious. She said, "She's much bigger than he and just towers over him." Apparently this girl, Charlene, was romantically interested in Ed. She would come up to him and say things like, "I'm gonna beat you up." This scared Ed, and he was very uncomfortable about it. Sometimes she would chase him, and he did not like that either. Finally . . . one day she took him aside after she had been threatening him and said, "It's OK, Ed. I just want you to chase me." Since that time, she has stood up for him and protected him when he was made fun of . . . by other black children.

Finally, it is important to recognize that a romantic or sexual partner is often valued not only for his or her own sake, but as an indication of the attractiveness of the other half of the couple. Erikson (1950) makes this point when he argues that during adolescence romantic involvements are not likely to lead to real emotional intimacy but rather function to help build a sense of identity. This aspect of romantic relationships among preadolescents was clearly reflected in the boasting about conquests that was discussed earlier. One eighth grader caught this aspect of heterosexual relationships in an insightful remark about romance among her peers:

Elaine (white): Most of the kids here are too young [to have boyfriends or girlfriends] , but lots *pretend* they are friends because it makes them feel older.

Given the traditional status relations in our society, to the extent that preadolescent romances function to bolster students' sense of self, one might have predicted that white girls would show little interest in black boys, although one might also have expected black boys to be interested in white girls. However, to the extent that black boys were perceived as stronger and more masculine than white boys, their value as desirable catches was enhanced. Further increasing the black boys' desirability relative to white boys' was the fact that quite a number of the black boys seemed to have more personal style than most white boys. By this I mean that many of them appeared to pay unusually careful attention to creating an attractive and eye-catching image. This is illustrated by the following excerpt from field notes taken during the eighth grade dance:

Two of the black boys are dancing with great style, using very wide and fluid body movements. They are dressed rather elaborately with wide, fancy belts and stylish shoes with high platform-type heels. When the music stops, one of these students turns around and slaps palms with a friend who has been watching. Then he does the same with one of the black girls who has been standing in the circle of onlookers surrounding the boys as they danced.

The traditional status ordering in our society, which may have increased white girls' attractiveness to the black boys, worked to decrease black girls' attractiveness to white boys. Even if black girls were attracted to white boys, because of this status ordering, several factors conspired to make such attraction fruitless. As previously discussed, black girls, being more mature than white boys and being perceived as relatively aggressive, were not particularly attractive as romantic partners to white boys. Since traditional sex roles were strong enough at Wexler for boys to take the initiative in asking for dates and the like, even in cases where black girls were attracted to white boys it was unlikely that any mutual public relationship would evolve.

The fact that white girls were more likely to be involved in romantic relationships with black boys than black girls were to be involved with white boys created some friction between black and white girls. Friction between the boys over this issue was much less apparent, perhaps because the boys, especially white boys, seemed less interested in romantic relationships. Friction between black and white girls had two distinct elements. First, there was the rivalry and jealousy that often led to mutual hostility or even fights between girls who both wanted the same boy whether the girls were both of the same race or not. Compounding this friction, which Vice-principal Cooper indicated in Chapter 4 was one of the major sources of fights among girls, was the resentment of black girls toward whites who they felt were stealing *their* men. Some black girls felt much more intensely about this issue than others, and these girls made their resentment known.

Mrs. McCloud [parent of a white seventh grader] said that she was concerned about a seventh grade girl who was being "harassed" by black girls. The black girls accused the white girl, who is quite pretty, of trying to attract some of the black boys and made it very clear that they did not like her behavior.

In summary, the romantic and sexual behavior of Wexler's students was influenced by the fact that Wexler was a desegregated school and the existence of interracial romances affected relations between blacks and whites of the same sex. In general, students restricted their choice of romantic partners to someone of their own racial group. However, the attraction that some white girls felt to black boys and the black boys' moderately frequent reciprocation of this interest was a source of concern to school staff and of friction between black and white girls. Furthermore, whereas the widely shared perception of blacks as tougher than whites enhanced the attractiveness of black boys, it tended to undermine that of black girls, leaving these girls in a somewhat difficult position that some of them deeply resented. Thus although the growing romantic and sexual interest of Wexler's students led to some diminution in segregation by gender as the students moved from sixth through eighth grade, it had little effect, or even the opposite effect, on racial segregation and created a new source of friction between black and white girls.

6

TIME AND CHANGE

As a model integrated school, Wexler was clearly intended to create a positive interracial atmosphere in which black and white students would come to learn how to work together and to like and respect each other. Most of Wexler's faculty and staff believed, as discussed in Chapter 2, that such a goal could be attained quite easily and naturally. People of this persuasion emphasized the fact that the students had chosen to attend Wexler. They argued that the volunteer student body and the careful selection of the faculty combined with the innovative plans for team teaching and individualized instruction made Wexler a school of extraordinary promise. Less than two weeks after the school opened, a 30-minute TV program called "The Birth of a New School" praised it as "one of the best — the most integrated and innovative school in this area."

On the other hand, some people worried that Wexler would be plagued by serious racial problems. An excerpt from an interview with Mr. Little illustrates this perspective.

> *Interviewer*: What did the . . . teachers [at your previous school] think of your decision to come here?
> *Mr. Little*: It was a mixed thing, some teachers thought it was a dumb thing to do. . . . There were negative images of what was going to happen over here. . . . Imagine the problems you are going to have racially. . . . You are going to have a lot of confrontations. This was their feeling. . . . I had a lot of apprehensions coming in because of the racial thing. . . .

Even before school opened, a completely unfounded rumor circulated through a nearby white community that, because of bad behavior, over 100 children, mostly black, had been expelled from a summer day camp program designed to familiarize students with each other and the school. The belief on the part of some that serious racial problems were inevitable was strengthened by the fact that in the late 1960s another local school that had been much praised for its innovative programs and racial mix unexpectedly experienced serious racial clashes.

DECREASING AVOIDANCE AND INCREASING ACCEPTANCE OF OTHER-RACE PEERS

Study of Wexler during the course of its first three years suggested that it fulfilled neither the optimistic prediction that it would quickly and easily lead to very major gains in interracial harmony and friendship nor the pessimistic one that racial strife would be widespread and disruptive. There were extremely few serious and overt racial conflicts. However, there was also a relatively slow increase in interracial friendship and understanding. The purpose of this chapter is to describe and analyze the extent and type of change that occurred in intergroup behavior as children progressed through Wexler. This analysis is based, as is most of the rest of the book, on the study of two separate groups of students — Wexler's sixth graders during its first and second years. The first group was studied during a three-year period, from enrollment in sixth grade through graduation from eighth grade. The second group was studied primarily in the sixth grade, with a few data-gathering activities continuing during their year as seventh graders.

Since change over time in relations between black and white students was of central interest to this study, this topic was covered in detail in repeated interviews with both students and faculty. One fact that became clear from these interviews was that black and white children did not always agree about either the actual state of intergroup relations or the amount of change that had occurred in such relations. Thus discussion of these topics becomes quite complex since conflicting perceptions must sometimes be reconciled not only with each other but also with conclusions stemming from other types of data. Further complicating the matter is a rather striking disjunction, especially noticeable in white children, in the amount and direction of change in interracial behavior and certain important interracial attitudes. Finally, it must be noted that because they came to Wexler with different backgrounds and different concerns about how students of the other race would act toward them, the interracial attitudes and behavior of black and white students often differed in significant ways at any particular point in time. Thus some statements about the evolution of intergroup relations have to be carefully qualified since they will apply more fully to one group than to the other. To simplify matters, the discussion of change over time in intergroup relations will begin with some issues on which there was wide agreement. Later sections of this chapter will tackle those issues on which there was disagreement, looking both at the nature of the disagreement and at possible explanations for it.

One general conclusion that emerged from analysis of both the interviews and the observations at Wexler was that a definite, but relatively modest, improvement in relations between black and white students occurred at Wexler. Roughly two-thirds of the students interviewed, both black and white, perceived some improvement in black/white relations when queried about changes over time in such relations. The vast majority of the remaining students saw no change, with only an occasional student feeling that intergroup relations had deteriorated. The excerpts from student interviews presented below are quite typical.

Interviewer: Are things different now [June] between black and white kids than they were in September?
Pat (black): No. It changed a little bit but not that much. First when they came here they were scared and they was tight. . . . They was afraid. They wouldn't talk to nobody until people started coming over and talking to them. . . . Last year they didn't know you that well. This year they do.

Lina (white, responding to the same question as Pat): Well, I think the kids are friendlier towards the end of the year. I think there's been less fights and the kids are messing more and having fun.

Observation of the students confirmed the gradual improvement in intergroup relations indicated in the interviews. Most noticeable was a decrease in the amount of avoidance of members of the other race. During their first few months at Wexler students often tended to avoid those of the other race and to watch each other very carefully. The rather striking avoidance behaviors in the field notes excerpted in Chapter 4 occurred in the sixth grade. Initially the behavior of white children, especially, was quite cautious.

> *Lorrie* (white): I used to live in the suburbs until fourth or fifth grade. I didn't have any idea about black people. That was the farthest thing from my mind. . . . When I came here, I didn't have any opinions until I learned pretty quick. My first year, I just tried to stand my distance and watch to see what happened.

Another white child, capturing the same aspect of intergroup relations in their earliest stage at Wexler, remarked, "There's a lot of watching going on here." Some children said they watched primarily to *find out* what out-group members were like. Most children, though, had at least some preconceived notions about what the other group was like and watched for confirming or disconfirming behavior.

Although many black children at first cautiously avoided out-group members as whites did, some used a more active strategy than just watching to find out how out-group members would behave. Specifically, these children engaged in behavior that seemed designed to test just how white students would respond. Such testing behavior was especially apparent when it consisted of assertive or mildly aggressive acts. In Wexler's first year, in which the following field notes were taken, whites very frequently responded to such behavior by ignoring it or, if possible, moving away from the person initiating it, as discussed in Chapter 4.

> Karen (black) suddenly lifts her arm and grabs a handful of Ellen's (white) long straight light brown hair. . . . She twists it a little. She doesn't twist it enough to make Ellen move her head or cause any apparent pain but she does clearly have control over the other child's physical movements. . . . After a few seconds she drops her hand. . . . Ellen immediately gets up and heads over to the doorway. . . . Then she takes the seat near me (a white female observer) . . . which she had occupied earlier for quite a while. About thirty seconds later Linda (black), who was at the table Ellen left a few minutes ago, comes over and says, "That's my seat." Ellen gets up without protest and moves away.

Toward the end of their first year at Wexler and during their second year, students began to be somewhat more willing to initiate and accept friendly contact with members of the other race. The study of seating patterns in the school cafeteria mentioned in earlier chapters illustrates this trend. For example, in the seventh grade, only about one-third as many children sat next to someone of the opposite race in February as did so in June. Although the trend was clear, it must also be noted that the absolute amount of change was not great because of the very small number of children who initially sat in interracial pairs (Schofield and Sagar 1977). Avoidance of racial out-group members did not completely disappear with time, but it did become both less frequent and less blatant as the students got to know each other.

> *Vice-principal Kent* (black): At the beginning of the [first] year, there were a number of children both white and black who were somewhat standoffish to the other race. You would notice it in the cafeteria. The blacks would sit together, the whites would sit together; they would play in their various groups isolated from each other. . . . I think you see more togetherness now [April of the first year]. You see a lot of horsing around . . . among youngsters of both groups, playfully enjoying each other . . . and I like what I see. Perhaps there are still youngsters who have not reached this point, but . . . they get along . . . in the classroom . . . feeling more comfortable working with another youngster of a different color or nationality, creed, or what have you. . . . I think initially you didn't see this.

The relatively friendly and relaxed interracial atmosphere that often prevailed after the students got used to each other is illustrated in the following excerpts from field notes on events occurring between children in their second or third years at Wexler.

> Mr. Cousins (white) is walking around the room checking students' work. . . . At Table 2, Jeff (white) and Henry (black) are still acting playfully. They occasionally whisper, do some talking, show each other their papers and all of a sudden they have given the "gimme five" handshake to each other. They lean very close together as they continue to whisper and giggle.

> Today in Ms. Hopkins's (black) class, there will be a speaker. . . . Two girls, a tall black child and a long-haired white one, who came up to this room together from their last class . . . are talking and holding hands.

Many children felt that although the atmosphere became more relaxed and friendly over time, there were real limits to just how friendly black and white children were likely to become.

> *Interviewer*: Some people say that black and white kids in schools like Wexler get to know each other real quickly and easily. Others say that this isn't always so. What do you think about that?
> *Rebecca* (white): I don't think it's always true. I mean, you learn to know who they are but you don't really get to know them. . . . You're hardly ever with them because they're with their own friends, so you really don't know what they're like. . . .
> *Interviewer*: How would you characterize how you get along together?
> *Rebecca*: You don't really talk with them too much, but it's not like you never speak to them.

> *Stephen* (black, responding to the same question as Rebecca): They get to know them. They just don't hang with them. They will assign you to a class. You go around, shake everybody's hand, meet everybody, and ask them what's their name and talk to them. Pretty soon you start to know them and to talk to them [but] at lunch time you are not with them; you don't hang with them. You see them and say "Hi" or something like that.

In spite of the relatively superficial level of acceptance that many children saw as characterizing most interracial relationships, some at least slightly deeper friendships did spring up across racial lines. Frequently, these friendships were restricted to the school setting and the students did not go to each other's homes or do things together on weekends. Sometimes black students expressed regret or even hurt to interviewers because whites whom they considered friends had never invited them to their homes. Such feelings existed even when the black child had never extended a similar invitation because of fear of rejection, embarrassment about home circumstances, or the logistical difficulties involved if the friend lived at a distance. Nonetheless, by the end of the students' second or third year at Wexler some children were occasionally doing things with friends of the other race outside school. For example, one white girl invited a black classmate to a performance of a nationally known black dance company that was given in a downtown concert hall. Other children fantasized about friendly interracial relationships continuing well into the future.

Shirley (black) is now sitting at the table with Lisa (white) and Karen. Sue (black) nearby, says to Shirley, "I dreamed about you," and she describes an unpleasant dream that she had. Shirley says, "My dream wasn't nothing like that. It was a good dream. I dreamed about Lisa and you. We all went to the same college and we had an apartment together. I had a car − " Lisa interjects, "A Corvette." The three girls continue in a social conversation. . . .

DIMINUTION OF WHITES' FEARS OF BLACKS

A substantial majority of both the black and white students interviewed were well aware that as time went on, most whites became more accepting of contact with blacks.

Interviewer: Do white kids act differently to blacks now than when they first came?
Stacy (black): Yes, they didn't want to be around blacks. I guess they . . . was prejudiced or something, too cute for the blacks. But now they are nice, you know. They are friends with mostly everybody.

Margaret (white, responding to same question as Stacy): Yeah, they have adjusted to them. I mean, before they hardly saw them, now they work with them and everything like that.

Their perceptions certainly agreed both with those of Wexler's faculty and administrators and with the observational data.

The conclusion that whites became more willing to interact with blacks as they spent time at Wexler may at first seem inconsistent with the focus in Chapters 3 and 4 on the ways in which the achievement gap and blacks' more rough-and-tumble play style tended to reinforce racial stereotypes. Indeed, answers to specific questions about the ways in which being at Wexler had changed white children's *ideas* about blacks suggested that the white children, in general, perceived little or no positive change in this area.

Interviewer: Has being in a school like Wexler changed white kids *ideas* about what blacks are like?
Martin (white): It's still the same old stereotype. Parents tell you what to believe, and then you probably believe it. . . .
Interviewer: I see. Do you think that being in a school like Wexler makes *any* difference?

Martin (white): It doesn't make any difference.

A significant minority of white students even said that their ideas about blacks had become less positive over time. One of the most striking examples of this phenomenon was the boy who told one of his parents that he had become a racist at Wexler.

> Mr. Rider (white) has a son at Wexler. When he heard I was doing a research project there he said that something had happened recently that greatly upset him. His son came home from school one day and said, "Dad, I know you won't like this but I think I'm becoming a racist." When Mr. Rider pursued the matter it turned out that his son was angry about the way he felt black kids at Wexler acted. In particular, he felt the black kids were overly aggressive and were neither academically talented or motivated.

Obviously, then, the question that arises is why most whites became more willing to interact with blacks as they progressed through Wexler even though their assessment of what blacks were like showed little if any positive change and in some cases became quite negative. One possible key to this rather perplexing phenomenon was that although whites' ideas about what blacks were like changed little, if at all, for the better, the white children did become somewhat less automatically and immediately afraid of blacks. For example, student responses to the question, "How often do you think kids here feel afraid of other kids here?" showed a marked and statistically significant change over time. The first time white students were asked this question their average answer was just above the point on the response continuum provided that was labelled "Most of the time." One year later, when they were eighth graders, their average response fell just above the point on the continuum that was labelled, "Sometimes." Since this diminution of fear was an important outcome for the white students and significantly influenced their behavior, I will discuss the factors that seemed to lead to it.

As indicated in Chapter 2, a great many students, black and white, initially felt nervous and apprehensive about attending Wexler. However, the basis of some of their fears was different. First, in contrast to black children, white children were quite obviously made apprehensive by the novelty of an environment that included large numbers of people of another race. This sense of being overwhelmed by the sheer number of black peers came up again and again in interviews as white students used phrases like "I never saw so many blacks in one place before" and "wall-to-wall blacks."

> *Maureen* (white): White people, when they got here, probably thought, "There is so many black people here in one place!" It really surprised them.

Black students, in contrast, did not find just being in the presence of many white peers a situation that stimulated such comment. Since many of the students, both black and white, came from segregated schools, this difference may spring from the fact that blacks, being members of a minority group, are likely to have somewhat more experience than whites with environments in which the other group is heavily represented. Compounding this sense of strangeness for white children was fear about physical safety that was present in many even before the school started.

> *Sara* (white): All of the white mothers were kind of scared to send their kids here because of the blacks. Parents were afraid because they [blacks] are tougher. . . . They [blacks] don't take anything [from anybody].

> *Interviewer*: Do white kids have any trouble knowing how to act toward black kids? . . .
> *Marcia* (black): Yeah . . . they don't talk. . . . The white people don't talk to the colored people 'cause they think they're going to get beat up.

The black children too had their own fears connected with attending a desegregated school, but fears of a somewhat different sort, centering on whether others would treat them well or reject them as somehow inferior or inadequate.

Part of the decline in white children's fears may have been due to something as simple as getting used to an environment that contained large numbers of black students.

> *Interviewer*: Do white kids act any differently toward blacks than they did when you first came to Wexler?
> *Bob* (white): Uh huh. When we came here the first year [we] didn't know what it was like to be with people that are different. So there probably was a little fear involved for both, but now . . . it's a lot different. Now you are used to it.

Several factors were also important in leading to a decline in the whites' level of fear and to the decreasing impact of such fear on intergroup relations. First, many white students developed techniques for reducing or handling their fear. As discussed in Chapter 4, often white children initially responded to perceived danger or threat of danger with withdrawal or submission, which was ultimately not very effective. However, with time, many developed or took advantage of more effective techniques, at least occasionally. For example, while it existed, the white boys' club, the Mice, seemed to give its members an increased sense of security. Numerous students, white and black, took advantage of the seventh grade student council, described in greater detail toward the end of this chapter, to try to find solutions to some of the problems that created fear and resentment.

> [Today the student council is discussing how it can "help Team E."]
> A black boy, Don, raises his hand. Pointing to another black boy, Stan, he says, "Stan has a good idea, but he's afraid to say it." Ms. Hopkins (black) replies, "Don't be afraid. I'm not your teacher here." Stan says he thinks it would be a good idea to have hall monitors to take the names of the kids who litter the halls. . . . Another child, who is white, says, "And what about gypping in the cafeteria?"

The student council appointed some of its members to serve as hall and lunchroom monitors. The effectiveness of this monitoring effort was made clear when the council's own vice-president, a black child named Bill, was reported to the group for his disruptive behavior. After discussing Bill's misconduct, the student council voted to place him on probation for two weeks and to remove him from office if his behavior did not improve. The students thus applied sanctions for behavior that violated group norms, such as the often expressed idea that student council members should set a good example for others. In this way the council helped to control negative behaviors that were aversive to most children and potentially harmful to relations between blacks and whites.

Some white students managed to overcome their initial trepidation well enough to stick up for themselves when necessary.

> *Ms. Richards* (white): I was just thinking about John, one of the black kids . . . a big bully. One of the white kids, Sam — he has a crew cut

. . . [and] is real straight, and if you saw him you'd think kids picked on him — just went up to John one day and said, "The only reason you get everything you want is because you bully . . . everybody." Well, John was so taken aback he just laughed. He didn't get mad. . . . Sam told the class, "No one should be afraid [of John] . . . . " He almost got a standing ovation from every kid on the team; everyone liked him [after that] .

Interviewer: Do white kids seem to act any differently toward blacks now than they did when they first came to Wexler?
Betty (white): I got involved in a few things that I didn't like. Then I learned to stick up for myself. . . . There was a couple of black girls that tried to force me to fight this other one. I didn't know what to do . . . I got in trouble. . . . The teachers, the first year I came to Wexler, were really afraid of black people.
Interviewer: Do you think that black kids act any differently to whites now than they did when you first came here?
Betty: I think when they first came they had a pre-set idea of white people's behavior. When they got here they learned that not all of the white kids are going to roll over and play dead when they say "boo."

Many black students admired such a willingness to stick up for oneself.

Charlene (black): Some black and white kids get along, but some don't. . . . If they [white kids] show black kids they ain't scared of them . . . when black kids hit them, they could get along with blacks.

Some students, like Betty, learned from their own experiences the value of standing up for themselves. Others found, generally to their surprise, that black classmates who were friends might help defend them against other black students who caused them trouble.

Today at the Friends of Wexler meeting, part of the discussion revolved around the fear white children feel even in situations in which they have not been threatened and the ways students have found to cope with this problem. [This group, an informal coalition of parents, social agencies, and other local institutions, worked quite hard to promote a positive climate at Wexler and to build community support for it.] One of the group's black members, Mrs. Johnson, said that one day her daughter Kim discovered a bunch of black girls gathered around Jeannette, a very small white girl whom Kim knows and likes. The black girls were baiting and bothering Jeannette. Kim, who is large for her age, went up to the group and said, "Hey, stay away from her or I'll get you." Mrs. Johnson said that Jeannette has not had any trouble with these girls since this incident.

Another method for reducing fear that many white students employed was to avoid as far as possible those places or behaviors that were associated with intimidation by other students. Chief among the places to be avoided were the bathrooms and other basically unsupervised areas. Some white students were annoyed or frightened in the bathrooms by black students who teased or taunted them. Others, who had few or no such negative experiences, still felt uncomfortable and fearful there since adult supervision was virtually nonexistent and black students who cut class to smoke or gossip with friends found the bathrooms a convenient meeting place.

Other students learned that one way to avoid trouble was to be especially careful about gossiping or making derogatory remarks about out-group members. Although fights about gossip were quite frequent among girls even when both parties involved were of the same race, the black children's concern about rejection and ridicule from whites made them especially sensitive to criticism by white peers. Some whites recognized this and learned how to avoid confrontations stemming from it.

> *Interviewer*: What have you learned about being with blacks from your experiences here at Wexler?
> *Sally* (white): You have to watch what you say. . . . Don't talk about [them].
> *Interviewer*: What positive things did you learn?
> *Sally*: They can be nice. About fifty percent are nice.

One final factor that made possible the simultaneous reduction in fear and maintenance or buttressing of stereotypes about black aggression was the growing ability of white children at Wexler to differentiate between individual blacks. On the one hand, as discussed in Chapter 4, whites clearly believed that blacks as a group were tougher and more assertive than whites. On the other hand, they built up a lot of experience with individual black classmates who were not at all aggressive. Indeed, experiences like the student council discussions of discipline problems let them see that many of their black classmates were as disturbed as they were by aggressive behavior. Thus, at the same time white children came to see differences in average levels of aggression in their black and white peers, they also learned through experience that many of their black classmates were unlikely to be any special threat to them and deplored the behavior of the rowdier students. A black eighth grader talked to an interviewer about white students' reactions to different types of behavior on the part of black students.

> *Interviewer*: Some people say that black and white students in a school like Wexler get to know each other real quickly and easily. Others say that this isn't always so. What do you think?
>
> *Janice* (black): Well, it all depends on how you act, how your behavior is. If you act bad or tense, the white people don't want to be around you; but if you act nice and quiet they probably want to be around you. . . . You go sit by them or something or you just talk to them . . . I met a lot of white people.
>
> *Interviewer*: Did you get to know them?
>
> *Janice*: Yes. . . . Some black kids and white kids get along just like sisters, but some fight. . . .

THE SHIFT FROM INTERGROUP TO INTERPERSONAL BEHAVIOR

The initial sense of being overwhelmed by an undifferentiated group, by "wall-to-wall blacks," gave way for many white children to a clearer understanding that although their black peers did share some visible physical attributes there were important individual differences among them. Thus, in their second and third years at Wexler, white students were much more likely to differentiate between individual black children than they had been initially. The following excerpt from an interview with a white boy in the spring of his second year at Wexler illustrates this differentiation:

> *Interviewer*: Do you think black kids have any trouble knowing how to act toward white kids when they are in a school like Wexler?
>
> *Sandy* (white): They might. Some of the black kids think of white kids as enemies instead of normal people. It depends on the person.

Thus even students who continued to deal with their fears by avoidance had the opportunity to learn that general avoidance of all blacks was unnecessary.

Black students, too, seemed more inclined to think of white students as individuals as they got to know many of their white classmates. One effect of this increasing differentiation among members of the racial out-group was that the students seemed to engage in less *intergroup* behavior and more *interpersonal* behavior. In other words, the children began to react to one another more as individuals and less as members of racial in-groups or out-groups. Racial group membership certainly did not become irrelevant or go unnoticed as students got to know each other. Rather, it became one of many salient individual attributes instead of remaining a characteristic of such overwhelming importance that it often virtually determined behavior. Although this shift from intergroup to interpersonal behavior was apparent, it was far from completed in two or three years. Also of interest is the fact that even after such a time period, some school settings seemed to bring out intergroup behavior more than others. For example, some black students felt that race had more of an impact on peer relations in academic classes than in other settings like art or gym.

> *Interviewer*: Do black and white kids seem to get along better some times than others here at Wexler? . . .
> *Debbie* (black): Gym . . . and . . . art . . . 'cause that's a fun class; but in math and reading they don't get along because it's a white person and you are colored. But in art or something, a fun class, you get along.
> *Interviewer*: Oh, I see, so color becomes a difference more in certain types of classes. . . .
> *Debbie*: Yes.

Although this issue was not investigated closely enough to warrant any firm conclusions, it is hardly surprising that the classes that were most frequently nominated as likely to minimize an awareness of race were nonacademic ones in which the status differential between whites and blacks stemming from different average levels of academic achievement was less salient than usual. In fact, in nonacademic classes, most especially in gym, black children often outperformed their white peers. Such a reversal of roles set the stage for a generosity on the part of black students not unlike that of the white students in academic classes as described by Ms. Shore in Chapter 3. Perhaps because they had little reason to suspect that others might reject or ridicule them because of their race, white children were generally able to accept encouragement or assistance from black classmates without resentment. Excerpts from notes taken in two different gym classes illustrate the friendly interracial interaction that was common there.

Today in gym the students are learning a new tumbling stunt. . . . Four white girls and two black girls are doing it. . . . One of the black girls, Amanda, leads off doing the [difficult] stunt very well. One of the whites starts to applaud and within seconds the whole group is applauding and cheering. The next girl to go is white. She does it very well and gets applause and cheers [from blacks and whites alike]. Amanda says to one of the whites, who looks apprehensive, "Don't worry, she'll [a white girl who is standing by to catch anyone who begins to fall] catch you. . . . Watch, she'll catch you. You'll see." There are all kinds of applause and cheers whenever someone does ths stunt, whether or not it is done perfectly. . . . One short, slight white girl, Rose, is having a hard time. . . . She can't get over the buck. . . . She looks a little dejected. As Rose returns to the line, Amanda, who has been so successful at the stunt, puts her arm around Rose's shoulder and says, "We're getting better. We're getting better."

Three white girls are playing leapfrog. . . . The teacher scolds them saying, "That's not what you're supposed to be doing. You're supposed to be practicing." All three look at the teacher and stop what they have been doing immediately. The shortest of the trio, Alanya, jumps behind Lily, a tall black who is very agile and . . . who completed the head stand roll so well earlier today. Alanya pretends she's hiding . . . laughing and holding on to Lily's arms. Lily is smiling. Then Alanya rests her head against Lily's back for a moment. The two girls smile at each other as Alanya moves away.

Incidentally it is of interest that one event quite outside the school's control did seem to impede the transition from intergroup to interpersonal behavior, especially on the part of black students. That was the showing of *Roots* on television. A number of students spontaneously mentioned in interviews occurring as much as eighteen months later that black children who saw the series tried to get back at whites for the historical oppression of blacks, which it demonstrated.

Interviewer: Are things at all different between black and white kids now compared to September?

Donald (black): Some people have changed from seeing TV. This new movie came out, *Roots*. . . . It made blacks start hating whites like they did a long time ago.

Interviewer: How did that change white people's reactions? Did they change at all?

Donald: No, they stayed the same.

Interviewer: How do black and white kids get along here at Wexler?

Janice (black): I'd say pretty poor . . . because black kids don't like white kids. . . . Like when they saw the show *Roots*, a lot of black kids came back and beat at the white kids. . . . I don't like whites . . . 'cause they act . . . like they too good to be around black people. . . . Like, you say "Hi" to one of them and they just don't say nothing. . . . This white girl Martha, me and her is good friends; but most of them just don't say nothing. They be scared, I guess.

One student observed that the major effect of *Roots* was temporary, but that it emerged later as an issue when something went wrong between black and white students.

Interviewer: Do you think being in a school like Wexler has changed black kids' ideas about whites?

Jim (black): Yes. They used to be talking all [about] *Roots*, saying they was going to get back at them for *Roots*. And then they just stopped it, but sometimes they bring it back up when people get mad at them.

RACIAL DIFFERENCES IN THE PERCEPTION OF INTERGROUP RELATIONS

As discussed earlier in this chapter, most blacks and whites agreed that intergroup relations in general improved over time and that white students' behavior toward blacks became more accepting. There was, however, some disagreement over whether blacks' behavior toward whites changed. Although whites generally reported an improvement in intergroup relations and saw ways in which their own behavior toward black classmates had become more positive, they were rarely able to specify ways in which black children's behavior toward whites had changed. Instead, to the extent that there was any consistency in their responses to questions on this topic, they felt that even after spending two or more years at Wexler

black children still behaved too rowdily or aggressively when interacting with whites. In sharp contrast, blacks, by and large, clearly
perceived changes in their own group's behavior toward whites. First,
they thought blacks had developed a greater willingness to spend
time with out-group members. Second, they saw a tendency toward
less aggressive behavior toward whites. Both of these changes are
reflected in the comments of two black eighth graders.

> *Interviewer*: Have the black kids changed in their behavior toward
> whites since they came to Wexler?
> *Geraldine* (black): They be with them [whites] more often. Before
> they used to hit on different ones, shorter ones. Now that still goes on
> but not as much as when we first came.

> *Ellen* (black): When we first came to Wexler, they [blacks] was wild.
> They wouldn't even be near whites, you know. Now all you see is black
> people hanging with whites a lot. . . . Mostly all my friends are whites.

It is difficult to be completely sure whether the perceptions of the
black or white students were more accurate since it was, for example,
often impossible to tell which of two children engaged in a friendly
interracial interaction had initiated it. However, the weight of the
available data suggests that black children did exhibit more friendly
behavior to whites as time went on. Their behavior may have
changed somewhat less strikingly than that of whites, but this
appeared to be mainly because they were initially less likely to
exhibit the very obvious avoidance responses that some whites did.

Blacks not only perceived changes in their behavior toward
whites that whites did not, but they were also more positive about
the state of intergroup relations in general. This point can be illustrated by examining Table 3, which is based on interviews with 20
students just before they graduated from Wexler. Similar interviews
with these students and others as seventh graders yielded parallel
findings, as has another recent study of desegregated middle schools
in Florida (Damico, Bell-Nathaniel, and Green 1981b). Note in
Table 3 that blacks rated intergroup relations at Wexler markedly
more positively than did whites. Whereas the black students' average
answer to the query about how blacks and whites got along fell
near the point on the response continuum labeled "pretty well"
(+5), white students' average response fell on the negative side
somewhat below "just OK" (0). Also of note is the fact that the

TABLE 3
Student Perceptions of Peer Relations

Question	Respondent's Race	
	White	Black
1. How well do you think white kids get along with other whites?	6.1	5.6
2. How well do you think black kids get along with other blacks?	6.8	4.1
3. How well do you think white and black kids get along?	−1.2	4.0*

*A 2x2 analysis of variance was performed to explore the impact of race and sex on responses to each of these three questions. The only effect that even approached statistical significance was a main effect for race on question 3, F (1, 17) = 13.4, p < .005. Possible responses ranged along a 21 point continuum from very poorly (−10) to very well (+10).

Source: Compiled by the author.

black students' ratings of intergroup and intragroup relations were very similar. Whites, in contrast, saw relations between the two groups as significantly worse than relations *within* racial groups, black or white.

Although our data do not allow a definitive explanation of these rather puzzling differences in white and black children's assessments of the amount of change in black children's behavior and the quality of intergroup relations, the difference in behavioral style of black and white children discussed in Chapter 4 provides one quite convincing explanation. As indicated earlier, black students at Wexler were more likely to engage in rough-and-tumble play and to display a somewhat more aggressive personal style than were whites. There were certainly times when whites were on the receiving end of this behavior *because* they were white. However, such instances did not appear to be a large proportion of the interracial exchanges that were frightening or annoying to whites. It may well be that as black children came to feel more accepted by white peers the number of such instances declined, thus leading black children to see their behavior toward whites as becoming more positive and inter-group relations as being quite good. Whites, however, who were still on the receiving end of many behaviors that were threatening to them, may have interpreted such events as attacks linked to their race, not fully recognizing the extent to which many blacks inter-acted in a similar style with peers of their own race.

Such a misperception could stem from a combination of factors. First, it seems reasonable to argue that white students paid closer attention to blacks' behavior toward whites than toward other blacks since the former was of more immediate relevance to white students concerned and apprehensive about how blacks would act toward them. Such a focusing of attention might mean that, as discussed in Chapter 4, white children were not fully aware of the extent to which the behaviors they perceived as indicative of hostile intergroup relations were, in actuality, no different from the behaviors that some of their black classmates frequently directed toward each other. An experimental study conducted at Wexler resulted in a finding that may explain some of the differences in the rate at which black and white children engaged in certain behaviors that could be interpreted as hostile in intent. Specifically, white boys perceived some fairly common school and classroom behaviors, such as taking someone's pencil without permission, as more mean and threatening and less playful and friendly, than did their black classmates (Sagar and Schofield 1980). To the extent that black and white children perceived the implications of such behaviors in rather different ways, they would naturally come to different conclusions about just how positive peer relations were. In addition, the very fact that a particular behavior was directed from a black to a white may have affected its interpretation and made it seem more threatening than it would have otherwise. Experimental work by Duncan (1976) demonstrates the reality of such a phenomenon. Although a comparable experiment conducted at Wexler failed to produce similar results, the at least occasional occurrence of such a phenomenon is suggested by incidents such as that mentioned in Chapter 4 in which a white girl was frightened enough to cry when a black girl just touched her hair. Mutual grooming of hair between girls of the same race at Wexler was frequent and rarely if ever occasioned upset.

THE IMPACT OF SITUATIONAL FACTORS
ON INTERGROUP RELATIONS

The discussion so far in this chapter has focused on changes over time in the behavior of black and white children toward each other. Even more striking to an observer at Wexler were the variations in black/white relations in different settings within the school. This issue was introduced briefly in Chapter 3, which discussed, among other things, the impact of various instructional methods on interracial contact. However, I return to it here since the circumstances under which black and white children interacted with each other were so crucial to the nature of their relations that this chapter would be incomplete without some mention of two situational factors that had a major impact on such relations – the presence of effective adult supervision and circumstances that required or strongly encouraged cooperation between black and white students. Each of these factors will be discussed in turn.

The Importance of Effective Adult Supervision
in Reducing Negative Behavior

Overt problems between black and white students at Wexler took place in areas that were not constantly or effectively supervised by adults in clear disproportion to the amount of time the students spent in such settings. This fact reflects nothing unique about black/white relations since fights, extortion, and other types of hassling between members of the same race were also widely acknowledged to be most frequent in largely unsupervised places like the hallways, stairwells, cafeteria, and bathrooms. Rather, it merely reflects two other facts. First, the classroom norms for deportment were somewhat different from those applying elsewhere, as indicated in Chapter 2. Second, and not surprisingly, when adults were not around to enforce rules inhibiting rough-and-tumble behavior, such behavior was more frequent than otherwise. Two examples of the sorts of incidents that were much more likely to occur in unsupervised areas than in classrooms are presented below.

> Mike, a tall, black seventh grader, has cornered Ann, a short white girl. . . . He keeps her in front of him with one arm across her chest.

His other arm clasps her arm behind her back. She squirms but cannot get away. . . . Mike says, "You better tell me!" and Ann replies, "I don't know. I told you! Ask Harold." As Jim (white) passes by eating from a box of candy, Mike says to him, "You better give me one." Jim turns and without smiling or saying anything gives him a piece of candy. Mike and Ann are now close to the classroom door. When they reach it, Mike lets go and Ann immediately heads towards a table at which three other white girls are sitting.

Today I saw a tall, slender, black boy bump very hard into a tall, white eighth grader who was going the opposite direction in the hall. The impact was so great that the blonde boy's hat was knocked off and landed on the carpet. The black boy, moving rapidly, took no apparent notice of the collision and kept going down the hall. The white boy picked up his hat, turned and called down the hall after the retreating figure of the black, "You fucking nigger." I did not see the incident well enough to have any clear idea of whether it was planned or intended by either of the students.

Although incidents causing obvious hostility between black and white children were more common in unsupervised areas than they were in classrooms, white students frequently suggested that relations between black and white students were also affected by the extent to which teachers were able to keep order in their classrooms.

Interviewer: Do black and white kids get along better in classes with certain teachers than with others?
Maria (white): Yea. The more strict teachers.

Mike (white, responding to the same question as Maria): Yeah. A lot depends on the teacher, how well the teacher can control the class. Mainly the kids that jag around may be black. . . .
Interviewer: When you say "jag around" what do you mean?
Mike: Don't listen, start wrestling or stuff.

Black students generally did not mention supervision or discipline as important to positive intergroup relations, perhaps because many of them perceived "jagging around" as good fun, to be shared with blacks and with whites, if they were not too "goody-goody."

Danelle (black): It ain't fun with all them white people. They don't like to do nothing. . . . They're goody-goody. [I'd like more blacks here], the ones that don't start trouble, [don't] start fights, call you names, or throw stuff at you.

The Importance of Cooperation in Fostering Positive Behavior

Strict supervision prevented some types of problems between whites and blacks by minimizing the sort of high-spirited, rowdy, or even aggressive behavior that worried so many children but that seemed especially threatening to whites. Although it undoubtedly minimized negative interactions, such supervision in and of itself did little to encourage positive relations between black and white children. Many of the situations that fostered high rates of comfortable, friendly interaction between whites and blacks required or strongly encouraged cooperation. This conclusion is not unexpected in light of the research and theory on the impact of cooperation on intergroup relations, which were briefly discussed in Chapter 1. More surprising, however, was the fact that quite a number of students seemed well aware of this link. For example, about one-third of the students who were asked whether black and white children got along better at some times than at others spontaneously and specifically mentioned teamwork or cooperation, in sports or on academic tasks, as producing positive relations. Alan's comments below were unusually explicit but very much in the spirit of those of many of his classmates.

> *Interviewer*: Does it seem that black and white kids get along better some times than others? For example, in a particular class or in particular areas of the school?
> *Alan* (white): They get along better in gym, because they are on the same team and they cooperate together and they are working as a group.

Although sports and other play activities were mentioned frequently as leading to positive intergroup relations, especially by the boys, cooperating on academic activities was also singled out by some students as a contributing factor.

> *Interviewer*: Do black and white kids seem to get along better at some . . . times more than others here at Wexler?
> *Ellen* (white): Yes . . . when we're not really working. I mean, we're working but we can get into groups. . . . They get put into groups together and they work with them. . . . If they have to work in classes

in groups they get along better, and when they're in gym they get along better.

The impact of policies that encouraged academic cooperation between children was apparent to the eye, in spite of the fact that, as discussed in Chapter 3, differences in average achievement levels sometimes caused difficulties between black and white children. For example, in Mr. Little's classroom, in which integrated groups of five or six children were assigned to sit at round tables, the initial strong tendency for blacks to sit on one side of the table and for whites to sit on the other gradually gave way to a more mixed pattern as the children got to know each other. Such marked shifts in seating and other behavior patterns were not characteristic of classrooms that were organized in ways that did not encourage interracial contact and cooperation. However, in Mr. Little's classes friendly social interaction such as that described in the field notes excerpted below was commonplace well before the end of the school year.

> [Jack, who is white, is collecting papers for Mr. Little.] When he gets to Norman (black) the two of them start playing. Norman takes a pencil and holds it between the index fingers of his two hands; Jack then gets ready to dislodge the pencil by hitting it very hard with the pencil that he holds in his hand. They have done this once and are preparing to do it a second time when Mr. Little walks by. As they catch sight of him coming, both of them pretend that they are not engaged in this playing behavior. Norman takes the pencil and grasps it in one hand as though he is going to write.

One obvious question that arises is why cooperation, academic or otherwise, should be conducive to the development of friendly relations. A number of factors are undoubtedly involved. Two of the most striking at Wexler were the role of cooperation in fostering physical proximity and in promoting a shared sense of group identity. Cooperation, as it most frequently occurred at Wexler, required physical proximity between black and white students. Although physical proximity in and of itself is probably not enough to improve intergroup relations significantly, it did have some important side effects. Unfortunately, the types of behaviors that were most visible to children who were physically quite distant from each other were the very behaviors most likely to cause problems in black/white relations and to reinforce stereotypes. Gross motor behaviors (hitting, getting out of a seat, showing off), loud talk, and getting into trouble with the teacher were very noticeable, but more normative behavior, such as working quietly, was not as likely to gain attention. Also, these noticeable behaviors seen from a distance were likely to be perceived as discrete acts divorced from any context that could make them more intelligible. As discussed in Chapter 3, children were often required to monitor the academic performance of others, including those at a considerable distance from themselves. Distance makes it more difficult to differentiate between out-group members. Hence the academic and social behaviors of specific individuals were likely to be associated with their group in general, if only because individuals could not easily be identified or remembered. Thus the avoidance of out-group members combined with the close surveillance of them typical in classrooms that did not encourage proximity and interaction was likely to foster the development or maintenance of negative or otherwise divisive stereotypes.

Proximity in and of itself made it easier and more natural for students to get to know peers of the other race, vastly increasing what Cook (1969) has called the acquaintance potential of the situation and helping students to discover what Allport (1954, p. 267) referred to as their "common interests and common humanity." However, a work or play situation requiring cooperation gave students both the *opportunity* and reasonably strong *motive* to get to know each other. This motive was especially strong in situations like team sports with a cooperative reward structure in which an individual's success is closely linked to the success of his or her teammates.

> *Interviewer*: You say they [black and white kids] get along better in gym?
> *Debbie* (black): 'Cause they got to be on a team. Like, if they was playing baseball or something, if there is a good white person that could play they gonna pick them.

The need to observe others closely is less strong when individuals can succeed as individuals but must work together than when cooperating individuals win or lose as a unit, but it is still there. Accurate assessment of those with whom one is cooperating may be less crucial in the first case than in the second; it is nonetheless important since even in this case misjudging one's colleagues may delay or impede one's work. For example, white students who assumed that all black children were less adept at academic tasks than whites were slowed in finishing their work when they ignored talented blacks in their group and sought assistance only from other whites. Thus, the sorts of cooperative situations that students encountered at Wexler gave them the motive and the means to observe their classmates as *individuals* and to discover the variations in behavior among students who shared membership in a particular racial group. This focus on the individual was undoubtedly important in leading to greater acceptance of specific out-group members even if it had little impact on the children's ideas about what the other group in general was like.

Many types of cooperative efforts at Wexler not only encouraged proximity and dealing with others as individuals but also helped to develop a sense of shared group identity that, while not abrogating racial group membership, *cut across* racial lines. The importance of this outcome of cooperation is made clear when one considers the work of Tajfel and his associates, which suggests that individuals tend in a wide variety of ways to favor others whom they perceive as part of their own group, even when the basis for the division into groups is quite trivial (Billig 1976; Tajfel 1978a, 1978b; Tajfel et al. 1971; Vaughan, 1978). Racial group membership was clearly a basis for social categorization in the minds of Wexler's students. Considerations of practicality and the fact that a sense of ethnic or racial group membership can serve many positive functions lead to the conclusion that trying to change this might not have been wise. An alternate approach to handling the potentially negative impact on intergroup relations of children's use of race as a category for perceiving themselves and others is to create new, supplemental group identities that cut across racial ones. To the extent that this is achieved, black and white children then become in-group members for each other, at least in the contexts that make this new group membership relevant.

It is theoretically possible to create a sense of belonging to a group in a variety of ways. At Wexler, however, this sense of group identity seemed most likely to emerge from cooperation among individuals who shared some mutual purpose and/or a group name. Athletic teams and academic work groups are prime examples of such situations. Another important one was the student council, which was mentioned briefly earlier in the chapter and is described in some detail elsewhere (Schofield and McGivern 1979). It was founded and supervised by Ms. Hopkins, a black teacher, in cooperation with Mr. Elliot, who was white. Ms. Hopkins felt that one way of improving relations between black and white children on her team was to create a shared sense of belonging to a group.

> *Ms. Hopkins* (black): The problem here is the kids don't feel like they actually belong. I am thinking of setting up a student council for this team. . . . I think the team is the place to start. . . . When I asked students about this and told them that I would be having a student council as an in-school club, so many of the students wanted to sign up that I had to discourage them. I had about 80 that wanted to sign up. . . .

Ms. Hopkins spent much of the first meeting of the student council emphasizing the team as an in-group and explaining that she would depend upon the students to cooperate in organizing the council's business.

> We won't allow other kids to be in this. This is just for us. I am not going to act like a teacher. In two weeks I expect you to be on your own. All that I am going to do is to get you started and give you some guidance on the best ways to begin. . . . Within two weeks I expect you to be able to discuss your own business, conduct your own meetings, set up your tables and chairs . . . the way you think they should be set up. . . .

Committee work was emphasized, which, of course, fostered both cooperation and a sense of jointly belonging to a group. Involvement with and enthusiasm for the group was typified in the students' reactions to the idea that the student council organize a talent show. The show was written, directed, and organized by the council, but any student on Team E who wanted to present an act was included. One of the first items for decision concerned organizing a committee to produce the show.

> Ms. Hopkins (black) asked who would like to be in the show, and every single student raised his or her hand. To this, Ms. Hopkins responded, " . . . All right. We need . . . an announcement to sign up people. I think the first question that we should ask is whether the talent show

should be for all of the seventh grade or only Team E. . . . " A chorus of students responded in unison: "Only Team E. . . . "

The effect of the student council on the students on Team E did not go unnoticed by others. For example, during an interview, Mr. Jamison, a white teacher whose team did not have a student council, remarked on the way in which Ms. Hopkins had improved relations between blacks and whites by creating a shared sense of group identity.

> One of the things I'm concentrating on personally is building up this feeling of belonging. That probably could be a very important deed. . . . Ms. Hopkins and others [on Team E] set up this program. They were sending cards to everybody on the team . . . who missed more than five days, or who . . . was hurt or in the hospital or whatever. They planned talent shows and this kind of thing. It's the kind of thing that . . . fosters loyalty to a group like a team, almost like a group of athletes. . . . The blacks and whites, simply because they belonged to the same group, the same team, break down some of the resistance. . . .

A CONCLUDING NOTE

This chapter suggests that on the whole, black and white children became somewhat more friendly and willing to work with each other as they progressed through Wexler. Furthermore, children from each group learned something about how to deal with each other. These changes occurred in spite of the fact that the students' observations of and experiences with each other sometimes buttressed traditional racial stereotypes. Both the diminution in white children's fear of their black counterparts and the tendency on the part of both black and white children to shift from intergroup to interpersonal behavior significantly affected students' reactions to out-group members. The students' intergroup behavior was also clearly influenced by external factors, such as the showing of *Roots*, and internal school or classroom-level policies.

The search for patterns such as those summarized above was especially difficult since black and white children had somewhat different perceptions of just how good relations between them were and how much change occurred as they progressed through Wexler. These varying perceptions can be seen as stemming at least partially from differences in the behavior patterns discussed earlier in this book. Yet the discrepancies in the perceptions of black and white children, as well as the unusually large variation within groups in responses to some of these issues, make especially salient an important point made initially at the end of the first chapter — that the search for patterns almost inevitably obscures individual variation. Just to emphasize this point, I will close this chapter with a few excerpts from student interviews that suggest the wide range of individual responses to the issues discussed here. All the students quoted are responding to a query about whether or not black and white students at Wexler get to know each other quickly and easily.

Clark (black): I did. I just started talking to them, playing with them on my lunch time. . . . The black people play with the white people all the time. . . .

Dick (white): No, that's not the case. Black and white kids don't really get along in this school. . . . Well, black kids just don't like white kids.

Dolores (black): No, 'cause some [white] children don't want to be your friend.

Irene (white): They make friends pretty easily. . . .

7

WHEN DOES A MAGNET SCHOOL
LOSE ITS MAGNETISM?

As described in Chapter 1, Wexler's creation as a model integrated school was set in motion by a variety of political and social forces. Important among these were both longstanding pressure from the state for desegregation of the district and the School Board's policy of opposition to any plan that required students to be bused to achieve desegregation. These two factors, combined with the Board's decision to create middle schools for children in the sixth through eighth grades, made the opening of Wexler Middle School as a showpiece for the benefits of voluntary desegregation a logical step.

Just as Wexler's creation was an outgrowth of forces existing in the school district at large, so too was its evolution as an institution inextricably intertwined with forces over which it had little control. The primary focus of this book has been on exploring what life was like *inside* the school, on the sorts of experiences students had and on the ways in which these experiences affected their views of and their relations with students who were not of their own race. However, any analysis of Wexler that does not consider the ways in which what happened inside the school was affected by external forces would be sadly incomplete, for such forces had an important impact on the extent to which the school was able to meet the goals initially set for it. In addition to affecting *in reality* the extent of its accomplishments, such forces also influenced the *perception* of Wexler as an institution, which in turn influenced its functioning in ways that will be discussed later in this chapter.

nally, an examination of the ways in which Wexler's evolution was affected by forces in the school district seems worthwhile for the lessons it suggests about some of the difficulties of creating one or a small number of exemplary, racially mixed "magnet" type schools widely believed to provide an education superior to that in predominantly black schools.

THE FIRST YEAR

Wexler's first year was clear success. Although, as indicated in Chapter 6, there were some who initially feared that there would be racial problems, most of the school's constituents were quite satisfied with the way black and white children adjusted to their racially mixed environment. Agreement was widespread among the school's staff that overt racial problems were minimal or even nonexistent, as the following rather typical excerpts from interviews with two sixth grade teachers during the school's second semester suggest.

> *Ms. Winters* (white): I haven't seen any racial problems so far; if there are any I'm unaware of them.

> *Ms. Monroe* (black): In general, I'd say they [the students] have adapted very well [to being in a racially mixed school]. A small minority don't get along. . . . There are always those few who have social problems, who cannot get along with anyone. . . . Generally, I think the kids are doing rather well.
> *Interviewer*: In these few cases where there are problems, is it generally without reference to color? Is race an issue here at all? . . .
> *Ms. Monroe*: No, they pick on anyone. They don't care who it is.

Administrators also saw racial problems as practically nonexistent:

> *Interviewer*: You said that another thing that leads to suspension is fighting. What sort of issues usually bring on a fight?
> *Mr. Reuben* (white): As I see them it is . . . very seldom racial, very seldom. I have seen only one racial fight. [Usually it's] petty things, you know, someone bumps someone in line . . . that kind of thing. . . . Petty little things that kids will fight for. . . . [In] 90 percent of our fights the kids start out playing with each other and someone hits someone too hard and there is a fight.
> *Interviewer*: Do you have any problems or arguments between kids

which start out as non-racial and turn into a thing where they start calling each other names?
Mr. Reuben: I haven't seen it. . . . I haven't seen any of that at all.

The very favorable reaction of most of the school's staff to the events of the first year is reflected in the comments made by one of the school's vice-principals, Mr. Callahan, in testimony at an open hearing of the Waterford Board of Public Education toward the end of that year.

Wexler has succeeded — beyond the most optimistic hopes, Wexler has succeeded. . . . Every educator I [have] talked with said that the school opening in September was the best he had experienced in a long time.

Parents, also, were generally quite favorable in their reaction to the school's first year, as excerpts from further testimony at the public hearings suggest.

I am Susan Reiber (white), chairman of the Wexler Parent Representatives and the parent of a son enrolled in . . . that school. I am speaking in behalf of the Wexler parents, 43 of whom endorsed this statement at a . . . meeting last night. . . . Wexler was promised innovative educational programs, a well-prepared staff, and a racially-balanced group of students who would choose to attend a middle school. The promise was kept, and this first year has been remarkably successful. We believe we have found a model for solving some inner-city school problems.

In spite of the initial fears many students had stemming from both Wexler's size and its racially mixed student body, most felt that the academic program was challenging and that peer relations were reasonably good. In the interviews in both October and June of their first year, black and white students consistently rated the academic program as markedly better than those at their previous schools. They also indicated that they felt more school pride and that they liked coming to Wexler better than their previous schools. Student behavior and peer relations were the only areas in which comparisons between Wexler and the students' prior schools did not consistently favor Wexler. In these realms, consistent with patterns discussed in the previous chapter, black students tended to rate the situation at Wexler more favorably than that at their previous schools, whereas white students saw little or no difference (Schofield, Shaeffer, and Hopkins 1977).

In some ways Wexler's very positive image during its first year contributed to forces that made it difficult for the school to continue to meet its goals in later years. Specifically, Wexler's opening coincided with two other events that made its very success the focus of heated controversy. First, the Board of Education opened Maple Avenue Middle Grade Center, a converted elementary school that drew its student body from several virtually all-black feeder schools. Second, renewed controversy over the issue of city-wide desegregation threatened when the city School Board began to consider a new desegregation plan to replace one rejected earlier by the state as unsatisfactory. The opening of an all-black school in a converted building nearly three-quarters of a century old, in spite of previous orders from the state requiring the city to move toward racially balanced schools, made many blacks acutely aware of the relatively poor facilities available in some of Waterford's all-black schools. Furthermore, the fact that the School Board was continuing legal efforts to avoid the need to desegregate at the same time it was working on a new desegregation plan gave those favoring desegregation little cause for optimism. Given the uncertainty about city-wide desegregation in the near future and the opening of an all-black middle school in antiquated facilities, many black parents found their inability to get their children into the highly touted Wexler especially galling.

Such feelings were clearly reflected in heated testimony by black parents and community representatives at hearings held by the Board of Public Education in the months before the opening of these two schools. An excerpt from the testimony of Mr. Martin, a black parent, suggests just how passionately some people felt about the situation.

There will be a private school situation in white neighborhoods and crumbs and leavings are all that is left for the black neighborhood. . . . You lied to us. . . . Where is the financing coming from to make this school [Maple Avenue] as good as Wexler? . . . A terrible lie. . . . The Board is committed to keeping blacks in their place. . . . We are charging the Board with fraud and genocide by unscrupulous administration. You have . . . for over twenty years planned the death of black children. You have killed our children mentally. . . . We want our fair share of the schools, too.

The School Board argued that it had taken an evenhanded approach in trying to obtain a student body for Wexler whose racial mix mirrored that of the students enrolled in Waterford's schools, that is, 58 percent white and 42 percent black. Many parents in Rockville, an economically depressed area of the city that was to be served by the renovated Maple Avenue Middle Grade Center, saw the situation quite differently. They argued that it was inherently unfair to admit *all* white applicants to Wexler, as had been done because of the relatively small numbers of white children applying, while turning away literally hundreds of black children, some of whom had applied on the very first day on which applications were accepted. The imbalance was made even clearer when it became known that, although the official application period had ended over six months before the school opened, white children's applications were being approved up to the day school began because fewer white children applied than had been anticipated. Furthermore, although Wexler was built to serve up to 1,600 students, it opened with roughly 1,500 because the decision was made that it was better to operate under capacity than to open the school with a student body that deviated too markedly from the initially agreed upon racial quota system, which called for the majority of the students to be white. Making matters worse, many of the black students not accepted at Wexler were assigned to Maple Avenue. Vehement testimony by black community members at a public hearing did not change this situation.

> I appear tonight not only as a concerned parent . . . but as an outraged citizen. [The plan to open Maple Avenue with a virtually all-black enrollment] is sinister and biased against black people. [It is] monstrous, against morality. I tell you there is no way we . . . will accept [this] garbage. . . . What will happen to our children? You are willing to run some schools [Wexler] below capacity to keep them lily white. . . . We the concerned parents of the Rockville Area . . . say "No."

Rockville parents did more than testify angrily at School Board hearings. First, in August, just a month before both Wexler and Maple Avenue were scheduled to open, their picketing of the latter actually stopped the remodeling work that was in progress. More importantly, a number of parents living in Rockville banded together and brought a class action suit against the school district in the name of seventh and eighth grade students assigned to attend that school.

They charged that the school district did not have the right to open a new segregated middle grade center and that Maple Avenue's physical facilities and educational programs were inferior to those available elsewhere, specifically at Wexler. Testimony given in court made it clear that many Rockville parents believed the School Board had previously promised residents of that section of the city that their children would go to Wexler. Such promises were characterized by some as part of a deliberate deception by the Board perpetrated in order to gain cooperation in the years preceding Wexler's opening. Wexler's central role in the Maple Avenue controversy was well illustrated by the fact that the legal opinion handed down by the judge had an entire section entitled "Comparison of Wexler and Maple Avenue." The judge concluded:

> There are numerous differences between the Maple Avenue and Wexler programs, and every difference favors Wexler. . . . Because defendants' actions of devoting greater attention and resources to Wexler are contrary to sound educational policy and because defendants have offered no reasonable explanation for such actions, this Court finds that such actions have occurred because Wexler has a majority white integrated student body while Maple Avenue has an all-black student body.

Later on in the opinion, the judge further supported the contentions of the black parents with this conclusion:

> Defendants' decisions to select Maple Avenue as the site for a middle school . . . and to use a racial quota at Wexler to insure a majority of the student body will be white were based in part on community sentiment of white residents of Elizabethville [a largely white middle- and upper-middle-class area] and Hadleytown [a majority white middle- and upper-middle-class area of the city that does, however, serve as the home of numerous blacks of roughly similar socioeconomic status] and consequently violated the Fourteenth Amendment.

The judge, in February of Wexler's first year, ordered the school district to close Maple Avenue and to reassign its students to thirteen schools, one of which was Wexler.

The Waterford School District appealed this judgment and took no immediate action to implement the judge's order. Yet the fact that this order was handed down in February of Wexler's first year, after negotiations suggested by the judge between the school district and representatives of the Rockville community had broken down, could hardly help having a major impact on an issue that had to be settled within months of the judge's decision — that is, whether to keep open enrollment as the mechanism used in obtaining Wexler's students, or to shift to a plan in which all graduates of several elementary schools would automatically be assigned there.

Many parents, especially white parents, had assumed that open enrollment would continue at Wexler indefinitely, or at least for several years. Numerous arguments, however, were put forward in support of the alternative plan under which students were assigned to Wexler. First, and least controversial, were the issues of administrative convenience and cost. It was clearly easier to make plans for Wexler and for other Waterford schools if children from specific elementary schools were assigned to Wexler. The open enrollment plan meant uncertainty from year to year about the number of students at Wexler and at other schools serving children in grades six through eight. Second, as indicated in the preceding part of this chapter, there was intense pressure on the School Board to increase the number of black students attending Wexler. Yet many people felt that a substantially increased number of black students was not compatible with open enrollment since they believed that whites would be unlikely to enroll voluntarily in a school in which the majority of the students were black. Since Wexler had been set up just a year before with great fanfare as a model of integrated education, the prospect of its becoming heavily black if whites chose not to attend it was far from pleasing to the School Board. Thus a plan in which students from a variety of elementary schools were required to enroll in Wexler was attractive to many. It would allow an increased black enrollment and at the same time make white reluctance to enroll voluntarily under such conditions irrelevant. Certain whites would be assigned to Wexler and would have no option but to go there unless they decided to leave the public school system altogether. Although there was no logical requirement for open enrollment to be associated with a fifty/fifty racial balance in the student body, or for a plan involving assignment to Wexler to mean a shift in that balance, most observers recognized in practical reality an association between these two enrollment plans and the future racial composition of the school's student body.

Under such conditions, it is hardly surprising that white parents tended to support the continuance of open enrollment whereas many black parents, most especially those whose children were not already at Wexler, favored a shift to the alternate plan. Many of the whites who testified at public hearings on the matter predicted dire consequences if a change were made in the enrollment policy. In general, this testimony stressed the success of Wexler's first year and raised the specter of white flight from the predominantly black school which, it was believed, Wexler would become. Typical of such sentiments were those expressed by the executive director of the Elizabethville Urban Coalition at a public hearing.

> We feel the first year for Wexler was a success. . . . However, the proposal [to eliminate open enrollment] . . . would have the effect of taking a successfully integrated school and making it just another segregated facility in a two or three year period. . . . Since it is working, why consider changing the important element of voluntary enrollment?

In spite of the predictions that a change in the enrollment policy would ultimately turn a very special school into just another segregated facility, the decision was made to shift to an enrollment policy that assigned students from a number of elementary schools to Wexler. Although it was not possible to determine definitely the extent to which this decision was made on grounds relating to cost and administrative efficiency versus those relating to the political pressures generated by the Maple Avenue suit and the attendant controversy, it is clear that the latter factors did have some impact despite the perception on the part of many in the black community that the School Board was unresponsive to their demands.

THE SECOND YEAR

The second year in Wexler's seventh and eighth grades was much like the first. However, the relatively unchanged situation in these two grades was in stark contrast to the marked change that occurred in the sixth grade, where the first six weeks of the fall semester were characterized by teachers as "chaotic," "ridiculous," and "horrendous." The root of the problem was the fact that, because of the change in enrollment policy, the number of sixth graders attending Wexler increased by almost 50 percent, from just under 400 to almost

600. Adequate provision for this massive increase in the student population was not made, at least partly because delays in the decision about the enrollment policy left relatively little time for planning once the decision had been made. Thus class size in some cases reached 40, and there were not even enough chairs and tables to go around. The teachers' reactions to the situation were typified by the comments of Ms. Winters as she looked back on her experiences at the end of the school's second year.

> *Ms. Winters* (white): Last year, I really enjoyed it. This year could have been a lot better. The end of the year was very good. Our kids came a long way. . . . Some of the success this year . . . is in spite of what happened. . . . I hope next [year] is better . . . getting off the ground. It would have to be! They [the central administration] couldn't foul it up that much next year. . . . Never again! The [children] fought over those chairs. They were more precious than gold! . . . There are no materials to individualize [instruction] this year. . . . We ran out of ditto paper in February or March and . . . [it was] rationed the last two or three months.

It took the better part of six weeks for the school to make the adjustments necessary to accommodate all the sixth graders in a manner that was acceptable for the long term. New teachers were transferred into the sixth grade, large storage rooms were converted into classrooms, and schedule changes were made. Although most of these changes were accomplished by mid-October, some negative effects of the initial overcrowding persisted. For example, some teachers who were transferred to the sixth grade from other grades at Wexler continued to resent having such a change imposed on them after the school year had started.

Although the increase in the number of sixth graders was the most obvious change, several other important changes in the nature of the student body also occurred in the school's second year. First, since students were now assigned to Wexler, some children attended the school in spite of the fact that they or their parents would never have chosen it because of factors such as its large size, its somewhat individualized program, or its racially mixed student body. This fact did not seem to pose major problems. Indeed, our interviews with students entering Wexler during its second year suggested that virtually all of them had wanted to come and did not feel coerced. Nonetheless, some teachers felt the change was responsible for an increase in vandalism and discipline problems at the school. Also, the principal found the sixth grade parents in the school's second year less supportive and more contentious than those of the open-enrolled children, who he felt had, with few exceptions, been quite cooperative.

A second important change in the sixth grade population was the widely acknowledged decline in the average socioeconomic level of the homes from which Wexler's white students came with relatively little change in that of the black students. Many upper-middle-class whites still attended Wexler, but joining them were quite a number of white children from families with relatively low levels of income and education. Mr. Reuben summed up the situation with only mild exaggeration when he said, "Last year [the first year] I don't think we had a poor white kid in the school. This year we have a [big group of] white kids from a public housing project." This change in the background of the white students was far greater than that of the black students during the same time period, although the proportion of black children from middle- and upper-middle-class families at Wexler did decline somewhat. Thus the socioeconomic gap between black and white students was considerably narrower in the school's second year than in its first. Although it was not possible to get information that allowed quantification of just how major the change in the relative socioeconomic background of black and white students was, some teachers estimated, for example, that the proportion of white students getting free or reduced-price lunches nearly tripled whereas the proportion of black students receiving such income-linked subsidies increased only marginally.

The achievement gap between white and black students also declined markedly.

> *Mr. Reuben* (white): Our first group of sixth graders open-enrolled. . . . The whole class was 20 percent gifted; 40 percent of the whites in that first class were gifted. . . . It's a whole different population [this year] . . . . In this sixth grade class, 50 out of 600, close to ten percent, were gifted. [Most of these students were white.]

As Mr. Reuben's comments indicate, the marked change in Wexler's white student population was largely responsible for the narrowing of the achievement gap.

In Chapter 3 I argued that the achievement gap between whites and blacks was one important cause of friction in peer relations.

Consistent with this analysis, the sixth grade teachers interviewed were virtually unanimous in agreeing that black and white students got along better in Wexler's second year than in its first.

Interviewer: What differences if any do you see between the way last year's students adjusted to being in an interracial school like Wexler compared to this year's students?

Mr. Hughes (black): This year . . . academic-wise there probably weren't as [many] high achievers. . . . Social skills were better compared to the group . . . we had last year. . . . I think there was a better intermingling among the boys . . . and even among the girls too. . . . The black girls sat down and talked to the white girls. . . . I never seen any hate. . . . I saw more intermingling and exchange of ideas as compared to last year.

Interviewer: How would you characterize the relationship between black and white kids . . . this [second] year?

Mr. Little (white): I truly think it's better this year for some reason. . . . The competition isn't there anymore . . . and there seem to be very few racial incidents. . . . You still see black kids maybe picking on a white kid but not half as much as last year. . . . This group of kids . . . they're going to be together as a group. Somebody stole a book out of a white kid's locker. His locker partner, who was black and a very popular student, was going to take care of it for him. [Another time] there was a white kid going down the steps with two black kids and somebody [black] started picking on him. His two black friends helped him. . . . I didn't see that last year that much. I guess I saw more polarization last year. . . .

In addition to a lessening of the barrier posed in Wexler's first year by differences in socioeconomic background and achievement levels, the fact that whites were a clear minority in the second year also seemed to encourage more interaction between black and white children. In Wexler's first sixth grade, the attention paid to balancing the racial and sexual composition of each classroom combined with the balanced racial mix in the student body meant that students who were not inclined to make friends with those of the other race still had plenty of potential friends of their own race and sex within their classes. In Wexler's second year, such was often not the case. For example, there were occasional classes with just one white girl and numerous classes with no more than three or four white children of either sex. Initially this situation seemed to intensify the anxiety and fear stemming from a sense of being outnumbered or overwhelmed by black students that white students had felt even in the racially balanced sixth grade the previous year.

> *Ms. Monroe* (black): I think sometimes the white kids [in Wexler's second sixth grade] felt outnumbered. . . . Maybe in the beginning of the year it was a big problem for a lot of kids, but I think as the year went on they got used to it.
> *Interviewer*: Did you see anything that indicated to you that white students might have been feeling outnumbered or — ?
> *Ms. Monroe*: Yes, some parents called, concerned because their kids were nervous when they came home from school, scared to walk down the hall or something. . . . A lot of times I think there were misunderstandings. . . . Somebody bumps into you a lot of times, doesn't say "Excuse me" and they [white kids] didn't know they [black kids] didn't mean it.

Although fear of black children, especially unknown black children, remained something of a problem, many of the white students in the school's second sixth grade class seemed impelled to make friends or at least to become acquainted with their black classmates by the need for social relationships with those of their own sex.

> *Mr. Little* (white): I think last year's class was much more intelligent but this year's class is much more friendly toward each other. . . . The decrease in the number of white kids affected [peer relations] and competition. It's like 80 percent black this year, so that white kids just had to melt in with them. . . . This year the white kids had to go find black friends and they did. . . .
> *Interviewer*: Are you saying there may not be so much group competition now because one group is larger?
> *Mr. Little*: Yes.

The results of interviews with the two groups of students support the teachers' view that peer relations were somewhat better in Wexler's second year than its first. In fact, student ratings of almost all aspects of the sixth grade, even in the fall of the second year when crowding was a major problem, were essentially equal to or more positive than the responses of sixth graders one year earlier. The difference in the rating of the school by sixth grade students in the two succeeding years was not large and sometimes was not statistically significant, being no more than one or two points on a twenty-one point scale. Nonetheless, in every single case in which identical questions about the school or peer relations were asked of the two groups, the second group was more positive than the first.

White students were well aware of their minority status in the sixth grade. In fact, when asked how many of the approximately 600 children in the sixth grade were white, the white students interviewed were remarkably accurate, with an average estimate of 212, which came very close to the official figure of 205. (Black students were also extremely accurate, with an average estimate of 371 blacks in their grade compared to the official figure of 368.) It was clear that some, though far from all, of the white children would have liked more white peers. Just under one-half of the white sixth graders interviewed during Wexler's second year said they would like to have more white classmates. The reason given consistently for this preference was the belief, discussed previously, that blacks were less rule-abiding and/or more aggressive than whites. One of the strongest statements on this subject came from Edna, a white girl.

Interviewer: Do you ever wish there were more white kids in school?
Edna (white): Yeah . . . because the black kids . . . they want to fight people and they think they are the greatest people in the world and there's no one better than they are and stuff like that.
Interviewer: OK, so how would it make a difference if there were more white kids in the school?
Edna (white): There wouldn't be as many bullies.

The majority of the whites, though, said they were satisfied with the racial mix.

Interviewer: Do you ever wish that there were more white kids in the school?
Norma (white): No. . . . I'm friends with a lot of black girls. . . .

In summary, then, relations between black and white students in the sixth grade during Wexler's second year were certainly as good as in the first year. Most indications suggest that, if anything, they were slightly better in spite of the year's inauspicious beginning; students got along reasonably well and came to accept and like each other more as the year passed. The fact that white students were in a clear minority exacerbated some of their problems in dealing with the black children's physically rougher play style. However, this seemed counterbalanced by the positive impact of the less dramatic differences in home background and achievement levels. Furthermore, their minority status encouraged many white students to seek out or at least to accept black friends more readily than they might have otherwise.

Although peer relations are the focus of this book and are one important aspect of any school experience, the quality of the academic program and a school's effectiveness in improving children's academic achievement are clearly of more importance to the vast majority of parents and educators. Direct comparisons between the effectiveness of Wexler's academic program in its first and second year are difficult to make. Gain scores on standardized tests were not available for use in this research. Furthermore, even if they had been, comparison of these scores would be problematic since one might reasonably expect rather different rates of growth in two classes that started out at significantly different points on such tests. Thus more indirect indicators must be used in assessing the comparative success of Wexler's sixth grade academic program in its first and second years.

The faculty in the sixth grade remained relatively stable from the first year to the next although, as previously mentioned, some teachers who preferred to teach in other grades ended up in the sixth grade because of the increased number of students. In addition, personnel cutbacks in the school system as a whole affected Wexler somewhat more than many other schools since the school's handpicked faculty was relatively young and union rules allowed senior faculty whose positions were cut to "bump" younger faculty out of positions the teachers with more seniority wanted.

Given the relatively small change in the sixth grade faculty, it is hardly surprising that neither the basic curriculum nor the quality of teaching changed in obvious ways, although, as Ms. Winters pointed out above, some teachers found their efforts to individualize instruction hampered by paper shortages and larger classes. Most of the sixth grade teachers felt that the year was successful academically if one looked at the progress students made, although the absolute level of achievement was on the average lower in the second year than in the first. Indeed, a number of teachers maintained that the intellectual atmosphere in the second year was markedly better than in the first.

Ms. Winters (white): This year's class seemed to respect intelligence. Last year's class was on a different [higher] intelligence level, there weren't as many non-succeeders. . . . There was more competition . . . sort of waiting until the opportunity when someone doesn't know the answer and then being very snide about supplying it, or flaunting the fact that they have their homework or that they got an A . . . when somebody else didn't. . . . They weren't willing to give respect to somebody else because they were in competition for that position. In this year's class, there was less competition in the upper levels. In the middle levels, there was a lot of competition, to strive, to excel, to be the best . . . [but] their measure of success was not bragging but in terms of "Hey, I did as well as so and so." In one group where we had a lot of kids who thought they were intellectuals [I saw] snide remarks and snottiness. In most of the other groups there were only one or two or three that really stood out and they were respected.

Of course, students were not able to make the same sort of experience-based comparisons between the sixth grade in its first and second year that the teachers were. However, comparison of student responses to two sets of identical interview questions in the two succeeding years lends support to the conclusion that the academic program remained strong. First, students in both years found it somewhat harder to get good grades at Wexler than they had in their previous schools and their average rating of just how much harder this was turned out to be virtually identical. Second, both groups rated Wexler's teachers better than the teachers in their previous schools (Francis and Schofield 1979; Schofield, Francis, and Hall 1979).

In summary, then, although the sixth grade academic program labored under difficulties connected with the initial overcrowding, there is reason to believe that, all in all, the academic opportunities offered to Wexler's students did not change substantially from the first year to the second. A decline in the number of very high-achieving children was clear, but this change seemed attributable to differences in the student population served rather than to a less effective academic program. Furthermore, some teachers contended that this change led to an improved academic atmosphere in which children respected achievement instead of constantly trying to enhance their own standing by deriding the accomplishments of others.

Although the analysis of both peer relations and the academic program in the sixth grade suggests that the situation in the second year, with the exception of the first six weeks or so, was comparable to or, in the case of peer relations, somewhat better than the first year, one would never have suspected this from the public image of the school. Many whites, concerned about the shift in the racial balance and fearful that the school would become almost entirely black, began to use the term *tipping point* in their discussions of Wexler and to consider sending their children elsewhere. The principal began to have to contend with white parents who wanted to withdraw their children.

> *Mr. Reuben* (white): There are a lot of concerns and rumors going around Elizabethville [a heavily Jewish section of Waterford] that came from the fact that they [the Board of Education] changed from the open enrollment to the feeder pattern. People [in Elizabethville] are really afraid the school will become all black. Whereas last year we had kids leaving the private schools to come here, this year we have kids leaving to go to private schools. . . . As a matter of fact, there are five or six Jewish kids who are now going to the Catholic parochial school. . . . They want to go to a private school, but they can't afford the other ones.

Controversy about the school's future came to a head in the spring of the second year when the Board of Education had to decide whether to keep the feeder pattern it had set up just a year before or to drop it in favor of a return to open enrollment or a new feeder pattern. There was considerable support for a return to open enrollment, especially from whites who felt their children would be trapped in an increasingly overcrowded and black school. They argued that retention of the assigned enrollment policy would insure that Wexler would become overcrowded. During its second year, the school had been able to absorb the new big sixth grade although the sudden increase caused considerable annoyance and inconvenience. However, if the Board kept the feeder pattern policy in effect, Wexler would have more students during its third year than many people felt it could reasonably handle. Projections indicated that if the feeder plan were retained without changes, the school, which had originally been built for up to 1,600 students, would have a student body of over 1,800. Testimony by white witnesses also objected to the assigned enrollment plan on the grounds that the school would soon become segregated — partly because of the racial balance in the feeder schools and partly because they believed many whites would withdraw their children from the public school system rather than have them attend an overcrowded and predominantly black school. Opposition to any assigned enrollment plan was expressed by numerous white parents and community members at public hearings that the Board of Public Education held in the spring of Wexler's second year.

> *Mrs. McCoy* (white): I saw . . . the beginning of a dream come true — Wexler Middle School — its conception, construction, and philosophy. Now I see . . . without academic excellence Wexler surely will end up another all-black school, only this time, not in a black neighborhood. . . . We worked hard to achieve our dream — an improvement in the quality of learning, not just for black children or for white children, but for *Waterford* children. . . . We could envision a whole series of magnet schools, we could already hear the accolades and we could see the articles in *Time*. . . . Then, last year, the sixth grade was sent to Wexler on an assigned basis. The dream disintegrated. Like Martin Luther King, we have been to the mountain top, but we are not, it appears, going to be able to save public education in the only area in Waterford [in] which it can really work, because the people want it to work.

Less fervent testimony by many others made similar or related points, like those made by the head of a largely white community group from Elizabethville.

> We feel that the first year for Wexler was a success. . . . However, the decision to eliminate the voluntary feature [of] the school . . . had the effect of taking a school which had the potential to become successfully integrated and cause it to become just another of Waterford's segregated facilities in a few years. . . . Because the first-year image of Wexler was positive . . . and the second-year image was negative, we must make the necessary changes now to reverse this trend. . . . The voluntary enrollment plan . . . is the best way to achieve a successful demonstration of how well-integrated, innovative education can work.

The Board was in a difficult position. There was strong support for a return to open enrollment among whites directly connected with the school. On the other hand, such calls were often thinly disguised complaints from white parents who were unhappy about Wexler's racial composition under the new feeder plan, and the judge presiding over the Maple Avenue case had already concluded that racial quotas set just to please the white community were inappropriate. The Maple Avenue case was still being appealed, and the Board was not known for its immediate responsiveness to judicial orders relating to desegregation; yet it did have to deal with black parents and community members, many of whom saw the push for a return to open enrollment as stemming from whites' hostility to having numerous black students at Wexler.

> *Mrs. Montgomery* (black): This administration has failed to support the school [Wexler] miserably. And yet it's the children, specifically the black children, who are being blamed for the problem. Suddenly when there's an overabundance of us, everything starts to fall apart. Everyone keeps telling me how beautiful everything was last year. So the only logical conclusion is that the black kids have caused the breakdown; while no one has said that outright, that thought is intrinsic in the statement, and I find that utterly repulsive. . . . On overcrowding, what guarantee can you give that once those two hundred bodies are gone, things will really be any better? . . .

Thus the support that many whites gave to a switch back to open enrollment was counterbalanced by opposition on the part of many blacks.

Of course, the Board of Education had the option of continuing with the assigned enrollment plan it had adopted one year earlier. The problem with retaining this, as many blacks desired, was that there was no politically feasible way to solve the burgeoning enrollment. Cutting a white elementary school out of the feeder pattern would lead in the direction of resegregation, which was undesirable given the ballyhoo that had surrounded Wexler's opening as an integrated school and the pressures for desegregation coming from the state. On the other hand, cutting a black school from the feeder pattern was not feasible either since many blacks in the city were already aroused by the Board's opening of the segregated Maple Avenue school and its failure to build a new middle school in Rockville or an adjacent area for all of Rockville's children. In the end, the Board decided to stick with the feeder plan adopted for Wexler's second year and to make another school near Wexler available as an annex to relieve the overcrowding. This school, Comstock, had been an elementary school before it was closed because of declining enrollments.

Unfortunately for the future of Wexler, the rather bitter controversy at the Board's open hearings on the enrollment policy attracted a lot of attention in the local media. The strong arguments about overcrowding and racial tipping points made to try to persuade the Board to readopt an open enrollment policy confirmed the growing concern of many parents about the school's viability. The visibility the controversy gave to real or potential problems at Wexler can be illustrated by brief reference to articles that appeared in Waterford's major papers. One headline covering a story on one of the public hearings proclaimed: "Crowding, Racial Balance Cited As Wexler Problem Areas." An excerpt from this article quoted the chairman of the Wexler Parents' Committee as saying, "Wexler opened with an ideal situation last year. . . . " The article then went on to say that the parent alleged that "Now the school is becoming overcrowded . . . and is becoming racially imbalanced." Another article a few weeks later proclaimed under a banner headline on the newspaper's front page that "efforts to adjust racial balance at Wexler Middle School [have] simply collapsed."

THE THIRD YEAR

Wexler functioned in a reasonably viable way during its third year. Most of its teachers and its academic programs remained similar to those in previous years and, as in earlier years, there were very few serious racial incidents. Yet although Wexler was reasonably successful in its third year when compared to other similar inner-city schools, it did begin to fall noticeably short of achieving the perhaps unrealistically optimistic goals initially held up for it. No one gratified the dreams of citizens like Mrs. McCoy who had anticipated reporters from *Time* magazine coming to Waterford to chronicle an extraordinary success story in urban education. No one came from Washington to see how Wexler's success could be replicated elsewhere. Instead, a number of changes, both those imposed by the school district administration and those occurring naturally as time moved on and some of the initial enthusiasm and excitement of being part of a new experiment wore off, undermined Wexler's ability to serve as a model of academic excellence and carefully planned integration.

Wexler opened in the fall of its third year with over 100 more students than it had in its second year. Both its sixth and seventh grades had roughly 100 more students than in the school's first year.

A decrease of about 50 students in the eighth grade did relatively little to compensate for the growth in the other two grades. Comstock School was available as an annex to help ease the impact of overcrowding, but its utilization created numerous problems, which will be discussed in some detail shortly. Furthermore, the central administration instructed Mr. Reuben that he was to drop some of the practices he had instituted the previous year to handle the burgeoning student population.

> *Mr. Reuben* (white): They don't want us to use anymore . . . the storage rooms [and] the teachers' work rooms [for classrooms]. . . . The storage rooms in many cases are better than the regular space. . . . The way Mr. Martin (white) had his decorated, it was nice . . . and the . . . [one] upstairs was really nice. They [the central administration] don't like it . . . simply because it doesn't look good.

Although some of these practices, like holding classrooms in storage areas, posed potential public relations problems, their alternatives posed potentially serious, although perhaps less visible, educational problems. For example, some of Wexler's teachers became "floaters" who had no classroom of their own but went from one room to another when teachers and students normally using those classrooms were at lunch, gym, or art. On the one hand, such a practice seems a reasonable utilization of space. On the other, teachers complained that it undercut their ability to teach effectively since they had to carry all their materials with them; they couldn't post student papers or displays; and they saw less of other teachers on their team and hence were less able to plan as a group. Teachers maintained that the team teaching concept, which had been considered a central feature of Wexler's academic program, was further undermined when, for reasons associated with both the utilization of space and public image, the hour and one-half of planning and preparation time, which many teams of teachers had previously had in one large chunk during the school day, was divided into several smaller segments.

Another change imposed by the central administration in spite of the objections of Wexler's principal and teachers was the use of "vertical houses." Previously, Wexler had been organized into three "schools within a school," each called a house. As indicated in Chapter 1, the houses were physically separated from each other and each house served only one grade. The philosophy behind these physical and organizational arragements was clear — the houses were thought to ease the transition from the rather personal atmosphere of the small elementary school to the more impersonal atmosphere of a much larger middle school. The shift to vertical houses meant that children from all three grades would be put together in each "school within a school."

Central administration staff in favor of vertical houses argued (1) that all middle schools should be organized the same way and that Wexler's use of one-grade houses was out of step with other middle schools and (2) that vertical houses allowed more efficient utilization of space. This latter argument was clearly supported by events back in Wexler's second year. The school as a whole was not really overcrowded, since it had just about the number of students for which it had been built. Rather, the sixth grade house was overcrowded, having been built for about 450 students but serving 600.

Wexler's staff, however, generally felt quite strongly that vertical houses were not desirable.

> Mr. Reuben (white) then presented to the faculty some of the changes anticipated next year [the school's third] . . . . The first change, he said, is that we have been told we must have vertical houses. . . . [Vice-principal Callahan (white) then explained some of the details.] One of the teachers, Ms. Cohen (white) raised her hand and when called on shouted out, "It won't work. There is no way it will work!" Mr. Callahan replied, "Look, we've got to make a try at this. You are not going to have mixed grades in classes, just . . . in the houses. . . . " One of the other (white) teachers said in an angry tone, "What we are doing is going back to the old junior high school concept." Mr. Reuben came to the microphone and said . . . "This isn't a change I want; this has come down from above. . . . There are a number of changes we are just going to have to accept! . . . The Board thinks that we can make better use of the space we have. . . . It's a policy they've adopted. . . . They want all middle schools to be the same."

Teachers gave numerous reasons for their opposition to vertical houses, ranging all the way from minor ones like a disinclination to leave the classrooms to which they had become accustomed to more major ones such as concerns about who the vice-principal responsible for their new house would be. However, one belief shared by virtually all of the teachers was that vertical houses would lead to more discipline problems since children of very different ages and sizes would be brought into constant contact with each other. This concern seemed justified since Wexler's sixth and seventh graders themselves, when asked to comment on hassling and intimidation among students, indicated that both age and physical size played a role.

> *Interviewer*: Are there certain groups of kids who are most likely to do this [to intimidate others]?
> *Jo Ellen* (a black sixth grader): The eighth graders. . . . I'd say mostly blacks.

> *Interviewer*: Are there some kids who seem more likely to be picked on than other children?
> *Georgia* (white): Yes.
> *Interviewer*: Why do you think this is?
> *Georgia*: Because they're little . . . and people think they can get their way . . . because they're little and they can't do anything about it.

"Floating" teachers, vertical houses, larger classes, and a number of other changes all helped Wexler to adjust to its increased student population. However, the major change instituted to deal with the overcrowding was the opening of the annex at Comstock School. Although the annexation of Comstock, an older but physically attractive facility, undoubtedly relieved overcrowding at Wexler, many questioned whether the way Comstock was utilized was consistent with Wexler's avowed goal of being a model integrated school. For a variety of reasons including scheduling considerations, two types of special classes, remedial and accelerated, were housed at Comstock. The accelerated classes were for academically talented sixth and seventh graders, who spent some time each week on special advanced work. In addition, the room used for Wexler's "in-house" suspension program, to which suspended children went to carry on with their studies rather than being denied access to school, was located at Comstock.

Housed on the second floor with the accelerated classes were classrooms for a fine arts program for academically accelerated eighth graders. All of these groups of children were predominantly white. The first floor of the school housed the three programs that were predominantly black: the remedial math and reading programs and the in-house suspension room. Mrs. Lyons, a white woman who was a member of Friends of Wexler, the informal coalition of parents, social agencies, and other local institutions that tried to promote a good social and educational climate at Wexler, described the situation at Comstock this way at one of the group's meetings:

> "There are two very different groups of kids over there, and the white kids seem to me to be privileged. The white kids get on the bus first and . . . have a teacher on their bus. . . . The black bus [for children in the remedial program] goes next [with] no teacher. . . . There is only one carpeted room in that school and it's the accelerated room. . . . " Mrs. Lyons went on to say . . . that when she goes over with the suspended kids to Comstock she feels like a jailer. . . . The black kids go to suspension on the white bus . . . and the other students ask "Hey, are you going to suspension?" She said everyone knows that is what is happening.

These heavily segregated remedial and accelerated classes had, of course, existed before Comstock was opened. However, at Comstock the contrast in their racial composition was painfully highlighted. For example, whereas before the children walked to their classes as individuals or in small groups, now they boarded essentially segregated buses. The invidious comparison between blacks and whites that occurred at Comstock was just the sort of thing the school had tried so hard to avoid in its first year or two.

There were other signs that the high priority that had been given to the creation of an environment that was carefully planned to foster positive relations between black and white students was not translated as effectively into everyday life at Wexler during the school's third year as it had been initially. The most obvious of these was the brouhaha over the assignment of students to particular classes that arose at the beginning of the third year. As indicated in Chapter 1, in the first year or two administrators placed considerable emphasis on keeping racial balance in all but a few special types of classes. The first student scheduling plan for the school's third year drawn up by Vice-principal Callahan was consistent with this emphasis. However, it was never implemented. High-level administrators at the Board of Education insisted on a new schedule because the first plan, as in previous years, was not in compliance with federal guidelines for the scheduling of children receiving instruction funded through the Title I program. Wexler's administrators were unable to come up with a schedule that met the federal guidelines but did not at the same time result in heavily segregated classes. Thus they argued that the schedule they devised in response to criticism of the first plan should not be implemented, contending that the federal guidelines were widely ignored and were not, in fact, strictly followed in all of Waterford's other schools. Their protests were ineffective, and Wexler opened with its classes heavily segregated. Furthermore, some of the classes that consisted primarily of white students had no more than seventeen or eighteen members leading to what some school staff called "a private school situation."

Many white parents were delighted with the new schedule. Understandably, their black counterparts were not. Indeed, a number of black parents organized a group to protest it — the first virtually all-black parents' group to coalesce around a particular issue in Wexler's three years of existence. The controversy over the schedule was heated. In the end, the school shifted to a third schedule that emphasized academic and racial heterogeneity. Although the end result was similar to prior years, the controversy was divisive and fueled racial animosity. White parents who had accepted heterogeneous scheduling in prior years felt cheated when their children were taken out of classes with many other white students and put into predominantly black classes, which were often larger. Black parents were upset by the very fact that Wexler had started its third year with basically resegregated classes and worried about whether they could trust administrators to stick with the new schedule. Indeed, some were so upset that they called upon Mr. Reuben to resign his position if this schedule were not implemented and kept in place, as he assured them it would be.

The way in which the emphasis on Wexler's mission as a model desegregated school weakened over time is well illustrated by a comparison of the material displayed on a bulletin board, prominently placed near the school's main entrance, in Wexler's first and third years.

> When I walked into the school for the first time this [third] year I noticed immediately that things were quite different from previous years. First of all, the motto "This Should Be The Finest School" was no longer on the bulletin board. In its place was written "Scenes from Summer — Wexler Day Camp." Underneath this heading were over 30 color snapshots from the school's summer program. The most striking thing to me about the pictures was the difference between those displayed this year and those displayed at the beginning of the school's

first year. That year, *every single picture* was integrated. This year about one-third were not.

Later in the school's third year, the bulletin board display contrasted even more strongly with the carefully planned encouragement of racial mixing apparent in the first year.

> There was a new set of pictures on the bulletin board near the main office today. The pictures were color photographs of a skiing trip which Mr. Williams, a black teacher, led. There were 22 pictures, only 1 of which showed a black child. The other pictures were all of white children, although 1 or 2 included Mr. Williams.

The extent to which the school promoted cooperation between black and white children and discouraged competition also changed noticeably over time. First, the level of funding that the school was able to obtain for its in-school and after-school program was less in the third year than before. Thus these programs were curtailed. Since they were a very effective means of promoting acquaintance and cooperation among students, this was a real loss. Second, affective education (AEs), twice-weekly classes designed to help children come to know each other and to learn how to work together, were dropped in Wexler's second year and not reinstituted in its third. Although AEs were widely and perhaps quite accurately perceived as ineffective, it was telling that these classes, which Mr. Reuben felt were "desperately needed," were discontinued rather than upgraded and improved.

In Wexler's first year, Mr. Reuben had discouraged the display of academic honor rolls, feeling that they would promote competition and lead to invidious comparisons between white and black children. By the third year, honor rolls were a common sight.

> Today as I entered House F, I noticed that honor rolls were placed very prominently both in a number of classrooms and around the vice-principal's office. . . . This struck me as very different from earlier efforts . . . not to emphasize honor rolls. . . . Certainly in the last two years, I never saw displays prominently placed like this featuring honor roll students.

In a school that had once tried to downplay the potentially destructive effects of competition on peer relations, one teacher now posted a motto exhorting students, "Don't Knock Your Competitors. Just Beat Their Brains Out By Being So Superior That Anyone Can Tell."

Many whites argued that no matter what its programs or policies, Wexler, in its third year, could no longer serve as a model of integration because of the racial composition of the school's student body. The actual shift from 50 percent black to about 60 percent black was not all that substantial. This shift was frequently exaggerated, perhaps partly because the sixth and seventh grades were indeed two-thirds black by Wexler's third year. Many white parents, community members and even occasional teachers labeled the school as 80 percent black, well past the fifty/fifty figure that was frequently characterized as the tipping point.

> Next Mr. Reuben mentioned that the school now [November of its third year] is 61 percent black. The eighth grade is 45 percent black, the seventh grade is 69 percent black, and the sixth grade 67 percent black. [These figures are close but not identical to figures in official publications.] He went on to say that he thought it was very important that people really know the truth about the school, because many people think that the number of blacks in the school is much greater than it really is. He said, for example, that a white parent who had called him recently believed the school was 80 percent black.

Whether or not Wexler was racially balanced at the end of its third year is clearly a matter of opinion. A great many whites felt it was not. Proponents of this point of view argued that the racial balance in the school as a whole was less important in shaping the experiences of its students than that in their particular grade. The fact that the two lower grades were two-thirds black and projections for the fourth year indicated that 71 percent of the incoming sixth graders would be black gave weight to the arguments of those who saw Wexler as rapidly becoming all-black. As one white parent put it during a public hearing on Wexler:

> There is a defeatist attitude abroad . . . which holds that pretty soon Wexler will be an all black school anyway, so what does it matter if the process is hurried along?

Many blacks, though, felt that whites were overreacting to the presence of increased numbers of black children at Wexler. They pointed out that the school had intended to open with a student body that was 58 percent white and asked why, if 58 percent white were ideal, 61 percent black was racially imbalanced. Proponents of the other point of view argued that since the school system contained somewhat more white students than black, comparisons like the above were unfair. Second, they pointed out that the official racial balance figures did not count the children enrolled in various special education programs, most of whom were black. Since these students spent a substantial part of their school day in regular classes and constituted just under 10 percent of the school's total enrollment, the official figures, which have been used in this chapter, markedly understated the percentage of black students. For example, whereas the official figures indicated that the school was 69 percent black in the fall of its fourth year, the correct figure, including over 100 special education children, was 78 percent. Finally, those who saw Wexler as racially imbalanced pointed out that, even if one did not count the children enrolled in special education, the sixth and seventh graders came extremely close to violating the racial balance guidelines set up by the state agency that had ordered Waterford to desegregate its schools. That Wexler's racial composition should come close to violating these guidelines a mere three years after the school's inception was seen as proof that it was fast on its way to becoming segregated.

THE FOURTH YEAR AND BEYOND

It is not possible to relate in detail the changes that occurred at Wexler from its third year to the present since intensive data-gathering spanned only the first three years. However, some research activities took place during the school's fourth year, and informal contact has been maintained subsequently. Since the description of Wexler's first three years stresses the trend toward increased enrollment, a shifting racial balance, and an increasingly negative image of the school among whites, it seems appropriate briefly to present information about the extent to which these trends have continued.

Wexler's student body in the school's sixth year, at the time of this writing, was approximately 1,635, just a few more students than the 1,600 it was built for, but substantially more than the number it had in its first year. The school was roughly 70 percent black, including the children in special education. Thus the proportion of black students, after a substantial rise between the third and fourth year, remained quite stable, declining very slightly in subsequent years. However, Wexler was more crowded than it had previously been with a similar number of students enrolled because Comstock was converted from an annex used by Wexler's students to a separate school. In fact, a memo written by the chairpersons to members of the Friends of Wexler about the school's sixth year contended that "space remains a problem."

The enrollment figures presented above suggest that, contrary to many dire predictions, Wexler's student population remained relatively stable after the fourth year. Perhaps one of the factors contributing to this was that during the fourth and fifth years it became increasingly evident that the School Board would have to bow at least partially to outside pressures to desegregate the system. Furthermore, the state pushed for immediate desegregation of all schools serving students in sixth grade and above. Thus it became clear that in the very near future the option of essentially all-white middle schools would not be available to white students within the public school system.

The public image of Wexler remained somewhat negative, especially in white communities. In spite of the fact that in its fourth year it was the only one of Waterford's middle schools in which average scores on the standardized tests given to all students were essentially equal to or above the national norms, Wexler's principal was replaced. The widespread negative image of the school was reflected in the decision about Mr. Reuben's replacement. The position was given to another white, Mr. Stanwick, who, as one knowledgeable observer put it, "went to Fairmount Avenue School when it was falling apart and did a very good job putting it together again." Mr. Stanwick had only one year in which to institute his approach, which was somewhat more structured and discipline-oriented than Mr. Reuben's. Then, because of seniority rules and cuts elsewhere in the system, Mr. Stanwick was replaced by yet another white male, Mr. Van Buron.

In summary, Wexler's situation six years after its much publicized opening was neither as positive as the overoptimistic dreams of those involved in its creation would have wished nor as dire as some of those watching its evolution in the first three years had predicted. Although Wexler, with its still fine physical plant and good staff, was hardly "just another ghetto school" at the end of six years, it was a far cry from the model of integrated education it had set out to be. Its racial balance shifted enough to leave it in danger of being out of compliance with state guidelines. Its special programs were eroded and undercut by lack of funds and shifts in staff. Its burgeoning enrollment contributed to both educational and discipline problems, and the constant change in policies and practices, many made in response to problems listed above, undermined public confidence in the school.

8

EPILOGUE

This book was written to describe and analyze the development of peer relations in a desegregated school that made a real effort to provide a strong academic program in an environment designed to foster positive interaction between black and white students. Its purpose is to shed light on the development of peer relations in this school in the belief that a close look at the dynamics of such relations will be of use to social scientists as well as to educators or parents concerned about fostering positive academic and social experiences for students in desegregated schools. Thus this work has explored in some depth what happened at Wexler and has tried to suggest the factors that contributed to various outcomes. It has not attempted to serve as a "how to" manual designed to give detailed advice on running desegregated schools. Nor shall I undertake such a task in this epilogue since the research on which this book is based was not oriented toward prescribing specific solutions to educational problems. Rather, I would like to highlight here a number of observations about intergroup relations that grow out of the research and are of particular relevance to those concerned with desegregated schools. Since my goals are to heighten awareness of distinctions that need to be made in order to think accurately and effectively about intergroup relations and to draw attention to social processes that are likely to operate in racially mixed schools, this epilogue should be of interest to theorists and researchers as well as educators. Most if not all of the issues to be discussed here have been touched on to some extent in the preceding seven chapters. Thus this epilogue will serve as a selective summary of the book, not attempting to cover all the major points but rather pulling together, highlighting, and expanding on some of its conclusions relevant to both social psychological theory and educational practice. Although the conclusions presented here are based primarily on an analysis of Wexler, which is by no means a "typical" desegregated school, it is my strong belief that these observations are likely to be broadly applicable. This belief is based on a close reading of others' research in a wide variety of desegregated schools and on the fact that the atypical features of Wexler are not related in any logical way to most of the findings on which these conclusions are based.

RETHINKING THREE ASSUMPTIONS
ABOUT INTERGROUP RELATIONS

This research suggests that three of the assumptions commonly made in thinking about intergroup relations are erroneous. These are: (1) changes in racial attitudes and behavior are closely and inextricably related, (2) black and white students are likely to share a very similar assessment of the state of intergroup relations in any particular setting, and (3) racial attitudes or intergroup behavior in one specific domain of intergroup relations are closely related to those in another. Reliance on these mistaken assumptions may lead those involved with desegregated schools or interested in theory and research on intergroup relations to overlook complexities that must be addressed if they are to accomplish their goals effectively. Each of these mistaken assumptions will be discussed briefly in turn.

Racial Attitudes and Behavior May Change Inconsistently

Group stereotypes and prejudice seemed not to decline rapidly at Wexler, as some of the school's more optimistic supporters had hoped they would. In numerous cases, such stereotypes even appeared to be reinforced. Yet intergroup behavior certainly became more friendly and accepting over time. This suggests the rather surprising conclusion that interracial behavior may become more positive while beliefs about the racial out-group may show little change or become even more negative. The idea that attitudes and behavior are not as closely related as common sense might lead us to believe is hardly new. Discussions of this fact have been prominent in sociology and social psychology for over two decades (Liska 1974; Schuman and Johnson 1976; Wicker 1969). However, the phenomenon observed at Wexler was more startling than the mere lack of a strong positive correlation between attitudes and behavior. Rather, the data suggest changes on one dimension, behavior, that were in the opposite direction from those occurring on the other, presumably somewhat related, dimension.

The data available give no definitive answer to the question of exactly how one can reconcile the occurrence of these two rather contradictory trends. Yet this study did suggest one explanation for the puzzle: as students come to know each other more as individuals who can be differentiated from others in the same racial group, their behavior may come more under the influence of their interpersonal attitudes and less under the influence of their intergroup attitudes. Thus intergroup attitudes become increasingly irrelevant to the interaction of specific students who know each other reasonably well. If this is indeed the case, policies or practices that facilitate interpersonal as opposed to intergroup relations between members of different racial or ethnic groups should be helpful in those many situations in which intergroup attitudes are somewhat negative. A wide variety of mechanisms to accomplish this goal are available. Choice between mechanisms would depend on many factors, such as the age of the students and the degree of negativity of their attitudes. Specific programs and practices at Wexler that seemed to encourage students to come to know each other as individuals ranged from the in-school clubs to the use in classrooms of small round tables rather than individual chairs with writing arms.

Perceptions of Intergroup Relations May Be Asymmetric

Prior research has not highlighted the possibility of asymmetry in black and white students' evaluations of intergroup relations, but there is reason to suppose that this phenomenon is not unique to Wexler. For example, one recent study found that whereas black children rated black and white peers whom they considered close friends very similarly on a variety of personality dimensions, white children, in contrast, rated their close friends who were white more positively than close friends who were black (Damico, Bell-Nathaniel, and Green (1981a). Thus the statement that one has a close friend of the other race appears to mean something rather different to white and black children. The implications of such asymmetries may be of more direct relevance to researchers than to educational practitioners. Specifically, this finding suggests numerous interesting theoretical possibilities, such as the idea that black and white students may focus on different areas of intergroup relations or have different standards for evaluating such relations. More generally, it raises issues of how one measures such relations. Although these asymmetries in perception may be of greater interest to researchers than to educators, their existence does point out the basic fallacy of the colorblind perspective, which many educators at Wexler and elsewhere see as so desirable. If students' experiences and perceptions really are influenced by their race, as this research so strongly suggests, then ignoring this fact can lead to problems. For example, educators who believe they understand the nature of intergroup relations after talking primarily with students of one race may be oblivious to problems that seem very real to members of the other group or take inappropriate action to deal with perceived problems.

Intergroup Relations Are Domain Specific

Researchers and educators often speak and act as if racial attitudes are relatively straightforward, so that one can accurately say that an individual's racial attitudes as a whole are positive, negative, or somewhere in between. A few researchers have begun to call attention to the true complexity of such attitudes, suggesting, as Woodmansee and Cook (1967) did some time ago, that individuals' attitudes toward some domains of such contact may be quite different from their attitudes toward other domains of contact. Making a similar point with regard to interracial behavior, Patchen (1982) has shown that there is little relation between the amount of positive interracial behavior students engage in and the amount of negative interracial behavior they report. Furthermore, Patchen's work indicates that quite different factors are related to change in different aspects of intergroup attitudes and behavior. The research reported in this book also strongly supports such ideas.

The complexity of intergroup attitudes and behavior and the surprisingly small relation between some of their different aspects suggest that both researchers and educators need to decide which specific components of intergroup relations are of most interest to them. For example, educators need to be aware that practices purported to increase positive interaction among black and white students will not necessarily decrease negative interaction. If the latter is of equal or more interest than the former, supplemental strategies designed specifically to minimize negative behaviors are required. Research suggests that whereas change in some aspects of intergroup relations appears relatively unrelated to many school practices, other aspects are quite clearly linked to variables over which educators have a reasonable degree of control (Hawley et al. 1982; Patchen 1982; Schofield 1980). Thus, an analysis of which components of intergroup relations are most crucial in a particular situation and of the sensitivity of these particular aspects to various intervention strategies may help educators to use their resources effectively.

THE DIFFERENTIAL MALLEABILITY OF INTERGROUP ATTITUDES AND BEHAVIOR

The results of this study suggest that relations between blacks and whites are reasonably responsive to the specific conditions under which contact occurs. Thus, in a general way, they support the basic assumption on which Allport's contact theory, discussed in Chapter 1, rests. Yet this research also suggests other conclusions about change in intergroup relations that have generally not been emphasized in previous theoretical or applied work.

First, at Wexler, students' negative ideas and feelings about out-group members seemed somewhat less open to change in a positive direction than did their behavior toward each other. Contact theory, with its focus on prejudice, that is, on racial beliefs and feelings, has directed attention to changing racial *attitudes*. Indeed, the vast majority of the research and discussion on race relations in desegregated schools and elsewhere has focused on such attitudes. I would argue that changing the interracial *behavior* of students may be a more realistic and readily obtainable goal for desegregated schools.

Theorists such as Allport (1954) and Cook (1969) have pointed out a problem that was clear at Wexler and that has too long been ignored by researchers and practitioners alike. Contact is unlikely to change beliefs about out-group members in a positive direction unless those individuals appear not to have the characteristics attributed to them in group stereotypes. Unfortunately, it is likely that this condition will often not be met in desegregated situations. Two major obstacles stand in the way. First, there may well be what Allport (1954) called a "kernel of truth" in many stereotypes, especially those linked in some way to the historical condition of particular groups. For example, blacks' perception of whites as conceited is not surprising given the role relationships that have historically governed black/white interactions in this country. Second, as discussed in Chapter 4, the very belief that a group has certain qualities, such as a tendency to be physically aggressive, may lead individuals to interpret ambiguous behaviors in ways that confirm this belief. Thus an important condition for the elimination of certain stereotypes will often not be present in desegregated schools.

Intergroup behavior clearly changed at Wexler over time so that students were more accepting of out-group members after spending a year or two there than they had been initially. More marked, though, than the relatively small changes in intergroup behavior that occurred over time were the rather striking changes in this behavior from setting to setting at any given time. Such changes are evidence of marked malleability in intergroup behavior and suggest that more attention should be paid to the ways in which specific situational factors influence it.

This research found that children with a given set of racial attitudes will act very differently toward racial out-group members depending on the structure of the contact situation. Indeed, certain situational factors, such as effective adult supervision and practices that fostered cooperation, had a clear enough impact on relations between blacks and whites so that the students were quite aware of their effect. The fact that situational factors have a very real impact on the nature of black/white relations has important practical as well as theoretical implications. From a practical standpoint, this conclusion suggests that educators must recognize that the decisions they make about classroom structure and process are not neutral in their impact but rather set a context that molds intergroup relations. Thus, for example, even teachers who have little interest in affecting peer relations nonetheless do so unwittingly. Teachers and administrators cannot attribute the state of black/white relations in their classrooms or schools solely to students' predispositions or attitudes but must recognize the role that they themselves play in structuring such relations, however unwillingly they do so.

Social psychologists and other researchers interested in intergroup relations are certainly far from unaware that situational factors influence intergroup behavior. The extensive work on the impact of cooperative and competitive environments on social relations between members of different groups is clear evidence of this (Aronson, Bridgeman, and Geffner 1978; Sharan 1980; Sherif 1967; Slavin 1980). Yet compared to the rich literature on intergroup attitudes, there has been relatively little attention paid to intergroup behavior and especially to the wide range of situational factors likely to influence it. My argument is not that racial attitudes are unimportant. It is, however, that intergroup behavior and the factors influencing it have received less attention than they deserve, since such behavior is reasonably malleable and is important both in its own right and as a mediating variable that may in the long run lead to attitude change.

RACE AS A LATENT IF NOT OVERT ISSUE

Most of Wexler's administrators and staff adhered to a basically assimilationist view that holds that integration will have been achieved when minority groups can no longer be differentiated from the white majority in terms of behavior, economic status, education, or access to social institutions and their rewards. This approach suggests no major changes in the school's social structure or operating procedures since the newly assimilated minority individuals will, ideally, be attitudinally and behaviorally indistinguishable from the majority. Such an approach appears common in desegregated schools (Sagar and Schofield 1982) and is well illustrated by a comment made by a staff member in the elementary school that Rist (1978, p. 83) studied during its first year of a token desegregation program.

> The teachers then began asking one another what they thought of their black students. . . . Mrs. Evans said, "My two little girls are just precious." Mrs. Brown said, "I've got one that looks like no problem at all. . . . " One of the secretaries . . . said, "I don't think with this small number of A.T. [Administrative Transfer] students that there should be any problems. Now if there were seventy-five or a hundred, it would

be different. But I don't think twenty-eight will make any difference at all. *We probably won't know they are here.*" This comment was greeted with nods of agreement from the other teachers. (Emphasis added.)

Consistent with this assimilationist approach is the colorblind perspective, which advocates treating students as individuals whose conduct will be judged by standards applied impartially to all and whose requests and needs will be considered without regard to their race. Wexler was somewhat unusual in the extent to which it was successful in creating a milieu that in many regards minimized the importance of racial group membership, but other studies of desegregated schools report similar attempts to embrace a colorblind perspective and to avoid even mentioning race (Rist 1978; Sagar and Schofield 1982; Willie 1973).

Even in Wexler's officially colorblind milieu, race had an important effect on peer relations, as discussed in earlier chapters of this book. However, the fact that Wexler had few if any overt racial problems does not mean that it was in any sense just like a racially homogeneous school. Awareness of race and of potential racial problems was widespread and influenced everything from the frequency with which assemblies were held to teachers' reactions to student romances. Thus, although it was possible to create an environment in which overt racial conflicts were rare and in which race appeared to be far from everyone's speech and thoughts, the often expressed belief that race did not play a role in shaping individuals' reactions to each other was more a comfortable myth than a reality.

When things were going well and individuals were satisfied with the way they were treated and their ability to achieve their desired goals, the myth that the interpersonal dynamics at Wexler were just like those in a racially homogeneous school could easily be maintained, especially since the colorblind perspective minimized the attention given to facts like the vastly different suspension rates for black and white students. However, when individuals felt that they or other members of their racial group were not getting what they wanted or deserved, race frequently emerged as an overt issue. (This was all the more striking because of the customary avoidance of the topic.) For instance, a black girl, on observing the all-white team that represented Wexler on a televised student quiz program, muttered, "Might as well call this White School." Furthermore, students sometimes mentioned the issue of race to their teachers when they were criticized or disciplined. Under such circumstances, students, especially black girls, occasionally defended themselves by accusing the teachers, be they black or white, of prejudice.

> *Interviewer*: Do kids ever try to get out of a difficult situation or punishment . . . by saying they're being treated unfairly because of their race?
> *Ms. Feldman* (white): Yes, just the other day, not even a week ago, I said something and the answer was, "You only say that because I'm black." That's nonsense. . . . We had a picnic last week, Team D and our team, and this kid wasn't allowed to go. All the teachers went over the kids we thought didn't deserve to go. One of the girls who was not allowed to go said once or twice to me, "You're just telling me that 'cause I'm black and you're prejudiced." So the mother called. . . . She was ripping and roaring around and carrying on that I was prejudiced. . . . I said, "That has nothing to do with it. . . . "

> *Ms. Partridge* (black, responding to the same question as Ms. Feldman): Blacks, definitely. They'll say, "You're picking on me. You're letting that whitey go." They do. The white students . . . are not very verbal when it comes to punishment. . . . They tend to accept [it or] let their parents come and discuss it. . . . Black students have been on their own for so long taking care of problems that they want to know immediately [the] why's and how's. . . .

One teacher told of a fascinating incident during which a black teacher with relatively dark skin who was accused of prejudice by a black student being punished for an infraction of classroom rules held her arm next to the child's to demonstrate that they were both black. The student said heatedly, "That don't matter. You're white!"

Since white students generally experienced fewer conflicts with school authorities than blacks, they did not complain so frequently of unfair treatment in this context. The most serious conflict between Wexler and its white constituents that persisted over a considerable length of time revolved around the issue of open enrollment. As discussed at length in Chapter 7, many whites felt betrayed when the decision was made to drop the first year's open enrollment plan. In response to this perceived betrayal, whites felt no compunction about introducing race as an overt issue, arguing that they would not tolerate a predominantly black school and would flee to private schools or suburban areas. As one white parent baldly stated at an open hearing, ". . . schools will not hold their white children if they become predominantly black." In fact, threats of white flight arose at public hearings virtually any time white parents felt their interests were not being served. Thus such threats occurred in response to issues as varied as personnel cuts, academic standards, and non-adherence to previously accepted plans for the district.

To many it may seem unnecessary at best to argue that a racially mixed school is not "just like" a racially homogeneous one and that race is a potent latent issue even when it is not constantly a focus of attention. Yet I feel compelled to make this seemingly obvious point here because it may be overlooked by those in relatively conflict-free desegregated schools that want to carry on with business as usual and that operate on the premise that acknowledging the continuing potential importance of race just *creates* problems. I would argue that rather than creating problems, sensitivity to and careful analysis of underlying racial tensions can help schools to avoid exacerbating such tensions and to better meet the needs of all their constituents.

THE PROBLEM OF FEAR

Desegregation involves by its very definition social change. Although change in and of itself is often unsettling and threatening, desegregation may be especially so. It not only challenges traditional ways of doing things but also puts children in a situation where, often with some reason, they may feel concern for their physical well-being.

Fear of physical harm, which was a problem for whites at Wexler, was not a major problem for blacks there, as it has been for blacks in many other desegregated schools; but fear of rejection, of not being wanted or respected, most certainly was. These twin fears of an attack on the integrity of the physical and social self profoundly influenced individuals' perceptions of what occurred at Wexler and why these events transpired. These factors also clearly affected the actual course of events.

The difficulties created by white students' fear of blacks in general, and of their more assertive and physical style in particular, have already been discussed at some length. Similarly, black students'

fear of disdain or rejection and their anger at white students' sometimes arrogant behavior have also been discussed. There was,
however, an important consequence of these twin fears that has not
been mentioned heretofore: both whites and blacks were in some
realms predisposed to think the worst of Wexler or its students and
this propensity fed the spread of rumors.

> *Interviewer*: What do you think was the biggest problem you faced
> this year with people outside of Wexler?
> *Mr. Reuben* (white): The biggest problem I had was [that] there was so
> much distortion about what goes on here at Wexler. People just don't
> know. The facts are twisted; rumors fly. . . . A woman came in the
> other day . . . and said that she heard two people were raped in the
> halls, and they believe stuff like this. . . . That's our biggest problem,
> rumors. . . .
> *Interviewer*: Do you hear these rumors from both whites and blacks?
> *Mr. Reuben*: Oh, yeah!

A large proportion of the rumors that circulated in the white
community concerned rule-breaking and physical aggression on the
part of blacks. A great many of these rumors appeared to have no
specific foundation.

> Ms. Fowler (white) said that last year she received a call from a (white)
> parent asking if Mr. Reuben was out of the hospital yet. . . . The parent
> said, "I heard he was attacked by a [black] student and is recovering
> in the hospital." Mr. Reuben added that there hadn't been anything
> that happened before that call that . . . could reasonably have been the
> source of the rumor.

Other rumors had some foundation but were so distorted that they
completely misrepresented the actual state of affairs.

> Some of the teachers . . . have heard some fantastic rumors. Ms. Fowler
> (white) . . . said, for example, that one rumor was that kids were beaten
> with chains in the school. She said, "Now this illustrates the way a
> rumor can grow. . . . " Apparently, a few months ago, some seventeen-
> and eighteen-year-old boys from a nearby high school were playing on
> the basketball court a couple of hours after Wexler had been dismissed
> for the day. They got into a fight and one of them . . . used a chain on
> the other before the other fled. However, there were no Wexler stu-
> dents involved.

Whereas school staff and members of the Friends of Wexler could produce numerous examples of the rumors that abounded in the white community, they seemed much less aware of the nature and extent of rumors in the black community. Examples given of such rumors often were not so much rumors in the strict sense of the word as shared beliefs about why things happened that were different from the perceptions of school personnel, especially white personnel. Not surprisingly, these perceptions seemed much influenced by the fear of rejection and of not being treated as well as whites. For example, a black member of Friends of Wexler reported a widespread belief in the black community that a plan to move classes for the educably mentally retarded to Wexler's annex, Comstock School, like the scheduling plan that was in place at the very beginning of the school's third year, was "just another sign that blacks aren't wanted at Wexler." Mr. Reuben, with a different perspective, pointed out that accelerated classes, which were heavily white, were also held at Comstock. Other black members of the same group reported heatedly that blacks felt that Mr. Reuben "didn't care what happens on the buses, especially on the buses going to the black community." Mr. Reuben countered by saying that the bus drivers often failed to report incidents to him in spite of his threat to see that they would be fired for failing to do so. Since the drivers worked for an independent company, this threat was far from completely effective, and Mr. Reuben's first notice of a problem on the buses was often a phone call from an irate parent. His lack of knowledge, often interpreted as lack of interest, fueled beliefs that he and the school felt little concern over the sometimes serious problems on the buses.

Rumors were a real problem for two reasons. First, they contributed to parental dissatisfaction with the school and reinforced previously held fears on the part of parents and students alike. Such reinforcing of fears was hardly conducive to building positive intergroup relations or parental support for the school. Second, these rumors often reached community members who had no children at Wexler at the moment but who were in the process of deciding whether to enroll their children there in the near future. Mr. Reuben commented in the school's third year, after spending a considerable amount of time talking with the parents and teachers of fifth graders in Wexler's feeder pattern, "The PR in the elementary schools is enough to make your hair stand on end." Although white flight from

Wexler did not occur to any marked degree, administrators and teachers both felt that the exaggeration of some quite real problems did contribute to the loss of white students to private schools. This research did not address the issue of white (or black) flight in any systematic way. However, frequent informal conversations with community members whose children were approaching middle school age revealed that most of these parents were well aware of rumors about the school and many were sufficiently concerned by their content to consider making other arrangements for their children's schooling when such was financially possible.

Because rumors were a widespread and important phenomenon at Wexler, the Friends of Wexler organized a special "hot line" service during the school's second year to provide parents with a phone number to call to get information and to check on the accuracy of rumors they had heard. Notices about the service were sent home to parents via their children. However, enthusiasm for the project, which was manned by volunteers, waned rapidly when few parents called. In fact, there were only two calls to the hot line during its first month of operation. Thus the service was soon abandoned. School personnel explained the failure of the hot line by pointing out that many parents were predisposed to believe the rumors that circulated because they reflected or confirmed underlying fears and concerns. Hence their accuracy may not have appeared problematic. Lack of effective publicity was also a problem since notices carried home to parents by children showed a remarkable propensity for being mislaid or lost. Finally, Mr. Reuben, who supported the idea of the hot line, pointed out in retrospect that some parents may have preferred to call him or other school officials, such as the vice-principals. Nonetheless, it is clear that many rumors were not brought to the administrators' attention but rather circulated widely with no attempt at verification made.

In sum, this research suggests that even in a desegregated school with a minimal amount of overt racial conflict and a generally positive atmosphere, fears can be a real problem. The colorblind perspective, which ignores the role of race in suggesting the particular kind of fears that black or white children are likely to feel, ignores important information that could be used to try to structure students' experiences. The existence of such fears not only affects children's behavior and their interpretations of their daily experiences but also facilitates the spread of sometimes quite fantastic rumors. Such rumors can undercut a school's public image and the willingness of parents to enroll their children there unless effective means of combating them can be found.

THE EROSION OF INNOVATION

There is much theoretical and empirical work on innovation that makes the point that innovations are frequently neither implemented thoroughly nor maintained consistently over a period of some years. (Gross, Giacquinta, and Bernstein 1971; Smith and Keith 1971; Sussman 1977; Weikart and Banet 1975). The experience at Wexler supports such ideas, and I would suggest that the same would be true in other desegregated schools that make efforts to change their traditional ways of doing things in order to better serve their racially mixed student bodies. There is little reason to believe that such organizations will experience less decay of innovation than other institutions. As discussed in Chapters 1 and 7, Wexler had some difficulty both in thoroughly implementing innovations dictated by its idealistic goals and in maintaining innovative policies and practices in the face of strong pressures stemming from practical realities, from custom, and from concerns about cost and administrative convenience. Although the decay of various innovations and the reasons for these changes were discussed in Chapter 7, one more example, that of the affective education classes, may be useful to illustrate the very real difficulties that are likely to arise both in the implementation and in the maintenance of innovations in desegregated schools.

As discussed briefly in Chapter 1, the AEs were intended to help familiarize the students with the school, their teachers, and each other. The basic goal was to provide a mechanism to help students overcome possible fears and anxieties and to get to know each other in an informal social context. Such a goal was, of course, highly consistent with the school's emphasis on fostering positive peer relations. During Wexler's first year, two forty-five minute class periods were devoted to AEs each week. Mr. Reuben was sufficiently concerned about the success of the AEs to include them as an agenda item for the in-service training held for teachers during the summer preceding Wexler's first year and as one of the major discussion items in the first year's very first all-school faculty meeting. The in-service training on AEs included a fairly lengthy presentation during which teachers were told that AEs were supposed "to develop communication and interaction between teacher and student and student and student through affective education type activities." The presentation then focused on specific goals and objectives consistent with this general overall goal. Only toward the end of the presentation were any suggestions made about how these goals might be accomplished.

> After exhorting the teachers to try to develop a positive self-image in their students by saying good things about them and avoiding criticism in the AE setting, the speaker emphasized the crucial importance of careful listening. He then continued: "A sense of purpose must permeate AE endeavors. This is the third attempt to do AEs. They failed the first two times [in other schools within the district] because teachers didn't believe this wise advice. Start with planned, structured, organized activities. . . . If you don't, you'll have a monster that you'll have to live with."

Teachers evinced considerable skepticism about AEs during the in-service training. For example, one whispered sarcastically to a colleague "What a riot!" as the presenter discussed the idea that teachers might feel anxious about their ability to handle AEs, and many of the questions asked of the presenter were openly skeptical or even mildly hostile.

The extent to which teachers utilized their AE periods to help students adjust to the school and each other as was envisioned in the planning for the program varied widely. Some teachers, almost from the start, used AEs as study halls or as a chance for extra instruction in their substantive areas. Two reasons were most commonly given for this deviation from school policy. First, consistent with the academics first, last, and only orientation, some of these teachers argued that school time was too important to be wasted on the rather amorphous and certainly nonacademic activities that were supposed to typify AEs. Some also argued, consistent with the natural progression assumption, that the students were getting along all right, that over time they would get along even better, and that attempts to force the pace of this evolutionary process were likely to do more harm than good, especially since teachers were not really trained in managing group processes. This viewpoint was exemplified by Ms. Sharp, who was quoted in Chapter 2.

In contrast to this first group of teachers, others started out utilizing activities suggested in the AE manual but retreated by the end of the first semester, if not earlier, to utilizing more familiar academic material or games not connected in any obvious way to achieving the original goals of the AE classes. Indeed, by December, it was unusual to see an activity in an AE that was clearly related to the goals of the program unless one considers the opportunity for free play or something like a kickball game as such. Ms. Monroe is a good example of a teacher who started out using the AE manual to plan for that class but gradually reverted to more familiar ways. During the first month of school she used ideas from the AE manual and developed other special activities that were obviously related to the classes' special purpose. So, for example, she had the students in her AE class make presentations on the things they liked to do in their spare time in order to help them get to know one another. Also, the children drew pictures of themselves that they then shared with their classmates. However, by mid-November Ms. Monroe was using puzzles and word games, which the students tended to work on individually. Before the end of the semester, she began to use some of the AE time for academic instruction.

The many teachers who, like Ms. Monroe, switched from using carefully planned AE activities to routinely scheduling regular academic or play activities explained their behavior by saying that they did not always have a chance to look at the AE manual, which was kept in a central location at the school, and that coming up on their own with new ideas twice a week took too much time away from more important academic duties. Some also cited other reasons similar to those given by their colleagues who had never really tried to implement special AE activities.

The fact that grades were not given in AEs, a policy adopted in an attempt to help students to feel comfortable and free in the class, was often cited as undermining discipline and implying to students that they need not take the AEs seriously. Thus some teachers fell into showing movies and scheduling other activities that, although they did little to promote interaction between children, were of sufficient intrinsic interest to keep the students moderately attentive and well-behaved.

The ability of the AEs to serve their purpose was further undermined by school administrators, who frequently made their public address system announcements during these periods. Although the utilization of the AE period for this purpose may seem like a small matter, announcements from the principal, the vice-principals and others often occurred over the course of ten or even fifteen minutes making it hard for teachers to get other activities underway. When asked in a faculty meeting to make announcements at some other time because of their disruptive effect on AEs, Mr. Reuben refused but agreed to restrict them to the last ten minutes of each AE period.

Given the types of activity that sooner or later came to fill most AEs and the fact that attempts at academic instruction in this context were not notably successful, it is hardly surprising that the large majority of teachers begrudged the time devoted to AEs and complained heatedly about the program.

> *Interviewer*: What about the AEs?
> *Mr. Reuben* (white): We need them. We need them desperately [but] there is a lot of teacher resistance. They don't know how to handle it. . . . I think they are afraid we will get into some very deep racial things or child development issues.

Thus it was with pleasure that many teachers heard that AEs had been dropped in Wexler's second year. Mr. Reuben contended that the reason for this was that scheduling problems connected with the increased size of the student body made them impractical. Indeed, he had initially developed a new plan for AEs based on a successful model at another school. However, even though this new plan called for 12-minute as opposed to 45-minute AE sessions, it was not implemented. The increased size of the student body did complicate scheduling, but other special activities, such as the in-school clubs, were maintained, indicating that AEs were not Wexler's highest priority for the use of nonacademic time.

Plans were also made to reintroduce AEs in Wexler's third year. Not surprisingly, when Mr. Reuben mentioned this at a faculty meeting after having announced several other changes about which most teachers were dubious, he met considerable resistance.

> At this point in the meeting, [right after the announcement about AEs] there is by far the biggest disturbance in the audience that there has been to this point. Previous announcements [about changes] were greeted with small ripples of discontent and comments, but the one about the AEs generated a very high noise level so that the principal, for the first time, actually moved up close enough to the microphone

so that it amplified his voice. . . . A (white) teacher yelled out, "Why? Why?"

Again, these plans to reintroduce AEs floundered for a variety of reasons, the most important of which appeared to be scheduling problems.

The history of the AEs at Wexler suggests, as does much of Chapter 7, the difficulties likely to be encountered in instituting and maintaining new policies or practices designed to help a school meet the challenges posed by an interracial student body. The lesson to be learned from the experience at Wexler is that considerable attention needs to be given to motivating staff to adopt new practices that seem desirable and to providing them with the training and resources necessary to help them effectively implement desired changes. Furthermore, it might well be useful to set up a monitoring system, which would serve two purposes: first, to diagnose problems that impede effective implementation of innovations so that the search for solutions can begin before such a negative attitude develops that rescue of the innovation becomes doubly difficult; and second, to make salient to teachers and administrators the extent to which innovations are being maintained. At Wexler, many of the staff seemed rather unaware of the extent to which some of the programs or policies that were part of the school's initial plans to foster positive race relations were eroded or undermined by the reemergence of old customs or by pressures to save time and money. A simple monitoring system that lists programs and policies designed to achieve various goals and requires some rudimentary evaluation of the extent to which each of the items is operative in a given semester could serve as a useful mechanism for alerting school administrators to problems in the implementation or maintenance of various programs and policies, the cumulative impact of which might otherwise be overlooked.

A CLOSING NOTE

This epilogue reflects earlier chapters of this book in that it has not shied away from focusing on the problems that arose at Wexler in spite of the special efforts made there to provide students with a positive academic and social environment. I have dwelt on these problems at some length rather than stressed Wexler's successes because any analysis of students' experiences would be woefully inadequate without attention to them. I also believe that awareness of such problems should be useful to both researchers and educators striving to understand the social dynamics likely to occur in interracial classrooms.

Careful attention to the problems that arose at Wexler is useful, but it may tend to lead readers to take an unduly negative view of what can be achieved in interracial schools. Although the school in the long haul did not completely fulfill the extremely optimistic predictions of its strongest proponents, neither did it fail miserably, as others thought it would. The extent to which it is judged a success or failure clearly depends on one's expectations and point of view. Since this book has focused heavily on students' experiences at Wexler, it seems appropriate to close this epilogue by briefly discussing the students' overall evaluations of and reactions to their experiences.

In order to explore students' feelings, we asked two groups of children whether, overall, they were glad they had come to Wexler. This question was put to the 20 students who were interviewed several times between the fall when they entered Wexler as its first sixth grade class and the spring three years later when they graduated. The same question was asked of 24 other students, who entered Wexler as sixth graders under the new enrollment plan in the second year, when these students had completed seventh grade. This discussion will focus primarily on the responses of the former group, since they were close to graduation when last interviewed and thus had had a more complete exposure to Wexler than the latter group. It should be noted that those students interviewed as seventh graders were not quite as uniformly positive as those interviewed as eighth graders. Nonetheless, more than half said unequivocally that they were glad they had come to Wexler, and the reasons they gave for both positive and negative responses were quite similar to those given by the eighth graders.

Almost two-thirds of the 20 eighth graders interviewed said that they were glad they had come to Wexler and expressed no serious reservations whatever about their experiences. The remaining group of students was quite evenly divided, with roughly half of them giving unemphatic responses such as, "I guess I'm glad" or mentioning serious drawbacks to the school as well as important positive aspects. The other half of the remaining group said definitely they wished they had gone elsewhere. One theme in these students' remarks was a preference for their old elementary schools.

> *Interviewer*: Are you glad that you came to Wexler or do you wish you had gone to another school,
> *Joretta* (black): Really, I wish that I stayed at Hanover Elementary School, but it only went up the fifth grade. . . . It seemed like I learned more [there]. The work here is less easier. . . .
> *Interviewer*: What about your relationship with other students. Does that figure into this [your preference for Hanover] at all?
> *Joretta*: Some. . . . You get along way better [there] than here. The ones here, all they want to do is fight and throw things at you. Some of them don't want to learn. . . .

Arlene was the most ambivalent of the group of students who saw both pros and cons to being at Wexler.

> *Interviewer*: Are you glad you came to Wexler – ?
> *Arlene* (white): [interrupting] In some ways.
> *Interviewer*: Or do you wish you went to another school?
> *Arlene*: In some ways I am [glad] and in some ways I am not. Like here, you meet a whole lot of new friends and then again I had a whole lot of fights with these friends. . . . This year . . . they put so much pressure on us, they don't make school any fun. . . . Last year [in seventh grade] at Wexler it was fun learning. . . .
> *Interviewer*: Are there . . . things . . . the school could do to improve?
> *Arlene*: I am not sure what. I was talking with a friend and he doesn't want his little brother to come here . . . in two years. He said it will be practically all black and that is all right, but not when you are a white person.

More representative of the responses of students who mentioned negative as well as positive aspects are the basically positive remarks of a white girl who, like a number of other students, saw participating in the accelerated program in the eighth grade as a real benefit.

> *Interviewer*: Are you glad that you came to Wexler or do you wish maybe that you went to another school?
> *Lilly* (white): . . . I am pretty glad I came here. I think getting into the accelerated program was one of the reasons. I – like in the sixth grade, I really hated the school, but I decided to stick it out. . . . Last year

we had a whole lot of fun. . . . This year I would say it was just about the same.

As mentioned previously, the majority of students interviewed were quite unequivocal in their positive reactions to the questions, although a few of them indicated that there had been times when they had felt less positively about the school. Students who were unequivocally glad they had come to Wexler gave a variety of reasons for their feelings, ranging from the fact, mentioned by several blacks, that they lived nearby to positive comments about Wexler's newness, its outstanding physical facilities, and the accompanying variety of special opportunities in athletics, the arts, and elsewhere.

Harold (black): I'm glad I came to Wexler . . . 'cause I like it. I don't want to go to another school. I don't! This school's new. . . . I like all my teachers. . . . I like my friends. I have a lot of them.

Miriam (white): I think I'm glad [I came to Wexler], believe it or not 'cause this is where I learned a lot. I can't think of any other school I would rather have gone to.

Sonia (black): I'm glad I came here. . . . Since I first heard it was going to open, I pleaded with my mother to come. I signed up and they gave us a tour [and] pamphlets. . . . [It is] fun meeting people from all over. . . . I just knew people in our neighborhood before.
Interviewer: OK. What has been your worst experience here at Wexler?
Sonia: Nothing, really.
Interviewer: OK, then what has been your best experience?
Sonia: Proving to myself that I could get into the accelerated academic classes.

Taken as a whole, the students' assessment of their years at Wexler suggests that attending a desegregated school, even under quite good conditions, is not a completely problem-free experience. Yet the large majority of students felt that, all things considered, their experience was a good one — good enough that they were glad they had chosen to attend Wexler. Many of the things that attracted students initially — the outstanding physical facilities, the wide range of courses and programs, the presence of accelerated academic programs — were the same things that students named in retrospect as accounting for their positive reactions to the school. Wexler's interracial student body was initially seen as an advantage by some students and as a disadvantage by others, especially some whites. Similarly, it was, in retrospect, connected in some students' minds with the things they liked about Wexler and in others' with things they disliked. Although the lessons to be learned about living in a pluralistic society by attending a school like Wexler did not always come easily, the words of Stan, a black eighth grader, capture beautifully one of the important things that interracial schools can teach.

> *Interviewer*: Are you glad you came to Wexler or do you wish you had gone to another school?
> *Stan* (black): I guess I am glad I came here. I learned a lot of things about people.
> *Interviewer*: What kinds of things, can you tell me?
> *Stan*: How people really are the same, and in some ways . . . different.

REFERENCES

Allport, Gordon W. 1954. *The Nature of Prejudice*. Cambridge, Mass.: Addison-Wesley.

Amir, Yehuda. 1976. "The Role of Intergroup Contact in Change of Prejudice and Ethnic Relations." In *Towards the Elimination of Racism*, edited by Phyllis A. Katz, pp. 245-308. New York: Pergamon Press.

———. 1969. "Contact Hypothesis in Ethnic Relations." *Psychological Bulletin* 71(5):319-42.

Armor, David J. 1972. "The Evidence on Busing." *Public Interest* 28 (Summer): 90-126.

Aronson, Elliot; Blaney, Nancy; Stephen, Cookie; Sikes, Jev; and Snapp, Matthew. 1978. *The Jigsaw Classroom*. Beverly Hills, Calif.: Sage Publications.

Aronson, Elliot; Bridgemen, Diane L.; and Geffner, Robert. 1978. "The Effects of a Cooperative Classroom Structure on Student Behavior and Attitudes." In *Social Psychology of Education*, edited by Daniel Bar-Tal and Leonard Saxe, pp. 257-72. Washington, D.C.: Halsted Press.

Bell, Derrick A., Jr. 1975. "Waiting on the Promise of Brown." *Law and Contemporary Problems* 39(2):340-73.

Billig, Michael. 1976. *Social Psychology and Intergroup Relations*. New York: Academic Press.

Blanchard, Fletcher A., and Cook, Stuart W. 1976. "Effects of Helping a Less Competent Member of a Cooperating Interracial Group on the Development of Interpersonal Attraction." *Journal of Personality and Social Psychology* 34(6):1245-55.

Blau, Peter M. 1964. *Exchange and Power in Social Life*. New York: John Wiley & Sons.

Bogdan, Robert, and Taylor, Steven J. 1975. *Introduction to Qualitative Research Methods: A Phenomenological Approach to the Social Sciences*. New York: John Wiley & Sons.

Brigham, John C. 1974. "Views of Black and White Children Concerning the Distribution of Personality Characteristics." *Journal of Personality* 42(1): 144-58.

Broderick, Carlfred B. 1965. "Social Heterosexual Development Among Urban Negroes and Whites." *Journal of Marriage and the Family* 27(2):200-3.

Clark, Margaret S.; Gotay, Carolyn C.; and Mills, Judson. 1974. "Acceptance of Help as a Function of Similarity of the Potential Helper and Opportunity to Repay." *Journal of Applied Social Psychology* 4(3):224-29.

Clement, Dorothy C.; Eisenhart, Margaret; Harding, Joe R.; and Livesay, J. Michael. 1977. "The Emerging Order: An Ethnography of a Southern Desegregated School." Chapel Hill: University of North Carolina. Manuscript.

Cohen, Elizabeth G. 1975. "The Effects of Desegregation on Race Relations." *Law and Contemporary Problems* 39(2):271-99.

Cole, Michael; Hood, Lois; and McDermott, Raymond P. 1978. "Concepts of Ecological Validity: Their Differing Implications for Comparative Cognitive Research." *Institute for Comparative Human Development* 4(34):34-37.

Collins, Thomas W., and Noblit, George W. 1977. "Crossover High." Memphis, Tenn.: Memphis State University. Manuscript.

Cook, Stuart W. 1980. "Unresolved Issues of Cooperative Learning." Paper presented at the American Psychological Association meeting, September 4, in Montreal.

_____. 1978. "Interpersonal and Attitudinal Outcomes in Cooperating Interracial Groups." *Journal of Research and Development in Education* 12(1): 97-113.

_____. 1969. "Motives in a Conceptual Analysis of Attitude-Related Behavior." In *Nebraska Symposium on Motivation* (Vol. 17), edited by William J. Arnold and David Levine, pp. 179-235. Lincoln, Nebraska: University of Nebraska Press.

Cusick, Philip A., and Ayling, Richard J. 1973. "Racial Interaction in an Urban Secondary School." Paper presented at the American Educational Research Association meeting, February, in New Orleans.

Damico, Sandra B.; Bell-Nathanial, Afesa; and Green, Charles. 1981a. "Effects of School Organizational Structures on Interracial Friendships in Middle School." *Journal of Educational Research* 74(6):388-93.

____ . 1981b. "School Climate Study: Howard Bishop Middle School." Gainesville: University of Florida. Unpublished technical report 1.

DePaulo, Bella M., and Fisher, Jeffrey D. 1980. "The Costs of Asking for Help." *Basic and Applied Social Psychology* 1(1):23-35.

Deutsch, Morton. 1949. "A Theory of Cooperation and Competition." *Human Relations* 2(2):129-52.

Dion, Kenneth. 1979. "Intergroup Conflict and Intragroup Cohesiveness." In *The Social Psychology of Intergroup Relations*, edited by William G. Austin and Stephen Worchel, pp. 211-24. Monterey, Calif.: Brooks-Cole.

Duncan, Birt L. 1976. "Differential Social Perception and Attribution of Intergroup Violence: Testing the Lower Limits of Stereotyping of Blacks." *Journal of Personality and Social Psychology* 34(4):590-98.

Dutton, Donald G. 1976. "Tokenism, Reverse Discrimination, and Egalitarianism in Interracial Behavior." *Journal of Social Issues* 32(2):93-107.

Ellison, Ralph. 1952. *The Invisible Man*. New York: New American Library.

Erikson, Erik. H. 1950. *Childhood and Society*. New York: W. W. Norton.

Fine, Gary A. 1981. "Friends, Impression Management and Preadolescent Behavior." In *The Development of Children's Friendships*, edited by Steven R. Asher and John M. Gottman, pp. 29-52. Cambridge: Cambridge University Press.

Fisher, Jeffrey D., and Nadler, Arie. 1974. "The Effect of Similarity Between Donor and Recipient on Recipient's Reactions to Aid." *Journal of Applied Social Psychology* 4(3):230-43.

Folb, Edith A. 1973. "Black Vernacular Vocabulary: A Study of Intra/Intercultural Concerns and Usage." *Afro-American Studies Monograph Series*, 5.

Francis, William D., and Schofield, Janet W. 1979. "Students' Changing Perceptions of a Desegregated Middle School." Paper presented at the American Psychological Association meeting, September 4, in New York.

Gaertner, Samuel. 1976. "Nonreactive Measures in Racial Attitude Research: A Focus on Liberals." In *Towards the Elimination of Racism*, edited by Phyllis A. Katz, pp. 183-211. New York: Pergamon Press.

Gerard, Harold B.; Jackson, Terrence D.; and Conolley, Edward S. 1975. "Social Contact in the Desegregated Classroom." In *School Desegregation*, edited by Harold B. Gerard and Norman Miller, pp. 211-43. New York: Plenum Press.

Glaser, Barney G., and Strauss, Anselm L. 1967. *The Discovery of Grounded Theory: Strategies for Qualitative Research*. Chicago: Aldine.

———. 1964. "Awareness Contexts and Social Interaction." *American Sociological Review* 29(5):669-79.

Green, James A., and Gerard, Harold B. 1974. "School Desegregation and Ethnic Attitudes." In *Integrating the Organization: A Social Psychological Analysis*, edited by Howard Fromkin and John J. Sherwood, pp. 291-311. New York: Free Press.

Greenberg, Martin S. 1980. "A Theory of Indebtedness." In *Social Exchange: Advances in Theory and Research*, edited by Kenneth J. Gergen, Martin S. Greenberg, and Richard H. Willis, pp. 3-55. New York: Plenum Press.

Greenberg, Martin S., and Shapiro, Solomon P. 1971. "Indebtedness: An Adverse Aspect of Asking For and Receiving Help." *Sociometry* 34(2):290-301.

Gross, Neal; Giacquinta, Joseph B.; and Bernstein, Marilyn. 1971. *Implementing Organizational Innovations: A Sociological Analysis of Planned Educational Change*. New York: Basic Books.

Hall, Morrill M., and Gentry, Harold. 1969. "Isolation of Negro Students in Integrated Public Schools." *Journal of Negro Education* 38(6):156-61.

Hawley, Willis D.; Smylie, Mark A.; Crain, Robert L.; Rossell, Christine H.; Fernandez, Ricardo R.; Schofield, Janet W.; Tompkins, Rachel; Trent, William T.; and Zlotnik, Marilyn S. 1982. *Strategies for Effective Desegregation: Lessons from Research*. Lexington, Mass.: Lexington Books, D. C. Heath.

Homans, George C. 1961. *Social Behavior: Its Elementary Forms*. New York: Harcourt, Brace, & World.

Jansen, Verna G., and Gallagher, James J. 1966. "The Social Choices of Students in Racially Integrated Classes for the Culturally Disadvantaged Talented." *Exceptional Children* 33(5):221-26.

Johnson, David W., and Johnson, Roger T. 1974. "Instructional Goal Structure: Cooperative, Competitive, or Individualistic." *Review of Educational Research* 44(2):213-40.

Krenkel, Noele. 1972. "Self-concept and Interaction Patterns of Children in a Desegregated School." Master's thesis, California State University (San Francisco).

Laosa, Luis M., and Brophy, Jere E. 1972. "Effects of Sex and Birth Order on Sex Role Development and Intelligence Among Children." *Developmental Psychology* 6(3):409-15.

LeCompte, Margaret D., and Goetz, Judith, P. 1982. "Problems of Reliability and Validity in Ethnographic Research." *Review of Educational Research* 52(1):31-60.

Lever, Janet. 1976. "Sex Differences in the Games Children Play." *Social Problems* 23(1):478-87.

Levine, John M. 1981. "Cooperative Learning: Unresolved Theoretical Issues." Pittsburgh, Pa.: University of Pittsburgh. Manuscript.

Liska, Allen E. 1974. "Emergent Issues in the Attitude-Behavior Consistency Controversy." *American Sociological Review* 39(April):261-74.

Lofland, John. 1971. *Analyzing Social Settings: A Guide to Qualitative Observation and Analysis*. Belmont, Calif.: Wadsworth.

Lortie, Dan C. 1975. *School-teacher: A Sociological Study*. Chicago: University of Chicago Press.

Maccoby, Eleanor E., and Jacklin, Carol N. 1974. *The Psychology of Sex Differences*. Stanford, Calif.: Stanford University Press.

Miller, L. Keith, and Hamblin, Robert. 1963. "Interdependence, Differential Rewarding, and Productivity." *American Sociological Review* 28(5):768-78.

Miller, Walter B. 1968. "Focal Concerns of Lower-Class Culture." In *Poverty in America*, edited by Louis A. Ferman, Joyce L. Kornbluh, and Alan Haber, pp. 261-70. Ann Arbor: University of Michigan Press.

Mitchell, Edna. 1981. "Children's Uses and Perceptions of Friendship." Paper presented at the American Educational Research Association meeting, April 16, Los Angeles.

Moe, Jeffrey L.; Nacoste, Rupert W.; and Insko, Chester A. 1981. "Belief versus Race as Determinants of Discrimination: A Review of the Evidence and Study of Southern Adolescents in 1966 and 1979." *Journal of Personality and Social Psychology* 41(6):1031-50.

Noblit, George. 1979. "Patience and Prudence in a Southern High School: Managing the Political Economy of Desegregated Education." In *Desegregated Schools: Appraisals of an American Experiment*, edited by Ray C. Rist, pp. 65-87. New York: Academic Press.

Ogbu, John U. 1974. *The Next Generation: An Ethnography of Education in an Urban Neighborhood*. New York: Academic Press.

Omark, Ronald R.; Omark, Monica; and Edelman, Murray. 1975. "Formation of Dominance Hierarchies in Young Children." In *Psychological Anthropology*, edited by Thomas R. Williams, pp. 289-315. Paris: Mouton.

Patchen, Martin. 1982. *Black-White Contact in Schools*. Lafayette, Ind.: Purdue University Press.

Patchen, Martin; Hofmann, Gerhard; and Davidson, James D. 1976. "Interracial Perceptions Among High School Students." *Sociometry* 39(4):341-54.

Petroni, Frank A.; Hirsh, Ernest A.; and Petroni, C. Lillian. 1970. *Two-Four-Six-Eight, When You Gonna Integrate?* New York: Liveright.

Pettigrew, Thomas F. 1975. *Racial Discrimination in the United States*. New York: Harper & Row.

———. 1969. "Racially Separate or Together." *Journal of Social Issues* 25(1): 43-69.

Riordan, Cornelius. 1978. "Equal-status Interracial Contact: A Review and Revision of the Concept." *International Journal of Intercultural Relations* 2(2):161-85.

Rist, Ray C. 1978. *The Invisible Children*. Cambridge, Mass.: Harvard University Press.

———. 1974. "Race, Policy, and Schooling." *Society* 12(1):59-63.

Rubin, Zick. 1980. *Children's Friendships*. Cambridge, Mass.: Harvard University Press.

Sagar, H. Andrew. 1979. "Stereotypes and Attribution: The Influence of Racial and Behavioral Cues Upon Social Perception." Ph.D. dissertation, University of Pittsburgh.

Sagar, H. Andrew, and Schofield, Janet W. 1982. "Integrating the Desegregated School: Problems and Possibilities." In *The Effects of School Desegregation on Motivation and Achievement*, edited by David E. Bartz and Martin L. Maehr, Greenwich, Conn.: JAI Press.

_____ . 1980. "Racial and Behavioral Cues in Black and White Children's Perceptions of Ambiguously Aggressive Acts." *Journal of Personality and Social Psychology* 39(4):590-98.

St. John, Nancy H. 1975. *School Desegregation: Outcomes for Children*. New York: John Wiley & Sons.

St. John, Nancy H., and Lewis, Ralph. 1975. "Race and the Social Structure of the Elementary Classroom." *Sociology of Education* 48(3):346-68.

Schatzman, Leonard, and Strauss, Anselm L. 1973. *Field Research: Strategies for a Natural Sociology*. Englewood Cliffs, N.J.: Prentice-Hall.

Scherer, Jacqueline, and Slawski, Edward J. 1979. "Color, Class and Social Control in an Urban Desegregated School." In *Desegregated Schools: Appraisals of an American Experiment*, edited by Ray C. Rist, pp. 117-54. New York: Academic Press.

_____ . 1978. "Coping with Desegregation: Individual Strategies and Organizational Compliance." Rochester, Mich.: Oakland University. Manuscript.

Schofield, Janet W. 1980. "Desegregation, School Practices and Student Race Relations Outcomes." Pittsburgh, Pa.: University of Pittsburgh. Manuscript.

Schofield, Janet W., and Francis, William D. 1982. "Interracial Interaction in Academically Accelerated Classrooms." *Journal of Educational Psychology* 29(5).

Schofield, Janet W.; Francis, William D.; and Hall, Barbara. 1979. "The Evolution of Peer Relations in a Desegregated Middle School." Paper presented at the American Educational Research Association meeting, April 12, in San Francisco.

Schofield, Janet W., and McGivern, Elaine P. 1979. "Creating Interracial Bonds in a Desegregated School." In *Interracial Bonds*, edited by Rhoda G. Blumberg and Wendell J. Roye, pp. 106-19. Bayside, N.Y.: General Hall.

Schofield, Janet W., and Sagar, H. Andrew. 1980. "Interactant Choice in an Interracial Environment." Paper presented at the American Psychological Association meeting, September 3, in Montreal.

———. 1977. "Peer Interaction Patterns in an Integrated Middle School." *Sociometry* 40(2):130-38.

Schofield, Janet W.; Shaeffer, David; and Hopkins, Charles. 1977. "Students' Perceptions of a New Magnet Desegregated Middle School." Paper presented at the American Educational Research Association meeting, April 17, in New York.

Schofield, Janet W., and Snyder, Howard N. 1980. "Effect of Intimacy on Co-Worker Preference in a Desegregated School." Paper presented at the American Psychological Association meeting, September 5, in Montreal.

Schofield, Janet W., and Whitley, Bernard E., Jr. 1982. "Peer Nomination Versus Rating Scale Measurement of Children's Peer Preferences." Paper presented at the American Psychological Association meeting, in Washington, D.C.

Schuman, Howard, and Johnson, Michael P. 1976. "Attitudes and Behavior." *Annual Review of Sociology* 2(1):161-207.

Sharan, Shlomo. 1980. "Cooperative Learning in Teams: Recent Methods and Effects on Achievement, Attitudes and Ethnic Relations." *Review of Educational Research* 50(2):241-72.

Sherif, Muzafer. 1967. *Group Conflict and Cooperation: Their Social Psychology*. London: Routledge & Kegan Paul.

———. 1935. "A Study of Some Social Factors in Perception." *Archives of Psychology*, No. 187, 1-60.

Sherif, Muzafer; Harvey, O. J.; White, B. J.; Hood, W. E.; and Sherif, Carolyn W. 1961. *Intergroup Conflict and Cooperation: The Robbers' Cave Experiment*. Norman: University of Oklahoma Book Exchange.

Shibutani, Tamotsu. 1961. *Society and Personality: An Interactionist Approach to Social Psychology*. Engelwood Cliffs, N.J.: Prentice-Hall.

Silverman, Irwin, and Shaw, Marvin E. 1973. "Effects of a Sudden Mass Desegregation on Interracial Interaction and Attitudes in One Southern City." *Journal of Social Issues* 29(4):133-42.

Singleton, Louise C., and Asher, Steven R. 1979. "Racial Integration and Children's Peer Preferences: An Investigation of Developmental and Cohort Differences." *Child Development* 50(4):936-41.

———. 1977. "Peer Preferences and Social Interaction among Third-grade Children in an Integrated School District." *Journal of Educational Psychology* 69(4):330-36.

Slavin, Richard E. 1980. "Cooperative Learning." *Review of Educational Research* 50(2):315-42.

Smith, Louis M., and Keith, Pat M. 1971. *Anatomy of Educational Innovation: An Organizational Analysis of an Elementary School.* New York: John Wiley & Sons.

Sussman, Leila. 1977. *Tales Out of School: Implementing Organizational Change in the Elementary Grades.* Philadelphia: Temple University Press.

Tajfel, Henri. 1978a. "Interindividual Behavior and Intergroup Behavior." In *Differentiation Between Social Groups*, edited by Henri Tajfel, pp. 27-60. New York: Academic Press.

———. 1978b. "The Achievement of Group Differentiation." In *Differentiation Between Social Groups*, edited by Henri Tajfel, pp. 77-98. New York: Academic Press.

Tajfel, Henri; Flament, Claude; Billig, Michael; and Bundy, R. P. 1971. "Social categorization and intergroup behavior." *European Journal of Social Psychology* 1(2):149-78.

Thorne, Barrie. 1980. "'You Still Takin' Notes?' Fieldwork and Problems of Informed Consent." *Social Problems* 27(3):284-97.

Tikunoff, William J., and Ward, Beatrice A. 1978. "Conducting Naturalistic Research on Teaching: Some Procedural Considerations." Paper presented at the American Educational Research Association meeting, March 31, in Toronto.

Triandis, Harry C., and Davis, Earl E. 1965. "Race and Belief as Determinants of Behavioral Intentions." *Journal of Personality and Social Psychology* 2(5):715-26.

Triandis, Harry C.; Loh, Wallace D.; and Levin, Leslie A. 1966. "Race, Status, Quality of Spoken English, and Opinions about Civil Rights and Determinants of Interpersonal Attitudes." *Journal of Personality and Social Psychology* 3(4):468-72.

Vaughan, Graham M. 1978. "Social Categorization and Intergroup Behaviour in Children." In *Differentiation Between Social Groups*, edited by Henri Tajfel, pp. 339-60. New York: Academic Press.

Waldrop, Mary F., and Halverson, Charles F., Jr. 1975. "Intensive and Extensive Peer Behavior: Longitudinal and Cross-sectional Analyses." *Child Development* 46(1):19-26.

Walster, Elaine; Berscheid, Ellen; and Walster, G. William. 1973. "New Directions in Equity Theory." *Journal of Personality and Social Psychology* 25(2):151-76.

Wax, Murray L. 1980. "Paradoxes of 'Consent' to the Practice of Fieldwork." *Social Problems* 27(3):272-83.

Webb, Eugene J.; Campbell, Donald T.; Schwartz, Richard D.; and Sechrest, Lee. 1966. *Unobtrusive Measures: Nonreactive Research in the Social Sciences.* Chicago: Rand McNally.

Weikart, David P., and Banet, Bernard A. 1975. "Model Design Problems in Follow Through." In *Planned Variation in Education*, edited by Alice M. Rivlin and P. Michael Timpane, pp. 61-77. Washington, D.C.: Brookings Institution.

Wicker, Allen W. 1969. "Attitude versus Actions: The Relation of Verbal and Overt Behavioral Responses to Attitude Objects." *Journal of Social Issues* 25(4):41-78.

Willie, Charles. 1973. *Race Mixing in Public Schools.* New York: Praeger.

Woodmansee, John J., and Cook, Stuart W. 1967. "Dimensions of Verbal Racial Attitudes: Their Identification and Measurement." *Journal of Personality and Social Psychology* 7(3):240-50.

Worchel, Stephen. 1979. "Cooperation and the Reduction of Intergroup Conflict: Some Determining Factors." In *The Social Psychology of Intergroup Relations*, edited by William G. Austin and Stephen Worchel, pp. 262-73. Monterey, Calif.: Brooks-Cole.

Zelnik, Melum; Kantner, John F.; and Ford, Kathleen. 1981. *Sex and Pregnancy in Adolescence.* Beverly Hills, Calif.: Sage Publications.

Ziomek, Robert L.; Wilson, Morris D.; and Ebmeier, Howard H. 1980. "The Effects of Integration on the Social Class Structure of the Elementary Classroom." Paper presented at the American Educational Research Association meeting, April 8, in Boston.

INDEX

ABOUT THE AUTHOR

Janet Ward Schofield is an associate professor of psychology and a research associate at the Learning Research and Development Center at the University of Pittsburgh. She has also served as a research psychologist at the National Institute of Education and the Office of Economic Opportunity and as a member of the psychology and sociology departments at Spelman College in Atlanta, Georgia. She is a reviewer for a wide variety of journals and has been a consultant on desegregation issues for both local and federal agencies. Her research has been supported by grants and contracts from the National Institute of Education and the National Institute of Mental Health.

Dr. Schofield, a social psychologist, has published extensively on topics ranging from children's friendship patterns to race relations and research methodology. Her papers have appeared in the *Journal of Personality and Social Psychology*, *Social Psychology Quarterly*, the *Journal of Educational Psychology*, and in numerous other journals and edited volumes.

Dr. Schofield received a B.A. magna cum laude from Radcliffe College, where she was elected to Phi Beta Kappa, and an M.A. and Ph.D. from Harvard University.